SONNY CLARK - FRAGILE VIRTUOSO

DEREK ANSELL

Copyright © 2024 by Derek Ansell

Layout design and Copyright © 2024 by Next Chapter

Published 2024 by Next Chapter

Edited by Elizabeth N. Love

Cover art by Jaylord Bonnit

All rights reserved. No part of this book may be reproduced or transmitted in any form or by any means, electronic or mechanical, including photocopying, recording, or by any information storage and retrieval system, without the author's permission.

AUTHOR'S NOTE

Sonny Clark was a unique jazz piano soloist. Initially inspired by Bud Powell and Art Tatum, his mature style, once fully formed, was like no other jazz musician. Although I've tried to cover everything known that happened to him and carefully researched, there are gaps. Because of his heavy dependence on heroin and his continued on-off addiction over ten years of his productive life, he would disappear from the scene for long periods of time. Sometimes a month, sometimes two, and on one occasion, thirteen months. It was impossible to pin down accurate dates for these disappearances, so I have used some speculation to produce a fully rounded story. Known and respected by other musicians, he never received the following and recognition he deserved from the jazz-loving public. Indeed, he is much better known, and his music loved far more today, in 2024, than ever in his lifetime. This is his story. The story of a unique talent, a fragile virtuoso and a great jazz tragedy.

PROLOGUE

A TRANQUIL INTERLUDE

IT IS A VERY DULL, GREY DAY IN SAN FRANCISCO THIS MORNING. Smoky. Difficult to describe or talk about unless you've been there and seen it, sensed it, felt it in your nostrils. Foggy, yes, a grey mist maybe, but no, the only way to describe it is smoky. The young jazz pianist Sonny Clark doesn't really care about the weather or, indeed, take much notice of his surroundings. He does not find them unpleasant, quite the opposite, in fact. After the black, soot-inflected bleakness of Herminie, a coal town in Pennsylvania, where he was born and spent the first twenty years of his life, this place is paradise. A place to thrive and earn a good living; make a good life all round. Now he is here and having a few days off from his gig with the Buddy De Franco band and, unexpectedly, has an extra one-night gig that he never saw coming. One that will suit him very well indeed.

He saunters down the road to a bar he likes and goes in for a drink. Maybe two but no more. He is determined to be fresh and alert for the gig tonight because opportunities like this do not come often. If at all. Not for young, twenty-four-year-old jazz pianists, of which there are a multitude in San Francisco and all over California for that matter. All chasing the same few, good gigs and record sessions. Not that he is complaining, he reflects as he sits on a stool at the bar, sips his first beer and lights a cigarette. When he arrived here two years ago in 1953, confident of his ability as a trained pianist, a boy wonder back in Herminie, and sought out the jazz scene, he still had no idea how things would pan out. Well, he did get gigs after a fairly short time; if it wasn't easy, neither was it too hard. And getting to play with Art Pepper and Dexter Gordon, how much of a thrill was that for a boy from the backwoods of Pennsylvania?

OK, so he did plunge right into the scene head-first, dressing like the other cats as soon as he managed to make a little money, hanging out with any of the men that accepted him, and getting into hard drugs almost straight away. Well, the drugs were everywhere, the scene was submerged in them, and all the cats were taking them. It was part of the culture, the lifestyle, and if you were going to join it, there was no point in only taking half-measures, was there? That heroin was tough though, hard, harsh, bitter, life-enhancing one minute and destructive the next, lifting you to the heights then plunging you to the depths. Playing with great musicians you had admired as a young teenager though, and producing wonderful music, that was the prize.

He has been very lucky; he admits that now. Thanks to the advice and help he had received early on from the older, wiser musicians, he had soon decided that the drugs were destructive, and he needed to get off them now, while he was still young and had the strength to do so. He had gone to the medical centre and sought help. Hard, almost impossible, agonising for a week of abstinence but finally coming through and seeing the daylight at the end of the tunnel. Now he is clean and feeling good. The cats had all told him that he would go back to the drugs eventually. Once a junkie, always a junkie. Well, no, there was no way that was ever going to happen. Not now he has a wife, a home, a shiny new car and a dog, a big shaggy mongrel mix of part chow and part German Shepherd that he affectionately calls Lulu.

Sometimes his wife says he shows more affection to that animal than he does to her.

Sonny smiles. He orders his second beer from the bartender and lights another cigarette. This will be his last drink, at least until tonight at the gig. It will be a big one; he will be able to show his prowess as a jazz piano soloist with a supportive bass player and drummer who both admire him. How many young cats are that fortunate?

It is good for a musician to receive praise and admiration from members of the public, but how much better is it to receive it from fellow musicians? That really is something special and not too many young musicians enjoy such praise. Sonny drinks his second beer slowly, leisurely. He smokes his cigarette and thinks about what he will do in the next few hours. He can't wait for the gig tonight but knows it will come soon enough. Calm and patience, that is what is required now. Calm and patience.

He really hadn't thought too much about it. Not taken it in. Of course, he had been pleased and flattered by the two young musicians he had met after the De Franco gig, both telling him how much they admired his piano playing and how they had been following his progress with the band. Jerry Good, the bass player brimming over with enthusiasm, asking him if there was any chance that he, Sonny Clark, would be prepared to play with them for a night, in a trio context. The words 'trio context' struck a chord, a loud one. Of course, he had said yes, anytime, anyplace. Well then, Good told him it could be arranged, no problem, leave it with him. Sonny noticed that Al Randall, the drummer, looked dubious and reminded his friend that it would depend on John Marabuto, the pianist leader. It's a week-long gig at the Mocambo club in Oakland, Good is saying. Just a long bar with a piano at the end and only just enough room to squeeze a full drum kit in. But John Marabuto is a good man and a happy cat; he will agree right enough.

Sonny smiles and drains his glass. He thought it was just wishful thinking on the part of two young dudes, anxious to experiment and improve their experience. When he bumped into Jerry next day, he had said it was all arranged. Marabuto was happy to take a night off and had even offered to tune the piano for them. Good had assured him it was a good gig, not too many in but an enthusiastic crowd. 'Floating crowd really,' Good continued. 'They come in, listen, have a drink or two, drift out, and some actually come back in later.'

Sonny's last thoughts on arriving at the Mocambo, coming to him late, he acknowledges, is how flexible and adaptable are these two young rhythm players. They will play standards all night, nothing new or tricky, that has already been agreed by all three. All being well, it will be ideal, just the type of set up he loves for an ad hoc performance. Just to be safe, he tells his colleagues that he will play an extended introduction and give them the nod when to come in. At the end he will take a coda. They've had no time for rehearsal of any kind. Sonny sits at the piano stool, raises his shoulders and hunches himself over the instrument. It is the way he plays. He plays a lavish intro to 'What's New,' enjoying himself already, right from the off. He spins out some lightning runs up the keyboard in the manner he's seen Art Tatum do it and includes some Bud Powell harmonic lines. Rhythmically he's flowing already, and as he nods to his bass man and drummer, they jump in tentatively but right on the beat. Then he is flying, bringing out his own licks he has already worked out and sounding fresh and original. His lines are his own, steeped in blues, sanctified sounding. A seven-minute workout seems to pass swiftly, and the boys are shadowing him faithfully, no problem at all. He has been compared in the recent past to Kenny Drew, the pianist he replaced in the De Franco unit and Horace Silver, and these are good role models, if you need them. Sonny doesn't need them. He is already shaping up nicely as his own man and he knows it. It is straight-ahead bebop and that is the music he wants to play, not the more usual cool jazz you hear in these parts. Right to the end of a long and complex improvisation on the song Clark knows he is swinging and is pleased to hear Good walking steadily and Randall using brushes discreetly with the added bonus that both men are contributing rhythm backing in keeping with Sonny's ideas and style of playing. Straight bop. In a flexible piano trio that gives him all the solo space he craves. His smile becomes bigger, broader and he nods to his bass-man and drummer. They lay out. Sonny knocks out eight bars of unaccompanied piano, increasing the volume one minute, dipping down to quiet notes the next. It is the way he plays, varying the dynamics effectively to generate a healthy swing. As he plays and sustains his final note the applause erupts. This is what he had hoped for.

Success breeds success, so he opens 'Willow Weep for Me' with another neatly constructed opening solo chorus. This time the tune is played a little faster than usual. Clark is swinging from the start, introducing some stride figures, and he nods towards Good to take a bass solo on the fourth chorus. His accents behind Good and his free-flowing backing enhance the bass solo before the three of them bring the selection to a smooth close.

Next up he calls 'There Will Never Be Another You,' a popular song these days. They keep it medium tempo but smooth and tripping along like the natural flow of a river. Sonny is warming to his gig. The smiles on bass man and drummer's faces indicate their satisfaction at the way the gig is going. Sonny uses chords well to rephrase the melody and develop his almost compositional improvised lines. Here he gives Good a short, effective, walking solo and trades fours percussively with Randall. It is all going even better than he had hoped. Next, they can dig into some tasty blues licks on the John Lewis arrangement of D&E.

The rhythmic momentum is picking up nicely. It was good to

start with but smoothing out wonderfully now. When it comes to 'All the Things You Are,' Sonny uses the introduction Dizzy Gillespie introduced on his 1945 Guild record, leaving no doubt in anybody's mind where Clark is coming from. He is solidly into first-wave bop although his improvised lines, as he warms up, announce a totally original jazz piano stylist. He can make old music sound new. Sonny's grooving solo is full of invention, the fresh melodic lines almost flowing into each other. He is fully engaged at this point. His brilliant inventions and the smoothness with which he executes them inspire the rhythm section with Good's lines stronger, more assured, and Randall whisking them both along confidently. The constant, effortless invention from the pianist and the thrusting rhythm make this medium-tempo opus positively glow. Good gets into a brisk solo, and the trio builds and builds and feels the urge to keep playing this one selection for ever. They continue, building and building, appearing to recompose this hardy standard until they all reach a natural, comfortable conclusion.

Sonny takes a slow, indulgent solo introduction to 'But Not For Me.' When they get into the song though, all three are swinging wildly. Not only is Sonny on top of his game now, but so are the rhythm boys. The pianist smiles as he heads into the next chorus. Just listen to them, he reflects. The bass is walking steadily, and drummer Al is kicking like Art Blakey or Philly Joe Jones. Clark slows the tempo down to a solid medium for 'Bags' Groove,' relishing the sound of the blues and creating new lines on the familiar theme. Time for a short bass solo, and Sonny fills in neatly behind him.

Time for one more standard, 'Between the Devil and the Deep Blue Sea' where the pianist frames the rendition between a piano solo introduction and ends it with a neat coda. In between, there are some clever inventive lines from Clark as he is now fully engaged with his material and the way he finds it so easy to embellish it and make it sparkle. Good solos then on bass, and the selection ends with Sonny and Al swapping four-bar exchanges. The applause roars out, partly because the bar has suddenly become full of people but mostly, of course, for the quality of the music being played. It is now time for some Dizzy Gillespie material, and Sonny counts the trio into 'A Night in Tunisia.' Clark gets into his own personal groove on this one, although some of the licks he plays during a long solo foray will be recognised as Bud Powell-inspired. Then the trio play 'Ow,' another Gillespie line, this time at a comfortable medium groove. By the time Clark has finished with this piece, anybody listening closely might be excused for thinking the pianist had composed it himself.

All too soon, it seems to the three contented musicians, the gig is ending. Sonny plays 'The Theme,' a piece gaining popularity as a sign-off tune for jazz musicians everywhere now that Miles Davis has recently picked up on it for his quintet. Usually credited to trumpeter Kenny Dorham as composer, it brings Clark's first recording with his own trio to a close. Jerry had borrowed a tape recorder and set it up near the piano to record the entire session. As he plays the last note of 'Dorham's Theme,' he glances over to the recorder and wonders idly if the music will ever be released commercially on an LP. Most unlikely, he thinks sadly, although he is pleased with the way the session has gone and grateful to his two colleagues for setting it up.

Now, though, it is time to wind down, and he is in no hurry to get back home. He swaps compliments with Al and Jerry and all three walk over to the bar where they are soon drinking beer and lighting cigarettes. As he drinks his beer, Sonny feels content after a good night's work, the first where he was in complete control and had as much solo room as he wanted. Now that everything is going so well and he can feel the adrenalin pumping through his body, it occurs to him that he would feel even more on top of the world with a shot of heroin in him. But no, no, he will never go back to that even though the temptation is often very strong and the desire to feel high and happy, even for a short time, is often almost overwhelming.

He can relax fully now, feel good about himself and his music and wonder what the next phase of his musical explorations will bring. It will be late when he finally makes it home, well into the next morning, and there will, most likely, be trouble with his wife if he drinks too much now and clumps into their home noisily and carelessly. Sonny Clark is on his way now to recognition as a top-quality jazz piano soloist, and he intends to make the most of it. So far everything has gone well, much better than he expected when he left home in Herminie, Pennsylvania, to visit his aunt in L.A. for a short spell that has now turned into almost four years. He is on his way; what could possibly go wrong?

Sonny Clark *Oakland 1955* Uptown 27.40 Sleeve note by Bob Blumenthal.

1

HERMINIE PA: THE BEGINNING: THE BOY WONDER

HERMINIE NO 2 IS A COAL PATCH A FEW MILES FROM THE BIGGER company town of Herminie, about sixteen miles east of Pittsburgh. Conrad Yeatis (Sonny) Clark was born on July 21st, 1931. The family moved from Georgia, and Sonny's father has worked most of his adult life as a miner there. Emory Clark is not a well man, he is suffering from what is known as 'black lung' in the family, and he has a permanent cough. Conrad Yeatis Clark is the youngest of eight children born to his mother. The family are surrounded by people from Italy, Poland, Austria, and Russia, as well as their own African American neighbours from Georgia and Tennessee.

The town has a school, churches, including one for black people, a store, a beer garden, and a black-owned hotel, the Redwood Hotel, where they hold popular weekend dances in the region for African Americans. People arrive from miles around for the weekend dances. On August the 2nd, Sonny's father Emory dies of what is described in the local newspaper as 'a lingering of tuberculosis' just ten days after the birth of his youngest son. It is a harsh blow, and from now on Sonny will be raised by his mother, Ruth, taking all and any menial jobs she can get, and his older brothers and sisters. The family move to the Redwood Hotel, belonging to John Redwood, as the house they were living in was owned by the mining company and could only be occupied by a working miner.

His mother started him on piano lessons at just three years old, so he gets just about the earliest start any youngster can receive. He takes to the instrument like a duck to water and needs no encouragement to practice regularly and keep at it.

In 1936, six-year-old Conrad Clark is getting on very well with his piano playing and will commence private instruction in two years' time. His older brother George is already a pianist and has his own band. Sonny listens to George playing, takes in what he hears, but already seems to have his own ideas about how the instrument should be played. Talking to jazz journalist Nat Hentoff many years later, he will recall, 'All the instruments were around the house. I fooled around on bass and vibes. I liked to figure out my own way of handling an instrument and was always bugged at studying because I wanted to do what I felt.' It was something that came early indeed to young, six-year-old Conrad Clark, soon to acquire the nickname Sonny, which he would be known as for the rest of his short life. He is an extremely small boy, lean, and will only grow to just over five feet tall as a fully grown man.

Sonny begins playing piano in the local hotel although he is still in elementary school. He causes quite a stir in the local community with his prowess at the piano at such a young age. His performance receives an enthusiastic write-up in *The Pittsburgh Courier*, the local newspaper. He wins a talent contest at the hotel and is carried home on the shoulders of his older brother, Emory. Even more exciting for Sonny is when he appears on a radio amateur hour show and plays some lively boogie-woogie. Everyone in the family is impressed even if one or two of his siblings are showing signs of envy. Sonny can sense it but somehow understands, young as he is, that his is a special talent, denied to the majority of the population, found in a very few. His playing on radio is a great success, so much so that the Pittsburgh Courier publishes an article about him.

It is listening to the radio that first alerts Sonny to jazz. He loves the music he hears and, particularly, Fats Waller, Art Tatum and Erroll Garner. Listening to these masters of varying styles of jazz piano, it occurs to him that he will have to keep studying, practice constantly and gain experience so that he can play the piano as well as these men. He listens also to Count Basie and loves the way he swings the orchestra along. Duke Ellington also. When he attends high school, he plays vibes and bass in the school band, but his real thrill is when he is chosen as piano soloist. The piano is his instrument, and he knows how good he is at playing it. At the age of thirteen, he feels he has studied enough and is now ready to take on the world. He has also received an offer to play in a local band that plays for dances.

When he talks about this to his mother, she stops him in his tracks. He needs at least another year of lessons, and he must take in everything he is taught and put it to good use. No giving up now that he is so near to achieving success. His mother tells him that he has a special talent for music, far in advance of any ability that his brothers or sisters have. Of course, she would never say that to any of them and he must never mention it, but there it is. And when you have such a special talent you must do everything in your power to nurture and control and make the best of it. He knows that already, of course he does so, there must be no more idle talk about giving up lessons.

Sonny knows the wisdom of his mother's words and carries on with lessons. For more than ten years he has practised regularly and has received lessons, first by his pianist brother George and then a qualified teacher. Even as he gets gigs to play in local dance bands, he keeps rigorously to his practice routines. All is going well above the surface, but underneath there is pain and trauma. As a young teenager, he is barely aware of the tragedies in his life, but they are there.

Struggle and tragedy have stalked the Clark family from the beginning. His parents Emory and Ruth grew up in the countryside of Stone Mountain, Georgia. Their first move was to Aliquippa where his father secured work in the coke yards of a steel company. Driven out of Aliquippa by frightening KKK activity, they settled in Herminie, another rural location, to raise their family and find security. But Emory's early death from a mining-related disease meant another move, this time to John Redwood's hotel. Sonny enjoyed playing piano there from an early age, but further trauma is to follow when his mother dies of breast cancer, and a short time later, the Redwood Hotel burns to the ground. The family move out to Pittsburgh.

Attending high school in Jeanette, Sonny is featured playing bass, vibes, guitar, and piano in the school band. Evenings and weekends find him playing in local Pittsburgh bands and earning a little money for himself and his family. At the age of fifteen, Sonny appears on the programme of the historic *Night of the Stars* concert held at the Syria Mosque to celebrate the music of Pittsburgh's jazz superstars. The show is presented by the Frog Club and *The Pittsburgh Courier*. Sonny is in important jazz company here, alongside Pittsburgh-born pianists, Erroll Garner, Earl Hines, Mary Lou Williams and Billy Strayhorn. He also shares the bill with jazz greats such as Billy Eckstine, Roy Eldridge, Maxine Sullivan and Ray Brown. It is a big moment for him, the culmination of a series of successful performances in public that began with his recital on piano at just six years old.

Could he make it as a professional jazz pianist? Sonny is just beginning to believe that perhaps he can, even if he is just a poor black boy from the rural backwoods of Herminie No 2. And if he can make it at all, the chances are slim indeed, here in Pittsburgh. Ideally, he would like to go to New York because that is the centre of most of the jazz activity in America. Always has been. But he knows from musicians he has spoken to in recent times that competition is fierce for every gig, every record date. According to one musician he spoke to, for every record date in

NYC, there are ten to fifteen musicians on every instrument clamouring to get on it.

New York is where he wants to be. That is where they play the sort of modern bop-fuelled jazz he wants to play. He intends to get there though, one day. Not just yet perhaps, not until he has gained more professional experience and has a list of known musicians he can say he has worked with. Also, although he hates to admit it, the size of NYC and the great number of jazz musicians struggling to make it there frightens him a little. The knowledge of this he has gained by talking to his brother George who is also a pianist, and he may have the answer to Sonny's dilemma. George is planning to visit their aunt in California but, if opportunity should be presented, he would like to live and work in California. He asks Sonny to go with him.

Sonny considers it and thinks it might be an extremely good idea. There is, he has heard, a lot of jazz in L.A., so it would be ideal to try and get a few gigs there for experience. Unlike George, though, he has no intention of staying long. A month, two, three at the outside? Then back home to see the family and reconsider his future options. After much thought and due deliberation, he agrees to go, so George and Sonny set off for Sunny California.

The Pittsburgh Courier
Sam Stephenson. *The Paris Review*

2

CALIFORNIA: THE CALM BEFORE THE STORM

SUNNY, YES, BUT MISTY, FOGGY AND WITH A STRANGE VAPOUR THAT shrouds all the buildings in the winter mornings. A mix of fog and smoke from chimneys and industrial buildings, Sonny supposes. But he loves the bright clean buildings and the wide streets and the colourful lights at night-time. He sets out to find all the jazz dives, the clubs and the after-hours joints where the musicians go to jam. It is quite a lively scene as he soon discovers. Not that they are that keen to let a new boy sit in, as he soon finds out after collecting a few refusals and being told to go home and woodshed in private. But he goes to all the clubs and hangouts he can find and listens closely to the music they play and the way they play it.

It is lighter though, less like the full-bodied, edgy bop he listened to on the radio at home and on records. Here the music is quieter, more gently melodic and more akin to classical music than the jazz he knows. Or a mix of jazz and classical, which jars a little with him although, he must admit, it is good music and pleasant to listen to. Sonny decides to spend time checking out every possible venue where jazz is played in an attempt to find out whether there are any musicians who play in the more hard-core bop that he is familiar with and wants to play. Not easy.

After a week of seeking and only finding the soft-focus, lyrical, classical-inspired jazz that he labels Chamber Jazz, he is ready to give up. Then he gets a break. Wandering into the more upmarket area of Sunset Boulevard, he stops off at a little club called the Hula Hut. There he hears tenor saxophonist Wardell Gray blowing up a storm on a blues with a tough rhythm section spurring him on. This is what Sonny has wanted to hear ever since arriving in L.A., and these boys are playing his music. He listens to two full sets, totally immersed in the music.

It is at this point and most likely at this venue that Clark will have most likely played his first music with seasoned jazz musicians like Gray and Teddy Charles. His enthusiasm, allied to his ability as a young, up-and-coming jazz musician probably gave him the courage to approach Wardell Gray and ask if he could sit in with the combo. It would not have taken long for Gray and his sidemen to see how good the young pianist was. A short time after his first visit to the Hula Hat, Sonny is reported as playing piano in Gray's combo, and he also gets to sit in and play his instrument in the groups headed by Art Pepper, Dexter Gordon, Art Farmer, Barney Kessel, Stan Getz, Zoot Sims and Anita O' Day. In fact, practically every jazz musician of note in or around California.

But the first night at the Hula Hut is one that Sonny will remember for a long time afterwards. He soon gets the feel of the band, and the tough bop style is the one he has been listening to since he was about nine years old, and it is very much the way he plays himself. He begins comping contentedly, tentatively for the first few bars and then let's rip. He strikes a dramatic pose, almost folding himself into the piano, and begins playing in a percussive manner, ecstatic as he hears Wardell pick up on a chord he has just planted underneath him to launch into his tenor solo. Sonny is flying. He moves to raise himself up from the piano stool at the end, content, pleased.

It isn't long before Sonny gets the call to play with Wardell again and finds himself in the clubs as part of the tenor man's regular combo. He is on stage with Frank Morgan the alto sax man, Teddy Charles on vibes, and Lawrence Marable at the drums. And not just club work: on February 20th, 1953, he is in the studio in Los Angeles recording with the tenor sax leader. His comping in the section is robust on 'So Long Broadway', but he does not get a solo. On 'Paul's Cause' and 'Lavonne', the latter his own composition, he plays introductory solos with a brisk, percussive flourish and sets up the band for their individual contributions. His melodic backing on the ballad 'The Man I Love' is impressive. Nobody would ever know that this was his first record date and that his previous experience was in local dance bands in Pittsburgh. Back in the clubs, he gets a gig with altoist Art Pepper and then an opportunity to record with him along with bassist Harry Babasin and drummer Bobby White. Sonny Clark has arrived in California.

The only downside is something he is told by one of the musicians he starts to hang out with at this time. The man wants to know if Sonny has tried heroin yet. When Sonny answers in the negative, the man spins out a long, sad story. A story of deprivation, bad treatment, bad food, bad accommodation after spending hours on tours on bleak unheated buses in deep midwinter. It gets worse. Having to go in the trade entrance rather than the front door at venues where you are providing their entertainment. Tours to the Southern States where you dare not arrive with a white musician in the band and white bands can never accommodate a black bass player or trumpet man.

The heroin can help so much, the man says. 'It lifts all the worries from your shoulders, and you go in there, wherever it is, a smiling, content man, ready to play. Not down in the depths and feeling like hell. It gives you a few hours of bliss and helps you play real good.'

Sonny isn't convinced. It's not what Charlie Parker said, advising musicians not to touch the stuff and claiming it never enhanced his playing. His mother instructed him never to go near the drugs, ever, and had drummed it into him ever since he played his very first paid gig in a dance hall. The man grins. Did Sonny ever hear Parker play a less-than-inspired solo? Sonny should look around him. All the best musicians playing now are on it. They know. 'It lifts you up, man, it gives you a real good feeling and makes it easy to go in anywhere, feeling great, ready and able to take terrific solos. Anyway, you can control the amount and frequency of what you use. Use it occasionally, like I do, and never get fully addicted.'

He is given the name and contact number of a connection. A dealer. He is told the man is reliable, safe, always available and he'll consistently sell you a bag without cheating you or overcharging. A good man. Sonny writes down the details reluctantly but vaguely thinking that it could help him occasionally if he uses the stuff sparingly and does not get addicted. Just when the going is tough. He can control his usage; he has always been streetwise, aware and determined to succeed, and he will use any method to do so.

The great bass player, leader, Oscar Pettiford is in town and the word is out that he is recruiting for a new band for gigs in San Francisco and some touring. Sonny has been working, for the most part regularly, gigs with Wardell, Art Pepper, Dexter Gordon and backing vocalist Anita O'Day. His prowess and reliability as a pianist is already out on the street, and he is becoming known as an original stylist. He is recruited for the piano chair in Pettiford's new band after playing just a few bars for the bass player.

Sonny is enjoying himself in San Francisco. His playing is brisk, lively, inventive and, above all, swinging. He and Pettiford mesh together extremely well in the rhythm section, and all the gigs are enjoyable. He spends two months with Pettiford, and he meets, during this time, fellow jazz pianist Kenny Drew who is working currently in Buddy De Franco's combo. These two are soon friends and spend most of their spare time when not playing with their bands at an after-hours joint where they play piano constantly and swap anecdotes. The joint is open at all hours, so they invariably end up there, becoming, virtually, a mutual admiration society of just two members.

The playing of Drew and Clark is very similar; both have the same love of early and current be-bop and tend towards playing in what they both refer to as the New York City style. Drew informs Sonny that he is leaving the De Franco band to form his own trio and expands on the merits of Buddy's combo to his friend. De Franco has a full diary of gigs and there are rumours abroad of a forthcoming tour of America and Continental Europe. He gets plenty of recording opportunities also, always a plus factor. Kenny wonders if Sonny would be interested in joining De Franco because, if he is, he would be able to recommend him as his replacement. Sonny is keen on this offer, as he has heard that Pettiford is always on the move and likely to break up his current combo and recruit a new one or to travel east, or west, or north, for that matter.

Kenny Drew has told De Franco that he has the ideal replacement lined up for him. He and the bandleader go to the Black Hawk in San Francisco, and there, seated at the piano stool, is Sonny Clark, beaming a big smile and anxious to show just what he can do. He begins to play. De Franco listens carefully and soon has a similar smile on his face to match Sonny's.

Much later he will recall hearing Clark play for the first time. 'I loved him right away,' De Franco recalled. 'He was interesting and intelligent and played with a happy, skippy feel. When I heard Sonny, I knew instantly we were musically compatible in terms of what we were trying to do in modern jazz. Drummer Bobby White and bassist Gene Wright joined around this time too.' Asked what was so special about Clark, he replied, 'It's the give and take. I might be improvising a line and Sonny would come through with an idea. And in a split second, he'd embellish it. Everything happened fast but in harmony, it was so exciting.' De Franco tells his interviewer that you have to think a lot while practising but not while playing. 'The idea is to play fluently among three separate upper structure triads. And create and invent ideas while you are doing so. Sonny was doing the same thing. He was feeding me the basic chord structures and alternates at the same time. He would know in a split second which alternates I was working on at the time. You don't do this stuff deliberately. It comes naturally. I used to practice six hours a day to ensure that it did.'

De Franco and Clark get along very well on and off the bandstand. Buddy describes Sonny as a lot of fun. He is light-hearted and happy according to his employer. Sonny settles in for an extended period as Buddy's pianist; it is the first time he has felt settled and not itching to move on, to go faster and seek change and new challenges. Not for the present time anyway. Gigs are plentiful. So much so that Sonny is pleased when there is a blank night, and he can relax and drink with the band members and other cats. Occasionally though, he has visited the connection his friend supplied and bought heroin. It is when he is alone and homesick, wondering when he will see his brothers and sisters again, that he shoots up. Not on the bandstand or when they are really busy. It is the thrill and exhilaration of playing in Buddy's quartet, feeding the leader juicy chords and hearing him respond, that turns him on.

The band gets a four-week engagement in Hawaii. It is a great location. The weather is warm and sunny, and during the day, before the gig, the band goes down to Waikiki beach to swim, lie on the sand and generally relax, completely contented. Buddy becomes aware that Sonny has a young lady friend, and he spends a lot of leisure time with her. He does not say anything about her, and Sonny does not respond to questions, frequently moving a hundred yards along the beach where the two of them can be alone together.

Buddy smiles. What Sonny does in his private, leisure time is up to him and nobody else's business. When Sonny, alone, does join them one bright morning, he finds drummer Bobby White giving Buddy lessons on how to snorkel. Buddy is a complete amateur, but White tells him that if he gets into any difficulties the best thing is to lie on his back, take deep breaths and recover. It is good advice.

Buddy goes swimming out to practice his snorkelling as the two friends watch him. Suddenly, Buddy appears to lose control and starts flailing his arms about desperately, as though he is drowning. He has lost his snorkel in his panic and thrashes away in the water in sudden, blind terror. Bobby and Sonny stand up, look concerned and throw their arms up in an attempt to attract the lifeguard. He does not see them.

Somehow, despite his panic, Buddy remembers the advice and floats on his back and calms himself down with a deep breath. Soon he is able to recover and swim swiftly back to the beach. When Buddy was back safely on the beach, Sonny asks him what he was doing out there. Buddy tells him he thought he was drowning so he was floating and trying to collect his wits. 'You were collecting the hell out of your wits,' Sonny says, and they all laugh.

These are good times for Sonny Clark, in the clubs, in the recording studios at Capital Tower with the band, on good terms with his bandmates, and a girlfriend he is keeping very quiet about. Even better, the quartet is recruited to take part in a touring package called Jazz Club U.S.A. They have many towns and cities to play in and then they will tour continental Europe, just as Kenny Drew had predicted. The quartet plays in Cologne, Germany; Paris, France; Sweden and Norway. He gets to play every night of the strenuous tour with Buddy, and occasionally the leader gives him a solo spot. There are opportunities, enthusiastically seized, to play in support of Billie Holiday, to jam with Jimmy Raney. Sonny is in his element, happily seizing these chances and especially the chance, as it comes up, to play solo piano at jazz enthusiast Randi Hultin's house in Oslo, Norway. Then, at the Penguin Club at the Sinsen Restaurant in Oslo, he plays a trio concert with Bobby White on drums and a local bass player, Ivor Borsum. In Paris, he plays a set in a quartet setting with a strong lineup featuring guitarist Jimmy Raney, Red Mitchell on bass, and colleague White.

The concert in Cologne, Germany, is a highlight for Sonny. Buddy, anxious to shake off his more recent work with the Woody Herman Orchestra and show his commitment to the new music, plays a stunning solo on 'I'll Remember April,' played at a brisk up-tempo, the way almost all boppers approach it. This defector to bebop plays a series of blistering choruses and receives a wild burst of applause. Sonny keeps the momentum moving smoothly as he takes over the solo spot; Bobby White is driving hard behind him, and Wright keeps the bass line firm. At the conclusion, Buddy introduces the band, Sonny receiving a wild burst of applause with whistles and foot stomping. Then he sails into his own feature on 'Over the Rainbow.' Unaccompanied. He opens with a flourish of runs that indicate he is still, at this stage, influenced by Art Tatum's lightning runs up and down the keyboard. Then he slows down the line and produces some delicate, melodic lines delivered with skill and soulful expertise. It is a much varied, attention-grabbing solo excursion, pulling out all the stops to bring about another appreciative burst from the crowd. Buddy begins an up-tempo reading of Charlie Parker's blues, 'Now's the Time,' a staple in the band's repertoire. Sonny comps crisply and stimulatingly behind him. Sonny's solo takes to the fast tempo easily and shows again his gift for playing with ease and without any sign of strain. Fast blues are meat and drink to him. Wright opens the next selection with a bass solo, spurred on by a staccato note from Sonny. The bassist indulges in some sing-and-play bass work, his voice humming the notes loudly as he plays. Sonny spurs him on with percussive supporting lines. Clark's piano gradually becomes more prominent in support, and the group are swinging brightly without the leader. The bass feature finishes with a blues chorus from Wright and Sonny. De Franco takes a lightning-tempo run at 'Sweet Georgia Brown,' Sonny's solo gliding along effortlessly, even at breakneck speed. White gets a workout on drums. The drummer produces a thundering, long solo in keeping with the ambience now electric in the concert hall. The drum solo, though, becomes overlong and repetitive, the one negative aspect of this wild performance. The audience, fully wound up by now, loves it. Sonny Clark, well-featured and now known in Germany as a future jazz soloist well worth watching, enjoys every minute. He will remember this particular concert for a long time afterwards.

It is, for the most part, a thoroughly invigorating, hectic, enjoyable tour where he gets to see many towns and cities that were previously just names on a map to him. If he takes the occasional fix of heroin, he persuades himself that it is just to keep out the cold and feelings of depression on long bus trips from one location to the next, in inadequately heated vehicles. Or to calm his nerves just before going on stage, tired and weary but still ready to play up a storm. With three pianists on the tour including Billie Holiday's accompanist, Carl Drinkard, he could wish there had been more trio and solo opportunities, but on the other hand, he did get a few very welcome impromptu sessions in Paris and Oslo. And a crazy concert in Cologne. And much of the music has been recorded for posterity.

He recalls recording with Billie Holiday and the fact that he had to pinch himself to realise it was actually happening. Really? Sonny Clark recording with one of the greatest jazz singers of all time? Well, he did and there is a recording out there to prove it. Holiday comes from a much earlier jazz time, usually known as the swing era now, but Sonny is learning fast that the best jazz from all eras is valuable. Holiday has a jazz voice that transcends time and style.

Even so, he is very pleased when Leonard Feather, the tour organiser and jazz critic praises him for his playing throughout. It has not escaped Feather's notice that, although Booker and Drinkard had more playing time, it was Sonny that caught the attention of all the younger members of the audience everywhere they went. He is making a name for himself.

SONNY CLARK - FRAGILE VIRTUOSO

It is freezing cold in Europe, in January, and Sonny will be pleased to get back to Sunny California where winter weather is much less harsh.

1. Sonny Clark-Buddy De Franco - Mike Myers Blog.
2. Jazz Club U.S.A. tour.
3. Past Daily sound Archive 2015.

3

BACK TO CALIFORNIA: FURTHER ADVENTURES OF A TOXIC NATURE

THE SUN SHINES AND THE CLIMATE IS WARM ENOUGH IN APRIL. Sonny is still with Buddy's quartet and happy enough to be there. The gigs are still frequent and mostly in good, bright clubs. He records regularly with the bandleader. The rapport between De Franco and Clark is noticeable on all the recordings, and critics are starting to notice and comment on the duo. On a slow version of 'Deep Purple,' the two musicians link up so closely that it is more like a duet than a soloist supported by his pianist. Sonny does not solo on this piece, but his fills and melodic countermelodies mesh so well with Buddy's clarinet lines that the listener's ear is frequently drawn to the supporting piano player.

Buddy's recording of 'Now's the Time,' is a lightning, up-tempo reading, far faster than composer Charlie Parker ever played it. Sonny is right there with him, providing skipping, challenging additional melodies that Buddy picks up on instantly. Sonny's solo is a gem of free-flowing melodic invention before a brief spot by bassist Wright and the leader's return. Sonny smiles broadly. He knows well enough that it is all part of De Franco's stated intention of bringing the clarinet back into the fold of modern jazz. If bop has never seemed compatible with clarinet soloists, Buddy is waging a virtual one-man war to change that. He plays bop lines with the fluency of any trumpet or saxophone soloist. Few clarinet soloists, if any, could play 'Now's the Time' at this tempo and keep it alive with a bopper's invention.

Sonny is trying to keep his use of heroin down to manageable proportions, but he does increase his use on tour and when he has a long period without a gig. Not that there are many lapses in the diary. Sometimes, though, he does feel depressed on the road, when he is obliged to use the trade entrance to a location where they are playing or eat meals separately, usually in the company of Eugene Wright. It isn't easy for him, and his increase in heroin use is becoming a problem.

On most of the tour gigs, he goes down to breakfast and enjoys a meal and conversation with Buddy. Most of their talk is about music and the musicians they have found most inspirational. Charlie Parker is at the top of the list for both men. They talk about music long into the morning before going their separate ways during the day, prior to the gig in the evening. Buddy does not talk about addiction to hard drugs, but he is, of course, aware of Sonny's problem. If Buddy has learned one thing it is that there are two subjects never to be discussed with Sonny, heroin addiction and his lady friend. Their association is purely a musical one, and the clarinet man is keen to keep it that way. Less contentious. What Sonny does in his leisure time is his own business and his alone.

They continue to work closely together on gigs and tours to different parts of the country. On the road, Sonny meets musicians like Johnny Griffin in Chicago and, on one occasion, Charlie Parker, although he does not get to play with Bird. Parker does hear him play though and encourages him, advising him to keep on playing. Clark is encouraged considerably by this but is disconcerted by the number of older musicians he meets who advise him strongly to give up drugs before it is too late and he is hooked irrevocably.

He still feels he is not fully addicted and can stop whenever he wants to. But he needs to prove this to himself and take action. One night he has a fix of heroin prior to a gig in a place where black people are often given a bad time. He is very sick after the gig and feels unwell and groggy for two more days. He decides that the time has come for action. He seeks help from the medical centre and gets it. He is given alternative substances and advised on how to approach his withdrawal symptoms.

Sonny is alone at home. His woman has departed to visit family and he has no gigs coming up for three days. It is an opportunity, and he feels that it is now or never. He must beat the threatened addiction. It is easier said than done, however, and now he is feeling very sick from the medicine he has received from the medical centre. It was there that he received advice to rid himself of any heroin he had before going into isolation. He did not do this.

On impulse, he springs up out of his chair, grabs the package of heroin and runs to the bathroom. Before he can stop to think about it, he empties the contents into the toilet bowl and flushes it. There is no going back now. Sonny returns to his room, grabs his beer bottles and cigarettes, and prepares for a long, grim two days alone. It is the darkest time he has spent in his young life, and he is surprised at how addicted he appears to be. He drinks, he smokes, he shakes all over, eats practically nothing and sleeps long, through the night and late into the next morning. Just when he thinks he can't go on and will have to go out, shaking and unkempt, to find his connection, he notices a change. He wakes from a long night of tossing and turning, shaking and feeling sick. He notices a bright light at the window, gets up, draws the curtain back and welcomes sunlight into the room. It is mid-afternoon, and he has slept right through but now feels hungry. And he realises suddenly that he is no longer feeling sick or shaking.

It is a new beginning for Clark. Work has always gone well for him since his arrival from Pittsburgh getting on three years ago. For too long now, the shadow of addiction has haunted his days, and he has been forced to confront the truth and deal with it. Now he is clean and feeling fresh. He dresses swiftly and goes out into the street and breathes in fresh air. The sky and buildings all round him look slightly darker and less sharply defined, but he takes that as a good sign. Drugs like heroin tend to bring objects all around you into sharp, illuminated definition. He stops at a store, buys a sandwich and consumes it hungrily, out on the street. He enters a bar, buys a beer and sits at the counter drinking and smoking a cigarette. A musician he knows only slightly walks in and greets him. Sonny beams. Asked how he is doing he forgets or temporarily abandons his usual reserved reticence and tells the cat he is doing just great, thanks very much for asking. He has a good gig coming up and a record session. He is living with a woman now and has his own small place, and he intends to buy a dog. Good vibes all round. The musician congratulates him, tells him that he himself has been scuffling lately but has a gig in sight and is looking hopeful. Sonny buys the cat a drink, lights another cigarette and stays for three more beers.

The days, running into weeks, then months that follow are some of the best that he has known since arriving in California. Up to now, he has been lucky with employment but always with the nagging discomfort of drug use dragging him down. He makes a resolution, on the spot, never, ever to be tempted back onto heroin use. The way he feels at this moment, if Charlie Parker himself offered him a bag, he would politely refuse. He can survive on a stable home life, regular gigs and alcohol. In moderation, of course.

He has money, a home and work. The tours and gigs with Buddy were frantic but not as frantic as the Jazz Club U.S.A. package. The hectic schedule of cross-country trips and gigs left little time for relaxation and virtually none for spending money. What is he missing now that would make his life complete? Sonny decides to buy a car. Never a man to do things by halves, he settles on a brand new, very large Oldsmobile. Sonny is in raptures as he goes to collect his new vehicle. He drives around the wide streets of L.A. all day, missing his meals, and is almost late for his evening gig with De Franco.

Sonny enjoys driving round the various parts of Los Angeles and waving to the girls he sees in the streets. One particularly attractive black girl waves back. And he has taken to arriving at gigs and parking his car right in front of the club door, or as near as he can get. This annoys club owners and particularly those that show him no respect. Or worse.

He is frequently pulled over by the police when out driving. Who owns this car, why is he driving it, is he the chauffeur for some big shot? Sonny keeps all the paperwork in the dashboard recess and his driving licence handy and realises that, however belligerent the particular cop is, he will have to let him go on, sooner or later. It annoys him though, makes him increasingly angry that he keeps being pulled over when he is doing nothing wrong and driving around in his own car.

On the second occasion that Clark meets bassist Jerry Good, the two men go to a familiar bar and settle down with beers. Good tells him he is looking fit and well and Sonny smiles. Everything is going so well that he can hardly believe it. He actually tells the bassist that he has a wife now and a new car and the gigs and record dates are flying in. He has recorded five times as Buddy De Franco's pianist, the last date as recently as September 1954. The first one back in '53 was a shouting big band which swung like hell, he recalls, although he adds ruefully that there wasn't much solo room to spare. Sonny still cannot believe Good's assertion that he can get him a night at the Mocambo club in Oakland, playing with him and his drummer pal. What an opportunity, Sonny thinks, if it does come off. Jerry Good is telling him about his previous gig with Al Randall where they were the rhythm section in the house band at a club called Jimbo's Bop City in San Francisco. 'Seven nights a week from 2AM to 6AM with no intermission,' Good tells him. 'All for just 5 dollars.'

Sonny nods, understanding because he has been in similar situations. 'We paid our dues there alright,' Good continues. 'Still, we did get to play behind Charlie Parker and Clifford Brown, so that was great.' The two musicians continue drinking, smoking, and talking music, and Sonny tells Good that he will understand if the proposed night at the Mocambo club does not happen. Good assures him that it will. The pianist on the gig, John Marabuto is a real nice guy, and he is sure he will agree to the arrangement.

When it actually does happen, nobody is more surprised than Sonny, and it is one of the most enjoyable gigs he has played, albeit low-key. He appears to be walking on air for days afterwards.

More good times follow. He will record on two further occasions in 1955 with the De Franco band. When he meets up again with Good in San Francisco, he asks the bass player if he can listen to the tape that they made at the Mocambo. Good takes him to his pad and the two musicians listen carefully to the tape, both nodding approvingly and tapping their feet. Clark speculates ruefully again on whether or not the tape will eventually be released as a commercial recording. Good shakes his head sadly. It isn't at all likely, he feels. Sonny nods and agrees. He says that he has done other quartet sessions which he believes were recorded but only privately by the people he was with and are even more unlikely to be commercially released.

Sonny has met up once again with Good and he introduces him to his good friend, a young alto saxophonist named Jerry Dodgion. This man turns out to be another admirer of Sonny Clark, someone who always goes to hear him play when the De Franco group is playing locally. He even goes into Los Angeles for a chance to hear the band. Sonny is flattered and asks Dodgion to keep in touch. Maybe there will be a chance to play together later.

Meantime, Sonny is busy with gigs, and when he has spare time, day or night, he frequents the after-hours joints and jams with Kenny Drew and other musicians he has met and come to know. Drew also wants to keep in touch, and he would like the opportunity to play with Sonny if the chance ever arises. Sonny grins. It could be done, he thinks. One of them playing piano and the other vibes. Why not? Good idea. Both musicians are competent on vibes and Sonny can add bass, organ, guitar and other instruments he managed to practice on back during school band days or those left around the house by his brother.

In June 1955, Clark receives an invitation to play on a Cal Tjader record session. It is amusingly titled *Tjader Plays Tjazz*. Sonny arrives on time, has a brief discussion with the leader, a run-through of a couple of selections, and then contributes his usual flowing contributions to the date. They play 'Moten Swing,' a familiar enough piece to the pianist and then one of his favourite standards,' There Will Never Be Another You.' This is followed by two recordings within the space of a month with Buddy De Franco's combo. He is invited by the leader to play Hammond organ on some selections and finds that he takes easily to the instrument although, as usual, his best and most inventive solo work is on the piano.

Work is positively overflowing. He receives an invitation to go to San Francisco, a place close by that he is more than familiar with due to his friendship with Jerry Good. This time it is from Jerry Dodgion, the young alto sax player he met there a short time ago. Jerry has a record date lined up and has remembered the conversation with Sonny. This is for part of a compilation album titled *Modern Music From San Francisco*, and he plays piano in the section alongside old friend Gene Wright, currently his colleague in the De Franco unit. Lawrence Marable is the drummer, whom he also knows. Clark makes blues-fuelled contributions to two originals named 'Miss Jackie's Dish' and 'The Groove.'

Finally, after an unusually intense period of work, recording and playing endlessly after hours in the joints that musicians frequent, it is quiet, for two or three days at least. Sonny heads home and falls into bed, exhausted.

It is dead of night, pitch black as he lies deep in sleep, when the bedroom is suddenly plunged into bright light. He wakes slowly, disturbed out of deep unconsciousness by strange sounds. He becomes slowly, agonizingly aware that he is no longer alone. His wife is kneeling on the bed in front of him, her face flushed and contorted with rage, and she is holding a knife to his throat. He cries out, a jumbled inarticulate sound, and she screams out to him not to move a muscle. He feels the icy cold tip of the knife just touching the skin of his throat. His terror shows in his widening eyes, and he is struck dumb with horror. He hears her voice, choking with rage, saying that she fully intended to kill him and would have done if the thought of the electric chair had not frightened her into pausing. Shaking, perspiring and still not fully conscious, he dares not move, but suddenly she pulls back the knife, tears streaming down her face, and is gone from the room, slamming the door behind her.

Confused, frightened and still shaking, he stumbles out of bed and dresses hurriedly. He will go, hurrying through the small hours of the night to a friend, a musician and junkie who he feels sure will take him in and get him a quick fix. He half walks, half runs into the night. The streets are mostly deserted. He is unaware of the time but guesses it to be around two or three in the morning. A solitary truck rumbles by, destined no doubt for some distant, early morning delivery.

The place where Sonny locates his friend is a large, dilapidated building, rough and none too clean. It is the refuge of several prostitutes, addicts and otherwise homeless people, but the dishevelled pianist is welcomed in by his friend who wonders, loudly, what has happened to Sonny. He is given the bare bones of the story as he prepares a fresh injector with heroin and hands it to the eager Clark. Once the drug starts to course through his veins and take effect, he can at last calm down a little and stop his body shaking.

He slowly, painfully, goes through the detail of the ordeal he has just been through with his pal. When he finishes, he is growing calmer by the minute as the drug takes full effect, and he finds himself wondering how what has just happened came about. He acknowledges the bad relations he had with his woman, to himself; the fierce, bitter arguments and unresolvable disagreements, the threats and counter threats and his tendency to stay out all night at after-hours joints frequently. But did he ever do anything to deserve his recent violent treatment? He does not think so.

It was necessary, he feels, to tell his friend exactly what happened and explain why he was in urgent need of a friend all at once and shelter for the night. He also felt the need of a quick fix of heroin, much faster than he could have obtained it from his old connection. Well, it is done now and over. He resolves that he will never, ever, under any circumstances, refer to or speak of this episode in his life again.

Buddy De Franco-Sonny Clark Part 1. Jazz Wax. Marc Myers.2010.
Sonny Clark, *Oakland 1955* - Bob Blumenthal's sleeve note.

4

WEST COAST BLUES (1)

BUDDY DE FRANCO'S CLARINET TRACES THE MELODY LINE OF THE standard song 'A Foggy Day.' Almost in partnership with the leader, Sonny Clark's sweet, melodic counter-line is heard. As Buddy moves into a boppish improvisation on the tune, the piano lines sing out, flowing easily and with no sign of strain. As Sonny moves into his solo the music moves along with such undiminished freedom and ease of expression that De Franco looks over at him and shakes his head, smiling. Then the clarinet player takes it out. As they finish playing, Sonny raises his hands and flicks his fingers up and down for a minute, reinstating flexibility again. Buddy calls 'I Should Lose You' and begins stating the melody. Once again, he is soon into a bop improvisation and those nourishing but gentle chords and occasional counter-melodies behind him from the piano encourage him to extend his solo run. Bass and drums supply steady rhythmic support although the pianist is swinging so powerfully and easily that they could lay out and the music would still have that wonderful, pulsating groove.

They relax for a minute or two and Sonny lights up a cigarette. De Franco smiles and says he was more than happy with that, and it was better than the version they put down on their recording. They take a relaxed run-through of 'Deep Purple,' the leader playing slowly and concentrating on enhancing the melody. As on their recording, they play it through with no piano solo, but Clark's close alliance with the clarinet player makes him almost a second soloist or duet player. Sonny hears De Franco say that will do for now. If they play it like that tonight on the gig, it will be fine. Sonny frowns and asks if they can try it one more time. De Franco nods and begins playing but notices that the pianist's supporting counterpoint is totally different. Just as fresh and free-moving but with new melodies and supporting interjections.

De Franco says that, on reflection, they should try playing it just like that on the gig. Sonny shakes his head and tells him that he will play a whole new set of variations tonight. Buddy looks over at him and shakes his head again, but the pianist is already running through a solo piano reading of 'Cooking the Blues,' another staple of their live concert performances currently.

They break up the impromptu rehearsal then and each man goes his separate way. Sonny traces the Charlie Parker blues line from 'Going to Chicago' in his own unique way, deep blue in flavour, his notes rich and warm, and then launches into his own slow, explorative investigation of the blues. He played something very similar on the band's Verve recording of 'Cooking the Blues,' but this time he is much more explorative, running through blues licks in slow tempo producing a ripe, full tone. He goes on playing until he has pretty much exhausted any more variations and stops, abruptly, in mid-chorus.

This is the time he dreads most. While his colleagues go about their business and pursue personal or family interests, he feels out on a limb, unsure how he will get through the next few hours. He decides to go to a bar, his usual choice of venue when not playing or when there is not a good after-hours joint around. Recent events are still so raw and painful that, in spite of his frequent attempts to shut out all memories that intrude, it is only the heroin or alcohol that can assist.

He buys a beer and lights a cigarette, feeling low now that the rehearsal is dead and gone and he is alone. He feels weary and hopeless and thinks he might have another beer but decides against it because he must be fresh for tonight's performance and too much alcohol can have a detrimental effect on his piano playing. And he lives for his piano playing. No, it is no use, another fix is the only way to steady his nerves and calm him down. He has gradually but very slowly increased his intake of heroin but only to the point where he knows he can still play without his music suffering. It is two hours away from his next fix, but he decides to have another one early. He needs it today. He walks out of the bar and seeks a quiet spot where there is nobody else around. He will shoot up and feel just a little, better.

Some days are better than others, perhaps inevitably so. When he meets up with Jerry Dodgion or Jerry Good and they discuss enjoyable, past musical times, he comes alive and talkative. Provided that neither of them intrudes on his grief and asks the wrong questions. Then, if that happens, he shuts down and becomes almost inarticulate. An after-hours joint is often the place for light relief, and if he meets up with old friends like Kenny Drew, so much the better. Their competitive but friendly rivalry always brings out the considerable best in his playing. The last time he saw Drew, he told him that there was the chance of them playing together in a concert critic Leonard Feather was organising that would also be recorded.

The recording session is on. Kenny Drew is a bit vague about it at first, but when Sonny presses him, he admits that it is a bit odd. Something different. A new attachment to an instrument he has heard on the grapevine but has no further details. Feather has assembled a band called 'Leonard Feather's West Coast Jazzmen' with a subtitle, 'Swinging on The Vibories.' Vibories? Neither Clark nor Drew is any the wiser.

Drew and Clark arrive at the studio within a few minutes of each other. Feather explains that the vibories consist of a small, three-octave keyboard attachment that is connected to a box that sits on top of the vibes. The box, Feather tells them, contains small cylindrical solenoids, one to each note, to which are attached small Bakelite mallets with cork tips. He tells the musicians that they were invented by someone called Jack Harris, and Feather himself named them. Clark and Drew frown and look doubtful. Feather would like them to play the instrument on the recording.

Sonny Clark raises his eyebrows. He likes Feather, the man who signed him up for the Jazz Club U.S.A. tour and praised him as being the most popular pianist on the three-piano-player tour. Also, he got to travel round European cities, which he could never have done alone. If Leonard wants him to play the vibes with this peculiar attachment, he will give it a go. Drew takes a bit more persuading, but he too agrees, finally.

Drew takes two solo spots, playing vibories while Sonny plays piano. Red Mitchell is on bass and Lawrence Marable is at the drums and the music swings along well enough. Sonny switches to the odd attachment instrument as Kenny plays piano. Clark gets a good groove going on 'Bluesology' and then the standard 'Body and Soul.' Once again, the music swings lightly along without anything special happening. At the conclusion, the verdict of most of the musicians is that it is a strange, metallic and rather hollow sound and not one that excites any of them, least of all Sonny. One musician says that he thinks it unlikely they will ever see that monstrosity in a recording studio again or, for that matter, in a club.

Leonard Feather is somewhat miffed, but he takes the trouble to chat amiably with Sonny and wish him the best of luck on future assignments. Sonny knows that Feather is a musician and composer and, indeed, has played piano on this session, but he thinks of him primarily as a writer and critic, a contributor to *Downbeat* and other magazines and an annotator of record sleeve notes. It will be more than a year before they meet again.

Sonny decides that, in future, he will only play straight-ahead jazz, straight-ahead bop and on straight-ahead instruments. He may play the organ occasionally, as he has at Buddy's request, but he accepts electric organ as a legitimate instrument in jazz. After all, Count Basie and, before him, Fats Waller played it and if it was good enough for them, it is good enough for him. It has been a nagging doubt in his mind for some time now that, here on the West Coast, they dumb the music down, dilute it somewhat. Ideally, he wants to play full-strength, red-blooded bebop every night. Every gig indeed.

That can't be done yet, and the only answer is for him to go to New York City. It is where he longs to be but resolves that the time is not yet right. When the unthinkable, unbelievable happened, he had to sell his precious car. That still hurts, but at the time he needed money, a lot of It, for getting a place to stay, everyday expenses and, most of all, to pay for the big increase in heroin usage. Well, alright, he is using a considerable amount now, depending on it to get him from day to day. But that can change. He has shaken off heroin addiction before and he can do it again. He knows he can. A little assistance from the medical centre and his own iron-willed determination. There are days when he just wants to curl up in a ball and give up because he has had enough, but not today. On this day he is ready to fight.

Serge Chaloff, the great baritone sax stylist, is in town. He has battled considerable bad health and fierce, debilitating heroin addiction in the not-too-distant past and is now making a comeback. He has secured a two-week engagement at Jazz City, a popular club, and is playing alongside Sonny Stitt. Kenny Drew is on piano. Leroy Vinnegar is the bassist and Lawrence Marable is on drums. On a few nights, Sonny sits in for Kenny on piano. He notices that Chaloff is listening carefully to his solo lines, snapping his fingers in time with the music, glancing across to the piano frequently. Serge has a record date at Capitol Studios shortly and he wants to get the best rhythm section possible. He knows that Philly Joe Jones will be in town shortly with the Miles Davis Quintet and is determined to grab him. Philly is Chaloff's favourite drummer. Next, he wants to secure the very best pianist and bass player available.

Sonny knows this record date is important. It is a recording that he is very much looking forward to. Serge Chaloff has chosen him as his pianist. He will be playing in the studio alongside Leroy Vinnegar on bass and Philly Joe Jones on drums. He has recently worked with Leroy and knows that he is now considered to be one of the top two or three jazz bassists to be found anywhere. Philly Joe, he has admired from a distance, loving his playing on records with the new Miles Davis Quintet and giving the kind of rhythmic support that he feels sure will be compatible with his own piano work. Philly Joe plays in that forceful, red-blooded bebop manner that is Sonny's ideal. So maybe this will be a more restrained West Coast date. He does not know what tunes will be called because Chaloff has indicated that he wants the session to be completely spontaneous, like a club date maybe? It will probably be standards, and Sonny is happy with standards, any-time, anywhere.

In the studio, Sonny learns that they will be playing material that neither he nor the other musicians have played much before. Standards though. All except 'Susie's Blues,' of course, which is Serge's own line and dedicated to the young woman who has helped him with his career and arranged bookings for him. Susie is there, in the studio. She has travelled a long way to be with Chaloff and lend help and moral support. Chaloff points out to the others one other exception. He wants to play 'The Goof and I,' a composition by his old colleague in the Woody Herman Orchestra, Al Cohn. He recorded it with Herman and wants to do it again.

Sonny smiles. He is happy enough with any set up at recording sessions because he is confident in his own ability. But this promises to be something else, a challenge really, and he likes musical challenges. It is mid-afternoon on a fairly dull California day. The producer appears to sense that the musicians are a little stiff, one or two of them more tense than others. There has been no rehearsal and the material will be, for the most part, unfamiliar. He tells them that he is going to dim the studio lights right down and try to create the atmosphere of a club. The musician's ambiance. It works well. Serge will call the tunes as they go through the session and they will go in cold, like a club date.

Serge calls 'A Handful Of Stars' as the opening track. He plays with light and shade, much attention to dynamics. Soft at first, then upping the volume, a little vibrato. Sonny and the bass and drums cruise in gently behind him; maybe this is a bit more West Coast in style than Sonny would prefer, but he is always adaptable, always ready to fit his flowing accompaniment to the leader's requirements. As indeed are Vinnegar and Philly. These are top bop professionals, players that Sonny has had all too little chance to play with up to now. He is quite content.

There is a lightness all round on the first selection, but after that, they all settle down and start blowing vigorously. 'The Goof and I' is a fast blues. Up tempo all the way. This is Sonny's music, and he digs in happily. Serge rides the fast tempo with ease with Sonny setting the rhythm section pace and adding little fills and additional melodies. His solo on piano glitters and gleams. Leroy and Philly also get short workouts here. They take the tempo down a notch for 'Susie's Blues,' but it is still up. Gliding along both Chaloff and Sonny are particularly inventive and melodic. Clark looks up after his spot, keeps the rhythmic flow going sturdily and notes the contented smile on Susie's face. This is her song and they have given her a smooth, pulsating reading. 'Thanks For the Memory,' by contrast, is played very slowly. Serge is all soft, breathy lyricism, and Sonny's piano solo spills out little jewels of glittering notes. Another ballad, 'Stairway To the Stars,' glides slowly along in similar fashion. Even before it is over, Sonny knows that this is a highly successful recording, and everything has gone exactly according to Serge Chaloff's plan. This is what Sonny wants, and he wants more of it, he reflects, glancing over to the drum kit and Philly Joe driving the set along.

They begin to play 'How About You' at a comfortable medium tempo where Clark plays one of his most consistently inventive and relaxed solos of the afternoon. Unfortunately, this piece does not appear on the resulting *Blue Serge* LP but will have to wait for a *Mosaic* collection of all Serge's leader dates in 1993. The recording session comes to an end. They all listen intently to the playback, and many heads nod approvingly. Chaloff thanks all the sidemen for their efforts. He tells them he is very happy with the results and thinks this will be one of his best, if not the best of his entire career. Sonny looks up from the keyboard and catches Philly's eye. They grin at each other. Maybe it would be good to get together with Philly, hang out somewhere and get high, ask a few questions about the New York scene that he would like so much to join.

It is with musicians like Philly Joe that Sonny would like to hang out, play clubs and record with. Along with all the other great New York City musicians he has listened to carefully, on the radio and the records he has heard. He wants to link up with the likes of Philly and bassist Paul Chambers. He has listened and been knocked out by the close rhythmic integration those two achieve along with pianist Red Garland. Or the wonderful combination of pianist Horace Silver with bassist Doug Watkins and Art Blakey on drums. These sounds are Clark's idea of how the music of Charlie Parker is being absorbed, integrated and expanded to what some are starting to call hard bop. He has been listening to it endlessly on radio and records ever since he was a small boy, fast becoming a boy wonder at the piano himself. So far, he has not had an opportunity to play with musicians like these, the ones he admires and feels in tune with.

This just completed session with Chaloff came pretty close, and at least one of his heroes was on the date. If only he could find an opportunity to get to New York and get started himself. Several musicians have told him of their experience in that city, the difficulties, how hard it is to break in and become accepted. The frightening number of musicians trying to get started and failing.

It does not deter him. He has enough faith in his own ability and knows that the constant work he gets in L.A. and San Francisco, along with occasional tours, means that he is gaining considerable, valuable experience and he is improving all the time. He decides that he will continue seeking work in the area for the next few months and maybe, just maybe, he will find a way and the courage to get himself to NYC and the action there.

1. Leonard Feather's West Coast Jazzmen—*Swinging on the Vibories*, ABC Paramount ABC-110
2. *The Complete Serge Chaloff Sessions*. Mosaic Booklet notes by Vladimir Simosko.
3. *Blue Serge* - Capitol T-742.

5

WEST COAST BLUES (2)

THERE IS NOTHING SPECIAL OR EVEN DIFFERENT ABOUT SONNY'S LAST gig with Buddy De Franco. They play together with the same intuitive integration and, as always, both musicians find new melodies and variations on the compositions they have been playing for the past two and a half years. The audience does not know that the band is breaking up because no announcement has been made. Nor will be. The music flows, reaches high points and is received enthusiastically by the audience. When Sonny asks Buddy after the concert why he is breaking up the band, he is told that it has just reached a natural ending. It is time to move onto new concepts and to play with fresh musicians. He is seeking new paths to follow, and it will be good for him to do the same. Clark can find no reason to argue with this, it sounds logical.

It is time to find a new band that will offer him full employment. He needs that to feed his drug habit, which is fast becoming acute. He shoots up heroin regularly. Occasionally, when he is feeling particularly low, he takes more than he should, which constitutes a mild overdose. Fortunately, his youth and healthy body mean that he can adjust to it, along with increased doses which come with bouts of severe depression. He is twenty-five years old now and able to absorb the drug into his system even if it means that he feels low and groggy for some time when the effects of the heroin wear off.

Meeting up with trombonist Frank Rosolino one day, he hears that the man has a record date coming up, and he offers the piano chair to Sonny. The offer is accepted immediately; Sonny likes Rosolino's style of playing, which is robust and not in keeping with most of the light-weight playing to be heard on the West Coast. Rosolino has chosen him because he has heard him on records and is an admirer of Clark's work.

In the studio, Clark sits at the piano stool feeling good. His mood always lightens as soon as he sits down to play and increases throughout the recording session. Assembled are Frank, blowing a few notes in preparation, Wilfred Middlebrooks on bass, and Stan Levey at the drums. He doesn't know the bassist, but he has played with Levey before and rates him as one of the best drummers in California. No problem. He is remembering that Levey was the drummer when Charlie Parker came west a few years ago for a resident stay at Billy Berg's Club, along with Dizzy Gillespie. Sonny is thinking about Parker, a great influence on him and regretting his sudden death at the age of thirty-four. He is thinking that alto sax and tenor players will have to work out their lines now and not rely on copying Bird. Rosolino calls the first selection. Sonny is alert.

Playing 'The Things We Did Last Summer' goes down well. It is a good standard tune and one he likes. Rosolino plays the melody, his trombone muted. Sonny keeps to the melody on his solo, embellishing it and adding a few runs up and down the keyboard. His relaxed approach helps the piece to flow along easily with no sign of strain.

'Doxy' is a blues by the new, highly-rated tenor saxophonist Sonny Rollins. It is a composition he has heard, and he introduces it at the piano with bright, juicy chords. Rosolino twists and turns in his solo playing with plenty of fire and demonstrating his considerable facility on his instrument. Stan Levey comes in next with a well-measured drum solo before Sonny begins. His lines skip along with ease, a natural swing building up. His variations enhance the basic melody, and he slips in a quote from 'Pop Goes the Weasel.' As Frank takes it out, Sonny is spurring him on with fills and counter melodies as Middlebrooks and Levey drive the quartet forward.

They play 'I May Be Wrong' and a lively 'Flamingo,' and the session ends with everybody happy with the music that has been captured. In conversation with the boys in the band afterwards, somebody mentions The Lighthouse at Hermosa Beach and Rosolino tells them it is a very good gig, long-lasting if they like you and the Lighthouse Café is right there, just a few steps from the beach. It's a great place to play, particularly in the summer. Sonny takes this all in and resolves to approach the bandleader, bass player Howard Rumsey, who runs all the sessions there.

Meantime, he has to go out into the sunshine and make his way back to the lodging where he is staying. He has no gig on this evening and it will be a long night ahead. He will make his way to a bar first and have a couple of beers and try not to take any more of the drug. As he sits, drinking slowly and smoking a cigarette, he resolves to make one more, positive effort to get off heroin and become clean again. He will need to get as much help as he can from the medical centre and hope that the medicine, they prescribe does not drag him down into despair even worse than when heroin addiction wears off. He has known that to happen in the past. It is a daunting prospect, but it is something he knows he must address if he is to move forward. Both his music and his life may be at stake.

Sonny makes a telephone call to The Lighthouse at Hermosa Beach and asks to speak to the manager, Howard Rumsey. The man has heard of Clark but can't recall hearing him play. He invites Sonny to come out to the Lighthouse on a weekday afternoon when things are usually quieter. Clark remembers vaguely a gig he did at the lighthouse in '53 with Art Pepper's combo, but he was driven out and back after dark and can't recall much about it. Sonny makes the journey out there and has a look around. It certainly looks like a good place to be in and to play music. He walks down towards the beach and notes the soft yellow sands stretching out as far as the eye can see. With a blue sky overhead, the colour is reflected in the sea, lapping gently at the shore. This reminds him of a gig with Buddy De Franco in Hawaii where they played every night and spent mornings on the beach. An enjoyable gig indeed.

He wanders around as he is early, passes the avenues of smart houses, the palm trees, goes down towards the long, narrow pier and walks back past the Ocean Aquarium. Everything he sees, he likes. The Lighthouse storefront is unassuming apart from a sign above it that is advertising jazz every night. And it is, as he has been told, just a short walk from the beach. He walks into the building and finds himself in a long, well-fitted room with a bar at the right, a considerable number of small round tables with chairs and a small bandstand. Above him are oblong light panels. Light, clean and bright.

Rumsey greets him and gives him a bottle of beer. He tells Sonny he came to the place in 1949 when it was run down and the owner, John Levine, was struggling. Patrons were mostly older men, longshoremen and other dock workers and fishermen. They liked to drink and were quite rowdy. They liked the older songs played in the old style but took little notice of it anyway. He was not making any money. Rumsey says that he made him an offer to start Sunday jazz sessions that lasted most of the afternoon and evening. He was warned that Sunday was the worst day for alcohol sales, but Rumsey asked him what did he have to lose? Levine told him to go ahead, and the jazz sessions now covered every day and Sundays from 2pm often running until 2am. He became manager of the club and played bass in the various lineups that appeared.

Sonny is impressed and likes the sound of this setup. He says so. Rumsey says he understands that he is a modern jazz pianist, and he is always on the lookout for really good ones. His idea was always to bring more young people in, college kids and young people from all over the area who want more modern sounds. Many of the musicians that play here, Rumsey continues, are from the Stan Kenton Orchestra, People like Bob Cooper, Shorty Rogers, Frank Rosolino and Stan Levey. 'This place is becoming known as the home of West Coast Jazz,' Rumsey says proudly. 'It is a modern sound,' he continues, 'light and melodic, cool, and the patrons love it.'

Sonny experiences his first doubt. He is no great lover of cool sounds in jazz but knows that they are playing bop and he must not be too particular. He is living in California, after all, and needs to play the music of the area if he is to survive. Then again, he reflects, the music of L. A. is mainly white folks' music. The people Rumsey mentioned along with Stu Williamson and Shelly Manne. Stan Levey too. He has heard Levey talk about Lighthouse gigs although he likes the drummer's style and the way he drives a combo. And Levey played with Charlie Parker, so if he was good enough for Bird, he is good enough for Sonny Clark.

On reflection, taking in everything he has just been told and everything he has heard about this place, he would love to play here. Rumsey tells him there are plenty of gigs available. All year round.

Rumsey invites him to play the piano on the stand and let him hear how he sounds. He can rustle up a bass player and drummer fairly swiftly if that would help. No, Sonny is quite happy to play solo. In fact, it is one of his favourite setups. He sits at the piano stool and plays a slow blues, fashioning it to his own way of playing, adding his own snippets of melody. Then he plays a standard.

Rumsey beams. He tells Sonny that there will be plenty of gigs if he wants them. He wants them.

Sonny makes an effort, as he did before, to get free of heroin.

He visits the medical centre and is counselled and given drug substitutes. He is told that he will get every help and available medicines but, ultimately, only he can give up taking drugs permanently. He is in agreement with what they say, he tells them he is determined this time; he has taken his last hard drug. He will take whatever they give him but will not attempt cold turkey at home. He suffered enough last time when he withdrew at home and knows that his addiction is far more advanced this time.

He is on his way to the Master Recorders Studios in Los Angeles. He has been chosen for the piano parts on a new recording by alto saxophonist Sonny Criss. On arrival, he meets Criss and is told that the saxophonist has heard him play and thought he would be right for his session. Sonny nods, talks briefly about the music to be played and prepares to play. He does not know what to make of Criss. The man seems arrogant to him, at first, but after further discussion decides that he is vulnerable as he talks about the amount of music he has played and recorded and feels he is still unknown, still underrated and badly treated by everyone. Criss rants on about the jazz community and everybody else for that matter, ignoring him. Sonny has heard of him but admits he has not heard him live or even on records. Criss tells him irritably that he has played all over Los Angeles, worked at the Lighthouse, and wonders if there is a conspiracy against him amongst record companies and the jazz community at large. He has, he tells Sonny, worked with Charlie Parker. In Texas, he stood on stage and blew saxophone with Bird and that little white cat, Chet Baker, on trumpet. Bird appreciated him. Clark is impressed and slightly envious. He wishes he had played with Parker in a small combo.

Today is different. He has been given a record date by Imperial Records, a company that are best known for pop and R&B discs. He calls 'Summertime,' and Sonny Clark plays a bright, melodic introduction on piano. Criss states the theme on alto and goes into a series of improvisations on it that are comprehensive to say the least. Clark hears a fat, billowing tone on alto that is striking, becomes rather shrill at times he thinks but effective. The saxophonist is close to Parker but has his own approach and uses vibrato. He seems to Sonny to be trying to fit far more notes in than he can possibly manage. He appears impatient. He slows down on 'Memories Of You' and Clark responds by supplying a rhapsodic, free-wheeling piano solo and then shadowing the leader with brisk chords. The quartet are working well enough with Leroy Vinnegar's big bass sound and Lawrence Marable stoking the fires on the drums. This is a bop session, and Clark hears that Criss is a bopper and not a typical West Coast-style player. For that alone he can forgive him any eccentricity, moodiness or whatever. He will provide the best piano accompaniment he can, as always, even if he gets the impression, as the session proceeds, that Criss is only interested in projecting himself out front and regards the rhythm section as merely an unimportant support unit.

Sonny traces a short, delicate piano introduction to 'The Blues For Rose,' and Criss seizes the theme and appears to be trying to squeeze more notes than are possible into his chorus. As Clark prepares to take his solo, the alto blasts forth again with another chorus. Then he takes his solo, gentle, melodic and in complete contrast to the frantic alto sax lines. As the recording session progresses, the pianist realizes that this is Criss's style, his way of playing, and it is up to him to adapt to it and give it his best whatever. At the conclusion, he feels that it is a good set overall, nothing special but a well-played recording.

At the conclusion, they have recorded enough material for an LP. He does not know the record company's plans but receives a call just short of three weeks later to return to the studio. The same musicians are on hand with the addition of Larry Bunker on vibes and Criss tells him that Imperial are going to put out two albums. Sonny thinks that will feed the alto player's ego a little, and he smiles as he sits at the piano stool to begin the next recording.

A month later, he goes to the Radio Recorders studio for a further album with Sonny Criss. This is to be a programme of music by Cole Porter, and he loves this composer's music. If the other two records were good, this one is something else. Sonny loves it from the first note to the last. If Criss was wild and frantic on the other discs he is measured and in full command on this one. Larry Bunker's relaxed, swinging vibes, Criss sounding more laid back himself, these factors help to put Sonny in a great mood for this album. 'In the Still of the Night' pulses along crisply. Criss is cool stating the melody then takes a complex bop solo that moves confidently forward. Sonny follows him on piano, swinging lightly and obviously enjoying himself. 'Love For Sale' is taken slowly, everybody relaxed and producing inventive solos. Sonny notes that there is nothing frantic in the leader's alto on this session. Bunker is prominent on 'Night and Day.' Criss is fully engaged but sounding in control and not rushing to get more notes in. Sonny comps smoothly and adds substance to the harmony. Criss is melodic and probing on 'Anything Goes,' his lines warm and fresh. Bunker follows with a short burst and then Clark solos briefly on piano. 'Easy to Love' receives a lush ballad treatment from the three front liners. The easy tempo is enriched by Sonny, and his solo is bright and slightly percussive, perhaps for variety. 'It's Alright with Me' gets a tear-up, fast tempo, Criss and Bunker lighting the fire initially. Sonny takes the first solo after the leader, happy and cruising with the up tempo. As the recording session winds down to conclusion, everybody looks content. After the playback, the smiles are broad, all around. The pianist chalks it up in his mind as one of his best record dates ever. Second only to the Serge Chaloff date that is his number one. Then he thinks, perversely, that it was, after all, just another recording and no big deal. When the LP is released, there is no mention of the pianist's name on the jacket or anyone else other than the leader.

He is congratulated on his performance by the studio manager and two quite young jazz fans. Both praise his work in the section and his solos. One young man tells him he loves to listen to him playing the blues. He has his own special blues sound tinged with melancholy and on some pieces, he hears deep sadness. Sonny is not aware of this. He mulls it over in his mind as he leaves the studio. He stops at a bar and has three beers and the same number of cigarettes. He has shaken off the heroin addiction once again, helped considerably by the medical centre people, and surprised himself with the success of his own determination. He has done it somehow; he does not really understand how. He has doubled his intake of beer and cigarettes. He determines in his mind to cut right down on alcohol, gradually though, having a little less each week. The cigarettes he does not regard as a problem although a cat at a gig recently told him they are just as addictive as heroin. Can that be true; he doesn't think so. In any event, he will try and cut down on tobacco too and get clean. If he becomes depressed, he will play his way out of it at gigs and recording sessions. He can do that. He knows he always feels great as soon as he sits at the piano stool. And he loves the gigs at the Lighthouse. Some days he arrives early, having been given a lift in a musician's car, and spends time down on the beach with just one bottle of beer and a packet of cigarettes.

Sonny is backing a particularly complex solo by Frank Rosolino. The trombonist has been playing variations of a popular song, 'When Sunny Gets Blue,' and the audience, hardcore jazz enthusiasts all, judging by their rapt attention, are enjoying it. The pianist feeds gently propulsive chords to him all through, varying the dynamics carefully to produce, along with Rosolino, a magical performance of a standard popular song. Some nights are like that in jazz. A soloist suddenly takes off, producing fresh lines on old material and once he is flying, his inspiration rubs off on the rest of the band and they tighten up the rhythm behind him. A performance to remember. This is such a night where the band is on fire and Sonny will remember it for long after the event.

Buddy De Franco has left a message for him. He has a record date coming up and he would like Sonny on piano. He meets Buddy at a hotel the clarinet man designates, and he is told about the recording. 'It's not just my gig,' Buddy tells him. 'It's Russ Garcia's orchestra and he wants me and Don Fagerquist on trumpet as main soloists. Don's a great trumpet man, so it should go well. But I want you on piano.'

The session is going well for Sonny, in so much as a commercial-sounding recording goes well. Buddy is featured along with Fagerquist and Howard Roberts on guitar. Standards are played such as 'Autumn In New York,' 'Come Rain Or Come Shine,' and 'Makin' Whoopee.' OK, so there is jazz content here, but somehow it is not quite the type of sounds Sonny is happiest with. It is great to see Buddy again though. He may be a different colour and culture, but the two of them know that jazz has no colour bar. They have always jelled splendidly in music and that is for sure.

When they get talking, after the gig Buddy asks Sonny how things are going. The pianist says that all is well, he is getting plenty of gigs and recording dates and he really can't complain. Gauging his mood carefully, Buddy suggests that, in spite of all the bookings, Sonny is not quite content with his lot. Sonny looks wistful. He says that he heard the Horace Silver Quintet recently with Louis Hayes and it is a great combo. 'All these guys play in my style.' It is the type of music he longs to play, and he can't do it here in L.A.

He has recently heard Art Farmer and, of course, the wonderful Miles Davis Quintet with John Coltrane, Red Garland and Paul Chambers. All these musicians are his heroes. He feels a great affinity with them but can't play their type of music on the West Coast. It was wonderful recently playing with Philly Joe Jones in the group, but it made him envious of the cats in that combo. His main influences, he tells De Franco, are Bud Powell and Thelonious Monk, as far as playing piano goes.

'You remember when we toured through Chicago?' he asks

and De Franco nods. 'I jammed with Wilbur Ware on bass there and he knocked me out.' He goes on to say that he loves the sound of John Coltrane, Paul Chambers on bass and, although he has only heard him on records so far, Hank Mobley. These are the musicians he longs to hook up with and play.

'The cats here have a different sort of feeling. They swing in their own way. People like Conte Candoli, Frank Rosolino and Stan Levey have helped me to enjoy some of my music though.' He goes on to say that those cats all played in the East for long periods. Their music has that steel in it. A big bop sound.

'They all worked for a long time in the East, and I think they have more of the feel of the eastern vein than you usually find in the musicians out west. The eastern musicians play with so much fire and passion.'

De Franco smiles and nods his head. He says he didn't realise how strong Sonny's feeling for the hard bop sound of New York was. He certainly adapted well enough to the De Franco band's music. And he never had to compromise or play in a manner that was alien to him. With Clark being so versatile and such a creative soloist, he will always be able to fit in wherever he goes, with any type of musical company. All things considered, if he feels so strongly about New York-style jazz, as they call it, that is the place he should try and get himself to. Sonny knows it. He smiles, looking thoughtful.

He says that he has a few gigs coming up and the promise of further record dates, so he will see those out and then make the change. By hook or by crook, he will find a way to get himself to New York City. He has been clean now for some time and is trying desperately to save some money. It is not that he isn't quite well paid; he is.

Unfortunately, Sonny meets up with another prominent jazz pianist at a joint in L.A. who persuades him to share a bag of heroin. Clark is caught at a bad time with a night when he has no gig and is thinking about the horrors of his recent past even though he attempts desperately to channel his thoughts in another direction. It does not work. The heroin is too big a temptation just now; it takes away his temporary depression and makes him feel good.

Sonny Clark Trio Blue Note 1579 Leonard Feather Sleeve note.

Stan Levey & Howard Rumsey - The Lighthouse Years.

Lawrence Marable Quartet - *Tenorman* - Jazz West JWLP 8

6

WEST COAST BLUES (3)

THE WORD IS OUT ON THE GRAPEVINE THAT THERE IS A NEW TENOR sax man who is going to surprise everybody. Jazz West is a small, independent jazz label located at West Pico Boulevard, Los Angeles 19. It is run and owned by Herbert Kimmel, a man who has put out some good jazz discs in the past. Drummer Lawrence Marable has been searching, without success for a new saxophonist, one who, in Herbert Kimmel's words, is 'an unspoiled rookie, whose corners would be rough and unpolished, free and clear of the restraints that tend to tie down and mould would-be jazzmen and make them hue the line of convention and sophistication.' Lawrence and Kimmel have discussed it frequently, and what they are seeking is a musician who is not afraid to blow, not overloaded with technique but plenty of guts.

At last, Marable thinks he has found him: James Clay, a young, slim, tall Texan who he heard playing at the Californian, an L.A. jazz club. The drummer reported that Clay had a big, hot, burgeoning sound, natural sounding rhythmic thrust, and he is sure that this is their man. He seeks out Sonny Clark at a downtown club where he is playing and tells him about Clay and the planned recording session. He certainly sounds good to

Sonny, the type of musician he loves to work with and not one of the cool school.

After Sonny's gig, the two musicians go to a bar and order beers. Marable is very excited. He really thinks this man is going to be the next great tenor sax star and will be in demand all over the country. The pianist smiles. He has heard claims like this many times before. Usually, the 'star' in question makes one, possibly two LPs and promptly disappears from sight. Or hangs out round the clubs and joints hoping to get a gig or a chance to sit in. This is not to say he isn't very interested in the Jazz West recording session. Marable wants Sonny on piano because he thinks he will give the young player a lift with his melodic yet propulsive comping and solos with such cute melodies.

He asks the drummer for details of the recording. He is told that it is at the Capitol studio in Hollywood and Marable is to be the leader. Clark nods. Jimmy Bond is the bass player he has chosen, and Sonny is happy with that, he has heard Bond and knows he has a strong, almost classical sound but is also a swinger. The two musicians look forward to recording together. Now that they have worked together several times, on records and gigs, they know each other's strengths and manner of playing.

Sonny Clark is struggling. In the studios or on gigs he seems fine, playing supportive piano to all manner of different lineups, smiling, confident, completely at ease. Many musicians have remarked that there is never any sign of tension in his music. The music, like the musician they see at the piano, is completely relaxed, unlike his stated influence, Bud Powell, who always sounds as though there is tension and disturbance in his music. Outside the locations though, Sonny is a mess. He is now very deep into heroin addiction, and every dollar he earns goes into feeding his habit and his desire for alcohol and tobacco. Usually, at least for the present time, he is neatly dressed, slim in build and appears in public to be in control, as far as the outside world observes.

At home, alone, which is the time when he takes a large dose of heroin to calm himself and his demons, he is strung out and often looks it. These are times when he does not wish anyone else to see him. He eats little, keeping cans of beer at hand and various things to nibble and keep him going. It is not the way he wants to be, but he has now fallen into a pattern of what he believes to be controlled addiction.

Sonny walks briskly through the hot August sunshine to the Capitol Records building in Hollywood. He is introduced to James Clay, a tall willowy young man wearing a small, coloured hat, by Marable. As soon as bass player Bond arrives, they get down to recording the music. Clay states the melody line of 'Between the Devil and the Deep Blue Sea' straight out, without introduction. Once the melody is stated, he hands over to Sonny, who plays a brief solo, light, bright, bubbly. Sonny is pleased to hear the tenor player's sound, it is clear, quite robust without being over-heavy, and he is an inventive improvisor. Sonny's chime-like solo provides a contrast to the strong tenor sound.

On 'Easy Living,' Clark is at his most rhapsodic, wrapping the tenor man in delicate piano notes all through his opening phrases. Sonny plays a solo here that includes his pet runs up and down the keyboard along with the most delicate of melodic improvising. 'Minor Meeting' is his composition and he is particularly pleased that he has been asked to write three pieces for the recording. He loves playing standards and putting his stamp on them, but lately has been composing his own material. Although there are not too many opportunities to play his music, and not too many requests to contribute material, Marable has, on this occasion, done so. The medium-tempo blues has the tenor player giving it a good run-through, his sound buoyant. Marable gets a workout on drums on this selection.

By the time they get to playing, a slow ballad version of 'Willow Weep for Me,' the pianist is feeling good about the session. Everybody is in synchronization, the music flowing along healthily, as does his solo on this piece. 'Three Finger's

North' is the second Clark chart to be recorded. It is an up-tempo romp begun by Clark's flying finger introduction. Clay has no trouble with the fast pulse and cruises happily through the chord changes. Sonny's piano solo is an exercise in effortless swing before Marable takes a lengthy drum solo.

The recording session draws to a close with a slow, rhapsodic reading of 'Lover Man,' where Sonny is sensitive in the extreme in his accompaniment and chime-like solo, followed by the pianist's composition, 'Marbles.' This is an extremely catchy melody of the sort that jazz musicians like to get their chops around. Clay pulses through it joyfully, Clark shadowing him closely and urging him forward along with Bond and Marable. Sonny plays a brisk, bouncing solo, quoting from a popular song before handing over briefly to Bond and Marable for exchanges with the leader.

Sonny relaxes in a chair as they listen to the playback. Everybody seems happy with the way it went, and the producer is congratulating young Clay on his performance. He is content enough with his contribution but, as always, thinks he might have been a bit more expressive on some of his solos.

The record, when released, will be called *Tenorman*, thus emphasizing the saxophonist's contribution at the expense of the drummer leader.

As to Clay, he does not know whether or not the young saxophonist will make it into the big time of jazz performances and recordings, but he doubts it. There are so many good and even great jazz soloists up and down the country that never really make it. Many of them never even leave the towns they were born in and remain unknown except to a few local supporters. As to his own performance and career up to date, he is happy enough that he is now being recognised by club owners, bookers and record company executives as a good, reliable player and getting more and more work. If he is still relatively unknown and unheralded by the fans in the jazz public, maybe that will change in good time. Maybe.

A jazz trio from San Diego are playing in the afternoon at the Lighthouse. It is Howard Rumsey's policy to bring in young musicians from Southern California to play on Sundays. It gives them an opportunity to play and show what they can do, and at the same time, it gives the resident band and subsidiary musicians a well-earned break. Playing from 2 in the afternoon to 2am the next morning is a long haul. Up on stage, the young musicians are wailing on a standard tune. A young drummer from another part of L.A. is asking Stan Levey if he will be able to sit in today. Stan tells him to stick around. Late tonight, he tells him, he will bring him up onto the bandstand to sit in with The Lighthouse All-Stars. It is what they do here.

Sonny Clark walks down to the end of the room where Rumsey has a table. He has just been playing with the band along with saxophonist Bob Cooper, Frank Rosolino on trombone, and Stan Levey. Two other musicians are at Howard's table as Clark joins the bassist. Rumsey hands Sonny a beer and he takes a swig and sits at the table. Rumsey shakes his head and tells the pianist he is still feeling shaken from listening earlier today to three great pianists playing. Lou Levey was one, Hampton Hawes the second, and Sonny the third. Where else can you hear three great piano players, one after the other, play on the same stage on the same day, Rumsey is asking. 'You were all great,' he says. 'And you all sounded different. Amazing.'

Clark tells him that they all have their own approach and takes another drink from his bottle. With barely a pause for breath, Clark had been back up on stage with Cooper, Rosolino and Levey, wailing with a quintet. Sonny reminds Rumsey that he was there along with Levey, and he had played even longer than he had. Rumsey smiles. He is running the show here and he loves playing anyway. Comes with the territory. They continue drinking and discussing the Lighthouse operation. Rumsey is getting into an expansive mood. He tells Clark that almost everybody of note in California and surrounding districts has been to the Lighthouse. Charlie Parker one night. 'Really?' Sonny asks.

'Sure thing. He walked in with four other men and went straight to a table at the front, facing the stage. The waiter asked him what he wanted, and he ordered a triple Hennessey.' Rumsey pauses and grins. 'Well, the waiter asks for payment and Parker waves him away saying that the band will pay. "Which one?" asks the waiter, and Bird just points to the nearest musician on stage and says, "That one."

They both smile. That was Parker. Rumsey tells Sonny that Parker could be generous. 'But he never paid for drinks.' The pianist nods. Rumsey tells him that they tried to get Bird up on stage to sit in, but he was reluctant. Eventually, he did go up but hardly played a note. 'We had to wait until he wandered off down the street and found some dive,' Rumsey goes on, 'and there he played for over an hour. We just stood there staring.'

Music is more or less continuous at the Lighthouse on Sundays. As one band finishes, another mounts the steps to the bandstand and begins to play. Sonny has just ended another long set and he comes down to the bar area and lights up a cigarette. There, suddenly standing next to him, is the pianist Hampton Hawes. These two are becoming friends. Both play in a solid bop style with a heavy injection of the blues in their music. Hawes says something to him about a joint round the corner and Sonny nods, agreeing. The two men walk out of the club together and find a spot where they can shoot up. When they return to the Lighthouse, both look relaxed and content. They have obviously found what they sought and taken full advantage.

It is getting late now, well past midnight. The audience has thinned out but there are still a fair number of hard-core enthusiasts sitting at tables, drinking, smoking and listening. Some are sitting there wearing only shorts or bathing suits, having come up from the beach in the afternoon and become hooked on the music. The young group are just finishing their last set. Sonny goes back on stage and starts blowing with Bob Cooper,

Rosolino, Rumsey and Levey. The pianist enjoys working with this band, particularly Rosolino, although he finds Bob Cooper's tenor sax a little too cool for his liking. His idols are Lester Young and Stan Getz, even if he also blows a smooth oboe on occasion. After two selections, Cooper invites his wife, June Christy, up to sing a couple of songs. She is a fine jazz singer, very laid back and melodic, and Clark always enjoys listening to her vocals. At times, he thinks Cooper is rather too brusque with her, for she is a gentle creature, but then it is really none of his business.

True to his promise, Levey invites the young drummer up on stage towards the end of their set and allows him to sit in with the group. It is now well into the early hours of Monday morning, but the musician's enthusiasm and measured playing is showing no sign of strain. Sonny comps away merrily, takes his solo spots with brio and hopes that the pleasant atmosphere at the Lighthouse and good companions on stage will continue indefinitely and he will get more and more gigs in this attractive location.

On a warm night in September, the Lighthouse All-Stars are in full swing. They play 'That's All,' and then a 'Mambo.' Rosolino is muted on trombone and Bob Cooper is playing oboe and English horn on this set. The music is being recorded for KABC-TV for television transmission. Sonny is carefully modifying his piano work knowing, as he does to lesser extent on recording sessions, that what you put down for a TV show can't be changed. You can manipulate a recording of course but not on a live broadcast. His playing is clean, fleet and only slightly subdued. The other musicians around him appear to be having the same thoughts for the music is slightly less spontaneous tonight, a little more refined.

The band play 'That's All,' and then June Christy steps forward. She sings 'Isn't this A Lovely Way To Spend An

Evening,' and then lends her silken, resonant voice to a slow reading of "Round Midnight.'

The gigs at the Lighthouse are coming thick and fast in September 1956. Clark has little time for anything other than a few hours, sleep in bed, followed by lying on the beach in the sun during the mornings. He can't complain. Being busy almost every night is just what he needs; it takes his mind off any other concerns and allows him to immerse himself in the music he loves.

They play a wide variety of music including Latin and Mambos, a particular favourite of the pianist. They play 'A Bit Of Basie,' and 'Taxi War Dance,' and Sonny is surprised at how easily he slips into the light swinging style of the Count. It is sparse, with few notes and a compete contrast to his usual bop fuelled style where he delights in playing countless notes, often at up-tempo. But it sure as hell swings easily.

'Love Me Or Levey,' works well for Stan at the drums, as indeed it was intended to do. And 'Swing House,' of course, does just that. On nights like this he is completely engaged in the music and his fellow players and if somebody called for 'Old Man River,' or an Elvis Presley tune he would most likely grin and say right then, let's do it.

Stan Levey and Howard Rumsey-The Lighthouse Years.
Howard Rumsey's Lighthouse All-Stars—Contemporary C 3528
Sonny Clark with Howard Rumsey's Lighthouse All-Stars
Vantage NLP -5004
Conversation with bassist Spike Heatley in 2016

7
WEST COAST SUCCESS

IT IS BACK TO THE RADIO RECORDERS STUDIO TO PUT DOWN FOUR final tracks of Sonny Criss' Cole Porter album. Sonny arrives just in time, minutes before they are due to start recording. Criss greets him and begins complaining about the record company and how long it is taking to get this disc out into the shops. He has nothing good to say about Imperial and is still feeling marginalised by the jazz fraternity and the fans that he thinks are ignoring his music. Clark, who is not exactly being feted by the jazz enthusiasts of California himself, agrees with the saxophonist.

The recording though goes smoothly enough. Four Cole Porter songs, starting with 'Easy To Love,' do not represent hard work for seasoned professional musicians like the two Sonny's. Clark's piano work flows effortlessly, as it usually does in these circumstances, as he listens to Criss out front. The pianist thinks Criss sounds like Charlie Parker with the fast-paced phrases he uses, but the tone of his instrument is still quite shrill and there are times when he resembles older alto men like Benny Carter and Johnny Hodges. At the end of the recording, they listen to the playback, everybody seems happy, and they all go their separate ways.

On the bandstand at the Lighthouse, they are playing a standard at a comfortable medium tempo. It is the last selection of a rather slow night when not too many people are in, and they are not exactly generous with their applause. Sonny shakes his head as he comes down towards the bar. You get nights like these, and you just have to forget them and get on with the next performance. He gets himself a beer at the bar and one for Stan Levey who is approaching. Stan though appears in jubilant mood notwithstanding a rather poor reception they have just endured from the audience. 'Noisy bunch tonight,' Clark complains. 'I hate it when they talk all through a cat's solo,' Stan observes. Even so, Stan does seem cheerful enough and his friend has picked up on his mood.

Stan Levey has got his own record date where he will be the leader. After playing on endless recordings and backing everybody from popular singers to Charlie Parker, it is good to have your own date. He wants it to be just right and has carefully selected the musicians to join him. Conte Candoli will be on trumpet. Sonny nods, he likes everything he has heard on records by the trumpeter. 'Rosolino on trombone of course and a young tenor sax player named Richie Kamuca.' Clark does not know much about him, but Stan tells him he will make a good contrast with Candoli. 'He sounds like a modern Lester Young,' Levey says, 'with a bit of Zoot Sims thrown in.' He adds that, of course, he wants Sonny on piano and the bass player will be Leroy Vinnegar. Sonny nods enthusiastically and thinks the lineup sounds great. Only Kamuca is an unknown quantity, but he trusts Stan's judgement. The drummer also asks him if he could contribute two original compositions to the date. He has heard, liked, and even played here at the Lighthouse the two pieces Clark wrote for his recent recording with Lawrence Marable.

Sonny beams. He enjoys writing music and has been told by other musicians that his charts are attractive, natural-sounding bop lines with plenty of melody, fizz and rhythm. Much as he loves playing standards, there is nothing like playing your own music. This is another opportunity and perhaps the beginning of his being recognised as a jazz composer.

Stan Levey is a big man in every sense. Tall, muscular, he is an ex-heavyweight boxer. At the Lighthouse, he is well respected and usually regarded as the nominal leader even though the band, the All-Stars, is a collective. At his record date, he commands respect. He is also a first-class jazz drummer. And he knows what he wants from his leader date. He has chosen three standards, one chart by Bob Holman, two by Bob Cooper and two by his pianist. He has also given a featured spot to all his frontline soloists including himself. Only bassist Vinnegar is left to provide a foundation with a solid bass line, something he will do very well.

Sonny Clark kicks off the standard 'Yesterdays' with a brief piano introduction, and the band play it at a brisker than usual tempo. Rosolino's trombone spirals all over the theme in his solo. 'Angel Cake' is Sonny's first original, which is a feature for tenor saxist Richie Kamuca. Richie is cool and laid back, but his solo is inventive, and he swings effortlessly. The theme is attractive and infectious, and Clark will return to it on future record dates and in the clubs. Sonny's feature is the standard 'Why Do I Love you,' a familiar popular song which he makes his own with a strong, up-tempo reading, faster than most musicians take it.

Sonny is enjoying himself here and plays some of the best music he has put on record to date. Always inventive, always swinging lightly but deceptively compulsively. This piano solo is a gem of improvised interpretation. 'Hit That Thing' is a feature for the drummer leader, and he turns in a well-thought-out, pulsating solo. Clark's 'Blues at Sunrise' features Conte Candoli, who acquits himself well. 'A Gal in Calico' is a tasty popular tune which the musicians, Clark included, give a fresh workout out to.

All the musicians are happy with what they hear on playback, and Sonny rates it as the second best of his career so far, following his favourite, 'Blue Serge' with Serge Chaloff. That record had such steady time that the pianist felt sure that working with Philly Joe Jones and Vinnegar presented his best chance yet of playing in a near perfect rhythm section.

If Sonny Clark's life consists of just playing music and sleeping, that is acceptable to him at the moment. He is aware that he is going through a hazy, drug-fuelled existence from late mornings when he rises at midday, moves out to Hermosa Beach and spends the afternoon on the sands drinking or in the nearest accessible bar. Except when he has an afternoon record date. For those, he rises earlier and attempts to make himself presentable before arriving, drug-and-alcohol-fuelled, at the studio. If he sees things through a foggy prism of blurred objects and time passing aimlessly, everything changes as soon as he sits at the piano stool. In the early years, it was a mild blur. Now, it is shaping up to be a heavy burden. His life outside the studio or club is becoming intolerable. At the present time, he is working regularly, as much and sometimes even more than he can comfortably handle. He is, in fact, becoming successful as a jazz soloist and an in-demand sideman. If he receives little recognition from jazz enthusiasts on the club scene, he still clings to the hope that the situation will change in time. He wants public recognition, craves it, but knows he must be patient.

Sonny would like a record date as leader of a small combo. So far, discussions with record company people, producers and others have yielded no results. Most of them have said that it isn't time yet, he is not well enough known. Others, including musicians, have told him bluntly that the decision-makers and producers see only an addict and not the gifted musician he truly is.

Night after night at the Lighthouse, he can lose himself in the music, swap phrases and solos with Cooper, Rosolino and, occasionally, guest soloists such as alto sax and flute man Bud Shank.

Or Shorty Rogers on trumpet or cornet. Vocalists like June Christy and Anita O' Day. Provide illuminating piano support behind Buddy Collett on flute and Bob Cooper on oboe. Play sparkling bop piano in percussive mode to counteract the more esoteric west coast sounds. All this he does with vigour and commitment, lurching from one gig to the next with the vague thought in his mind that soon and better sooner than later, he must make one more, third attempt, to kick his habit.

Cannonball Adderley is in the club tonight. Sonny arrives early, anxious to hear every note from one of his favourite East Coast combos. He is introduced to Cannon, a bubbly, effervescent, friendly man who treats him like an old friend and talks music to him for twenty minutes. Cannonball invites him to sit in for one selection and he is delighted by the offer. The song chosen is 'The Way You Look Tonight.' It is a familiar standard to the pianist, and he digs in vigorously. He is soon swinging easily, a big smile on his face, and enjoying listening to the bop band he is playing in with Cannonball on alto sax, his brother Nat on cornet, Sam Jones offering big fat, juicy bass lines, and Specs Wright driving at the drums. The selection is recorded. It is a night to remember.

He goes home on a high and then can't get to sleep thinking about the way a hard bop combo grooves and pulses and the way he was able to adapt to one almost immediately. These men are the sort of musicians he wants to link up with, play with regularly. Surely, he thinks, now is the time to make the trip to New York and take his chances. Lesser musicians have done it, he knows that. Money is short though. He gets good pay at the Lighthouse but most of it goes on drugs, beer and tobacco.

There must be another way surely? He suddenly remembers something he heard one of the cats say yesterday. Blues singer Dinah Washington is starting a tour round several cities and is looking for a replacement piano player. That tour would take in New York or end up there, wouldn't it?

He decides to seek out Dinah, audition for her, play the blues for her. Beg her if necessary to make him her accompanist. It can't be that difficult. Now he can get to sleep.

Stan Levey Sextet - *Grand Stan* Bethlehem BCP 71
Stan Levey & Howard Rumsey—You tube video

8

ON THE ROAD

IT IS TIME TO MOVE FORWARD AND SEEK NEW AVENUES OF expression. Working with Dinah Washington will keep him busy for several weeks, but he will end up in New York. That is where Dinah is based, and she never stays away from the city for long. She told him that when she hired him. She only had to listen to him play the blues for two minutes to know he was the one she was looking for. He will be working with her regular trio and leading it, in fact. She tells him that all he has to do is provide a solid, swinging accompaniment. And take good solos when she gives him the nod. She sings with a powerful, blues-based voice, she tells him, that is why she is known as the Queen of the Blues. When she sings in a club, audiences sit and listen quietly. They do not talk in loud voices, or she hurls glasses at them. She has been known to do just that on occasion. He will soon get the hang of the repertoire once they start, she informs him. After each gig there is a party backstage or in her dressing room, depending on the location. He will have fun.

Sonny has heard rumours about Dinah and her parties and her idea of fun. Some cats have told him she can drink any musician under the table and still go on for another two hours. She stands no nonsense from club owners or anybody else and puts them in their place, swearing like a trooper. She can be awkward, difficult, occasionally unreliable. On the other hand, she is a great singer with the ability to cover jazz, blues, pop, R&B, gospel or any other style you care to mention. Her articulation is precise, her intonation spot on. She has a big, blues-based voice and was once a gospel singing choir girl.

He wants this gig as it will get him where he needs to go and, he hopes, allow him to visit his sisters in Pittsburgh whom he hasn't seen for over five years now. Dinah has told him he can have at least three hours in Pittsburgh, visiting. He is pleased, if slightly ill at ease with his first impressions of Dinah. She seems big in every respect, brash and possibly overbearing. He is generally quiet and keeps himself to himself in the main, not too keen on drinking and partying in public.

Dinah introduces him to the other members of the trio. Jimmy Rowser is on bass and the drummer is Arthur Edgehill. They tell him that she is alright, she is very popular, usually has sell-out audiences and is fine unless anybody crosses her or tries to make her do anything she does not wish to do. When they go to after-gig parties, they are expected to bring some booze along. Although she earns a fortune, her new agent is restricting her weekly income to a set amount and busily investing the rest in property for her. In other words, Rowser claims, he is looking after her best interests. Both rhythm men say she is very generous when she has money. Sonny is partly reassured.

The trio play together for forty minutes to get used to each other. Clark finds that the bassist and drummer tighten up on medium- and up-tempo music in what he thinks is the New York bebop style. This pleases him and he responds by playing in his own, best, percussive manner. All three jell together almost immediately and realise that they will have no problems playing together.

Dinah plays a night at the Black Hawk in San Francisco. It is familiar territory to Sonny before they hit the road and cover a lot of miles. Dinah gives a well-received, lively performance, and the rhythm section slot in neatly behind her. Clark is a little disconcerted at her habit, frequently used, of going from one song into the next without a break and no indication to the audience. She will often change key on the new piece, more than a little disconcerting to even as alert a pianist as Sonny. Jimmy Rowser grins and tells him he will get used to it. He doubts that. As to the music, it is mainly jazz, this being a well-loved jazz club, but she will also sing rhythm-and-blues, popular, and even a country and western tune she has taken a liking to. At first, Clark is confused, but his experience and continuous playing over the past five years have given him both confidence and ability. Somehow, he manages to adapt to what is going on around him and the concert is a success.

Dinah has applied for a special marriage licence under her real name of Ruth Jones. She has met and been playing with Eddie Chamblee, a saxophonist, and fallen for him in a big way. Rowser smiles and tells Sonny she has been married four times before and the marriages never last. Usually about a year or slightly less. He says they will be all over each other for two to three months and then the arguments and fighting will start. He has seen it all before. On the road, Dinah has decided that they will have separate billing. Dinah Washington and her trio and the Eddie Chamblee Orchestra. He will bring his usual musicians.

Sonny Clark notices that his new employer is not just flamboyant in her music delivery but in almost every other way. She wears expensive gowns, jewels, mink coats and jackets. She is known, he is told, for giving away the latter to her close female friends, fans or anyone who helps her in any way. On the road, she can be difficult, disturbing, often cursing and swearing vehemently at anybody who fails to give her what she asks for or occasionally demands.

They stop at a gas station to refuel, and Dinah asks the attendant for the key to the restroom as she needs to relieve herself. He refuses, telling her it is for the use of whites only. Dinah curses and swears at him, but the man still refuses to hand her the key. Sonny watches in amazement and horror as she pulls out a gun from her bag and moves forward, pointing the gun at the man's forehead. Dinah receives the key to the restroom.

At most gigs on the tour, the band are received with noisy applause and plenty of foot stomping. In the more up-market rooms, the applause is restrained and polite, but they listen to her, the trio, and even to Chamblee's often raw rhythm and blues offerings. On a rare occasion when they find a high level of conversation coming from the audience, Dinah stops in mid-song. She lectures the audience on the need for silence while she and her musicians are performing, and for the rest of the evening, all is quiet out front. Sonny backs her R&B selections with percussive chords and solid blues licks and receives his own wild applause. On this tour, he is learning more about adapting to different musical expression than he did four years playing on the West Coast.

The package tour stops at the Rainbow Theatre in Denver and is very well received. Dinah shifts easily into jazz mode and varies it with straight-ahead modern blues. Then she sings two popular songs from her latest record release and again scores heavily with the audience. The rhythm section cruise along easily, this is their music, by and large, and playing it is a pleasure.

In Chicago it is all blues. Dinah hams it up, asking Masters of Ceremonies and club managers to introduce her as the Queen of the Blues and generally getting down and dirty with her most suggestive lyrics on her own compositions. Sonny is in his element playing the twelve-bar blues licks with relish and sometimes even hamming it up a bit himself. On one evening, he gets to jam at an after-hours joint with Johnny Griffin, the up-and-coming Chicago tenor saxist. Griffin is known as a speed merchant with a penchant for playing at killing tempos, and Sonny relishes keeping pace with him in support and his own solos. A feat he accomplishes with relative ease.

They arrive early in Pittsburgh, and Dinah keeps her promise, giving Sonny time to visit two of his sisters and a brother. They are delighted to see him after a long absence and make a huge fuss of their brother. He is given a slap-up meal and they tell him how surprised and pleased they are that he is making his way as a professional jazz musician. They hadn't expected that he would do so well; after all, George never made the big time as a jazzman. Sonny protests that he is still not that well known and not really appreciated by record buyers and audiences generally although he intends to do something about that in the near future. They will have none of it and tell him everybody in town talks about him and many have bought records he plays on.

One of Sonny's sisters has moved to Dayton, Ohio, and he gets to visit her too. Once again, he is a musical hero and famous beyond anything he ever envisioned himself up to this point. But he laps up the hero worship and vows that he will justify it in future. Then it is back on the road with Dinah.

Another town, another club. Dinah is singing 'Evil Gal Blues' and other pieces of a similar nature. It is easy enough for Clark to back her sympathetically and contribute his deep blue twelve-bar fills and solos but hardly stretching his ability as a soloist. He goes through the motions as usual, but in truth, he is getting weary of playing a wide variety of music that is less than interesting to him. New York is getting ever closer. For the first time, he is beginning to feel just a little apprehensive. After all, there is no way he can be sure he will make the grade in NYC. So many others have tried and failed.

He is also feeling a little guilty. Dinah has looked after him, paid him well and is getting used to having him behind her at the keyboard. He has often stayed behind at gigs and joined her raucous after-hours parties and drunk a lot of gin and other beverages, shot up heroin and felt great for a few hours. When he gets to NYC, he will jump ship immediately and leave Dinah needing to find another pianist. He consoles himself with the thought that there are hundreds of them, the good, the bad and the indifferent. She will soon get fixed up, but he will not hang around long to listen to her cursing and swearing about him. New York City awaits his presence, ready to make or break him.

He is more than ready to take the plunge.

9

THE NEW YORK SCENE

THE JAZZ SCENE IN NEW YORK CITY IN 1957 IS BRIGHT, BUBBLY, glittering at times. When Sonny arrives, he heads to the clubs that employ the musicians he admires most. Birdland, Café Bohemia, The Five Spot. A host of others, some that will survive, others that won't. He hears the bands of Art Blakey and the Messengers, George Wallington, Miles Davis, John Coltrane and, best of all, Thelonious Monk. Jazz is all around, and the jazz clubs are thriving.

It is, he soon realises, a jazz haven for bop, hard bop and progressive, modern jazz. And these are the golden age years for jazz. Most of the recordings that are made now come from the small independent jazz labels or those that put out a large percentage of jazz in their catalogues. Best of them all is Blue Note Records because this company looks after the musicians they record. Bands receive two days paid rehearsal before recording, and on the day they go into the studio to make their recording, snacks and drinks are provided. The company is a two-man organisation run by Alfred Lion and his friend and partner, Francis Wolff. These two are jazz lovers from way back who began their appreciation of the music in Germany and escaped from that country, Lion in 1926 and Wolff in 1939 just before the outbreak of war. These two, record jazz of the day because they love the music, not to make money. Some months it must be difficult to make any profit at all when you take into account the paid rehearsals, the food, and paying the musicians and highly regarded recording engineer Rudy Van Gelder. And after having most of their vinyl LPs pressed at the Plasticite pressing plant, a high-quality product.

No such luxury exists at Prestige Records, another independent company issuing jazz music of the current style. Musicians are expected to come in, record, be paid and depart. They do produce some classic recordings, perhaps more by accident than design. Sonny Rollins recorded his classic *Saxophone Colossus* in 1956 and Miles Davis completed a marathon of five LPs by what will be known as his first classic quintet in that year. He also makes his first LP for Columbia Records, who have signed him to a lucrative contract.

Other small to medium companies are active in recording jazz. Atlantic Records, also famous for R&B, is producing music by top jazz musicians. Bethlehem too. And Savoy.

Sonny Clark spends his first week in New York trying to make contact with the sort of musicians he wants to play with and checking out the clubs and the record companies. He goes to Birdland, the most famous of all the jazz clubs in town. He is pleased when he gets a gig playing piano for tenor saxist Stan Getz. It is to be at Birdland and is a two-week gig. Getz is very popular and plays in a warm, lyrical manner in what could be described as a modern jazz version of Lester Young. He is though, influenced heavily by Charlie Parker and knows the bop lines intimately. For Clark, it is a very good start and keeps him busy spinning out supporting lines behind the melodic Mr. Getz.

The next gig he secures is playing in a group supporting vocalist Anita O' Day. He has worked with Anita before, briefly, when he first arrived in California in '53 and they got on well together, musically and as friends. It is a weekend gig and goes well. Anita is friendly and they are mutually complimentary towards each other. To Sonny, it seems as if West Coast music, or something very much like it, is stalking him in New York City. It is what he is known for. Then he gets lucky.

He is approached and then booked to play piano on a Sonny Rollins record, here in NYC. He makes his way down to the Reeves Sound Studio in town and is greeted by Orrin Keepnews, the producer and part owner of Riverside Records. The producer is always early, often the first to arrive at record sessions. As the others arrive, he introduces Sonny. Percy Heath is on bass. Roy Haynes is the drummer. Then he shakes hands with the man many enthusiasts are calling the greatest tenor sax star of them all: Sonny Rollins. The pianist keeps calm somehow, shakes all the hands as if he has been doing it all his life regularly but he is very much aware, deep down, that he is now in some pretty fast company.

The first thing he must do is adapt quickly to Rollins' stop-start, staccato style on this date. The tenor man starts with 'The Last Time I Saw Paris,' an unlikely pop song. Mostly it consists of solo Rollins or a duet between him and drummer Haynes. Most of this performance though is disjointed, as Rollins no doubt intends it to be. 'Just In Time,' is much more straight ahead and he gets the chance to spin out a typical flowing single-note-style piano solo. 'Toot, Toot Tootsie' has more fragmented Rollins, but Sonny has settled in by now and is following the tenor in smooth piano accompaniment wherever he ventures. The piano solo fairly sparkles. Roy Haynes is impressive too with his colourful drum explosions.

By the time they get to 'What Is There To Say,' a cute ballad, Sonny is feeling extremely confident, and enjoying himself. He plays a pretty, chiming introduction and then shadows Rollins closely throughout his solo which sticks closely to the melody. By contrast, Clark's solo is melodic but based mainly on the chord structure of the theme. Rollins' solos, both beginning and ending, are inventive and tuneful although he might just be thinking that his pianist is a little too prominent here. 'Dearly

Beloved' is not used much in jazz these days, but Rollins can take any piece of music from anywhere, improvise on it and make it special.

He tackles 'It Could Happen To You' as a solo tenor sax excursion, just as though he is saying 'I can do it on my own without any rhythm section when I'm in the mood.'

More rare songs are included with 'It Could Happen To You' offering a good workout. At the end of the session, Rollins starts to play 'Funky Hotel Blues,' which will not appear on the album when released. Clark is bright and bluesy on his solo, moving gradually into a complex bop series of phrases. At the end of the recording, everybody seems satisfied with the results and they slowly depart without much further ceremony. Keepnews shakes his hand and thanks him for his contribution.

Clark likes Keepnews. Riverside is a relatively new company as far as modern jazz is concerned but they are doing well, musically at least. Financially not too clever, but that is the problem for several independents. The pianist has enjoyed his first recording in NYC with some of the musicians he most admires. Roy Haynes is one of the greatest of drummers, and he has worked with almost everybody of note in jazz including Louis Armstrong and Charlie Parker. Percy Heath is a much in-demand bass player, highly skilled. As for Rollins, his ability to improvise on anything and make it sound personal, interesting and full of bop phrasing, knows no bounds. Clark likes Riverside and, in particular, their producer because he took Thelonious Monk away from Prestige where he was unhappy and considered himself neglected and has relaunched his career with three stunning LPs, including his master work, *Brilliant Corners*. As far as recording goes, his first session has been a winner. The future looks promising.

Sonny's next record date comes just four days later, much quicker than he had hoped or expected and this time it is a Hank Mobley session for Blue Note Records. Mobley had heard him in a club downtown, liked what he heard and talked about him to

Alfred Lion, who had come down to hear him live. Lion had been impressed and looked forward to hearing what he would sound like on Mobley's date. This is also Sonny's first chance to have his music recorded by Rudy Van Gelder, the engineer all the cats are talking about. The general opinion, almost universal amongst musicians, is that Van Gelder gets just the sound of each instrument that every cat wants. He makes them sound on record as close as you can get, to live performance.

Sonny makes his way to the Van Gelder studio in Hackensack, New Jersey, where all Blue Note and, for that matter, Prestige records are now recorded. The recording studio is a converted room in Rudy's parent's stylish, contemporary-type bungalow out in the suburbs. Inside is a big room with modern lamps, venetian blinds and just one, big monitor speaker. The session is to be recorded in stereophonic sound or, as Van Gelder chooses to call it, two-channel mono. The sound engineer is not too fond of the new-fangled stereo and thinks monophonic sound gives a better representation of recorded modern jazz. But it is a sign of the times and is obviously going to be coming in more and more and Van Gelder is not a man to be left behind in his craft. He will master the recordings in mono anyway because, although they are recording in the new format, Blue Note are not yet issuing stereo discs. They will shortly put out just four, carefully selected titles in stereo. One of those titles will be John Coltrane's *Blue Train*, a future classic.

In the studio, Sonny shakes hands with trumpeter Bill Hardman, a brassy, direct player who sounds the way Clark likes to hear the instrument sound. He knows Hank's music from recordings he has heard and likes it very much. Curtis Porter is the other saxophonist, also known as Shafa Hadi. The tall, very slim bass player is Paul Chambers, another musician Clark has heard frequently on records and in person when the Miles Davis Quintet played on the West Coast a short time ago. He is pleased to meet this well-known and highly regarded bass man and looks forward to teaming up with him in the rhythm section along with the experienced, noted drummer, Art Taylor. This promises to be an extremely good, hard bop session.

Sonny likes the idea of a sextet. So much can be done in terms of sound colours with a three-man front line. The group play the slightly oriental flavoured 'Mighty Moe And Joe.' Curtis Porter solos first on alto and then Hardman takes over, his trumpet notes spilling out like bullets at up tempo. Mobley is his usual laid back, melodic self, his notes fitting neatly where he wants them with little or no regard for the harmonic sequence. The piano solo follows Hank's lead of relaxed but compulsively swinging sounds. Clark is back in harness, playing with a tough hard bop New York group and it feels good.

Sonny decorates 'Bag's Groove' with delicate, chime-like notes in his introduction. A slow to medium tempo appears to suit everybody. Even Hardman is more sparing in the number of notes he uses. Clark follows the trumpeter and produces easy-flowing blues lines in a thoughtful solo. Hank is as laid back as ever. It only remains for Paul Chamber to spin out a pizzicato bass solo in his usual competent manner and then the horns play the theme through to see the piece out.

The entire session goes quite smoothly with few stops or need to do more than one version of a composition. They do 'Mighty Moe and Joe' twice because Hank thinks it can be improved. During the recording, Alfred Lion is on the prowl, as he often is, not getting in the musicians' ways but listening carefully from a respectable distance. He does seem to be moving over to the piano frequently, Sonny thinks and begins to wonder if he is doing something wrong. Mobley assures him that is not the case. Quite the opposite, in fact. He is doing something right and Lion is very impressed.

Mobley and Clark are friends now. They have met up several times at gigs, and now Hank has recruited the pianist for his LP. They find they have similar ideas about music and, unfortunately, the same drug habit. They hang out together at gigs and Clark notices that Hank is very quiet and withdrawn almost. At gigs, he will play a long set, and when the band take a break, he goes off to sit in his car across the street until it is time to return to the bandstand. Well, Clark can understand that his new friend is shy and not very sociable. He himself is not exactly an extrovert and has never gone out of his way to make new friends. But as two individual musicians who have played gigs together and suffered police harassment from time to time without being guilty of any criminal activity, they get along together very well.

Another musician Sonny has met on gigs already is the young trombonist Curtis Fuller. These two have admired each other's musical styles and become friendly even though in this case their personalities and lifestyles are completely different.

Sonny is invited to call in at the Blue Note office in West 61st Street. He arrives on a hot July morning and climbs the staircase to the first floor of the building. The office is not quite what he was expecting. Alfred Lion and his partner Francis Wolff are in very casual clothing, in their shirtsleeves. The room is fairly untidy, and the window is open. Resting on the windowsill is an exceptionally large cat that looks overfed. Sunshine and dust swirl around the open window.

Sonny is invited to sit down, and Lion tells him he was very impressed with his piano playing at Hank's record session. He appears to be an individual piano player who sounds like himself and nobody else. Lion finds that very rare at a time when most pianists sound interchangeable. As do many saxophonists and trumpet players. Clark feels flattered but wonders why he is there. Lion tells him he wants to offer him his own record date as a leader. He can choose his musicians.

This is a special moment for Sonny Clark. Something he has wanted for some time now and never expected to achieve after being in New York for such a relatively short time. He thanks Lion, who smiles, and Wolff grins. He tells them that he fancies a sextet as the recent Mobley date went so well and he would like Mobley and Curtis Fuller in the front line. Along with Art Farmer on trumpet, if he can get him. Art is someone he worked with very briefly in Los Angeles and then lost touch. But he admires Art's soft-focus trumpet sound and thinks it would make a great mix with the trombone and tenor.

He is feeling light as air as he goes off, stopping at a bar for a drink and a smoke along the way. He is pretty sure he can trust Lion and Wolff because both Mobley and Fuller have spoken highly of them. Fuller told him that Lion came over in 1926 anxious to get away from the horrors he saw going on around him in Germany. He arrived in the U.S.A. with no money and had to sleep rough in Central Park for a while. When he managed to get a job, he set about trying to get his friend, photographer Francis Wolff, out of Germany. It wasn't easy as war was looming, but he got him out just in time.

Clark meets up with Curtis Fuller in a bar and they have a couple of drinks and some conversation. The pianist tells his friend he has all the musicians he wants for his upcoming first leader date. Wilbur Ware remembers the jam session in Chicago where they played together. He is in New York now and available to record. As are Hank Mobley and, of course, Curtis on trombone. Sonny has been listening intently to Horace Silver's Quintet and likes the drummer who was with him on that gig: Louis Hayes. He reminds Fuller that he first heard him play in the Dizzy Gillespie Orchestra and was impressed. Art Farmer is also on board although Lion had to get permission to use him from ABC-Paramount. Art is under contract to them.

Fuller wonders why the pianist left California; he was doing very well there, wasn't he? Well, yes but it was spasmodic, all over the county, and often not the sort of music he was really into to.

'Jazz is jazz wherever it's played,' Sonny says. 'The whole thing has to do with the individual and his conception towards jazz. The thing is that my way of playing jazz is different to the way most of the fellows out west play. I'd rather work in the East because what is played here is closer to the traditional meaning of jazz. They're getting away from tradition out west—

combining jazz with classical music and playing chamber music-type jazz. What they play is really very good, but it's just not the way I want to play. That's why I came back east.'

Fuller nods. He understands and feels great affinity himself with New York hard bop music. Sonny then tells him that he is really knocked out having his own record date. He thinks getting a leader date in California would have been well-nigh impossible because he was not in tune with the styles clubs and record companies were looking for. Even so, he enjoyed most of his stay there musically. When Fuller asks what Clark's private and domestic life was like in L.A., he says the climate was crazy, but he prefers not to discuss any of his domestic life. In fact, he clams up completely remembering things suddenly that he has been busily shutting out of his mind for months now.

At the studio in Hackensack, Rudy Van Gelder is setting up his microphones. Exact placement is important to him as is every aspect of his recording setup. Sonny watches as the engineer places the microphones near and for the piano. Van Gelder has assured Alfred Lion that it will be a stereo recording and he is using his two-channel mono system. Lion is puzzled but says nothing. He trusts Van Gelder, who obviously knows what he is doing. There is only one large loudspeaker in use so he can hardly play back tapes or listen to discs in stereo at this stage. Lion, thinking ahead, wonders if it will be possible to issue the LP in stereo at a later stage as the format is already catching on and is certainly here to stay. Van Gelder tells him it will be possible.

Sonny Clark sits on the piano stool. He is quite content. After six years, most of them in L.A., he is finally leading his own recording session. He has written four originals to play, and the cats have had a chance to play through them and become comfortable with his music. Art Farmer likes the music and Hank Mobley has praised his skill as a composer. Wilbur Ware said nothing, but he is a quiet cat anyway and Sonny knows he will do a great job. As will young Louis Hayes. To round off the originals, he has selected two favourite standard songs, 'It Could Happen To You' and 'Love Walked In.'

'Bootin' It' is a bright blustery piece, and after the opening ensemble by the three horns, Sonny takes the first solo, his fingers fleet as he spins out lively single notes. Curtis Fuller matches him with a full-blown trombone segment and then Hank Mobley blows a typical tenor solo. Art Farmer gives the record just a touch of lightness on his lyrical trumpet solo, just what the leader wanted. Sonny is gently rhapsodic on 'It Could Happen To You.' Art Farmer's lightweight sound as he takes the first solo sets the mood for the rest of the band. Clark is gently introspective and slightly melancholy on his solo, but he does insert some bouncy bop lines as well. At times, on this selection, the pianist's touch is as light as a feather but so melodic. When Hank Mobley follows him, he too is warm and almost caressing in his approach to the melody. Curtis adds to the melancholy mood Clark has sustained so far. 'Sonny's Mood' is a medium-tempo exercise with telling solos from Art, Hank, Curtis and the leader's piano bringing up the rear. On 'Love Walked In,' the horns are given a break and Clark demonstrates his skills as a ballad interpreter with just his bass player and drummer backing him. His piano stylings here are gently pensive on this one although he ups the tempo as bass and drums enter.

At the end, he is encouraged by the enthusiastic comments he hears at the playback. The sidemen are all happy with the results. So is Alfred Lion judging by his expression and then his smile. Francis Wolff has taken pictures of all the musicians which will appear on the back liner of the LP. The musicians have all had beer and snacks to eat and plenty of time to rehearse. Only Sonny himself will be seen on the front cover, at the piano, in his summer check shirt. He has made his first LP for Blue Note and knows, instinctively, that it is an impressive debut.

Sonny Clark – *Dial S For Sonny*. Blue Note 1570 Robert Levin's sleeve note.

10

1957 - A VERY BUSY YEAR

SONNY IS VERY BUSY OVER THE SPRING, SUMMER AND AUTUMN OF 1957. He has gigs in the clubs and either plays with or meets up with Thelonious Monk, Charles Mingus, Sonny Rollins and a host of others. Monk is a particular inspiration to the young pianist, someone whose work he has begun to listen to more and more and to appreciate considerably. Monk plays hard bop with a distinctive flavour of his own, a personal sound of jagged chords and percussive blues lines. After Bud Powell, Monk is the main source of inspiration to Sonny and he finds himself seeking out the man, to talk to. To listen to. He is pleased to find that Monk responds to him and treats him like a young musician in need of help and encouragement. Monk promises to introduce Clark to Nica de Koenigswarter, the woman known as the jazz baroness. He is certainly keen to meet this aristocratic English woman, a member of the Rothschild family and a jazz lover who has known and promoted the music of Charlie Parker and Monk himself over the years.

Sonny recalls that Charlie Parker died in the baroness' apartment back in 1955. He had called in to visit and been taken ill. She had looked after him, but he died as he watched television. Yes, he will look forward to meeting such a person. In the meantime, he works hard for every gig and has been watched as he played by Alfred Lion of Blue Note Records. Having just recorded his first leader session for Lion, he is pleased that the man is still keeping an eye on him. It looks good for the future. When Lion approaches him, however, it is not to record again as leader but to play piano on a new recording he is setting up for Curtis Fuller and a baritone sax player named Tate Houston.

It is, Lion explains, a gamble. He is promoting both Fuller and the baritone man as he is impressed with their playing, but there is no way of knowing if the record will sell well. To give it the very best chance musically, he wants Sonny on piano, as he has been very pleased with his work both on the earlier Fuller disc and his own session. He wants Sonny, Paul Chambers on bass, and Art Taylor on drums.

Clark is pleased to accept; he will play on anything with his friend Curtis Fuller. In the studio in Hackensack, he greets Paul Chambers, Art Taylor and Curtis again, and Fuller introduces him to Houston. They run down Algonquin, a medium-tempo burner on which Curtis plays the first solo. Houston follows playing a dark-hued, bop-style baritone which Clark admires. His pulsing single-note lines, along with Chambers and Taylor keep the music swinging healthily. Sonny is at his most elegant on the ballad 'Nita's Waltz,' where he gets an extended solo that manages to combine sweet melodies with a strong injection of the blues. Curtis takes a trombone solo that is bouncy and full of simple melodies. Paul Chambers gets a typical pizzicato workout on this one.

Although the session goes well enough, Sonny thinks he has done his bit to help both Alfred Lion and the two front liners and waits expectantly for the Blue Note boss to offer him his next leader date. Lion tells him he is anxious to bring out a new, young alto sax player called John Jenkins. He is making the musician the leader on his own recording but, to try and ensure his success, Lion is adding Kenny Burrell, the well-known guitar soloist, to the front line. Burrell will also be pictured on the front cover, which will give enthusiasts the idea that he is joint leader. Burrell's presence, plus Sonny's on piano, will, Lion thinks, ensure a first-class recording and set the young musician up.

On reflection, Sonny is happy to go along with Lion's plan and realises that his time is coming. He has learned to be patient over the years in California and now he is making it in NYC. It is also looking as though Alfred Lion has long-term plans for recording him and that is just what he wants.

In the studio, he accompanies the young alto man on 'From This Moment On.' He provides staunch, forward-propelling chords behind the extended alto sax solo. The piece swings compulsively with Chambers and Charles Mingus' drummer Danny Richmond completing the surging rhythm section. His solo continues the easy-flowing, hard-grooving mood he has helped to set up. He is inventive, adding bright melodies to the proceedings. Kenny Burrell's guitar takes the third and final solo, never letting up the momentum for one minute.

'Everything I Have Is Yours' finds everybody comfortable and swinging lightly but melodically at ballad tempo. After Jenkins and Burrell have played their solos, Clark produces one of his gems. A full flurry of notes to begin and then he moves into rhapsodic, melodic mode. His touch is ultra-light, as he builds purposefully towards a climax. The session continues with 'Sharon,' a medium-tempo selection with Burrell's blues-based guitar leading off the solo sequence. Sonny is fully engaged now with the leader's choice of music as he propels the soloists forward smoothly, Chambers and Richmond in full synchronization with his piano lines. Jenkins' sweet-toned alto is obviously Charlie Parker-influenced but without the hard, percussive, bluesy thrust of the master. Clark is thinking that he will find his own, full voice in the fullness of time, but in the meantime, he is swinging along nicely, and the recording will be a very good one. On 'Blues For Two,' he plays a forceful introduction and is the driving force behind this brisk tempo fuelled blues. He gets an early piano solo and is by now and until the last note of the set, at his brilliant best.

Sonny has been given a date for his next LP as leader. Now he is frantically running round trying to get the right musicians, the ones he really wants. He has decided on a sextet, recalling how well his last album went with Farmer, Mobley and Fuller. He considers the tone colours he can get with three horns. John Coltrane is a tenor sax man with a great, hard-edged sound he has heard and liked very much. Sonny remembers seeing the Miles Davis Quintet in California and being spellbound listening to Coltrane.

Curtis Fuller tells him he has been in contact with Coltrane who has indicated that he wants the trombonist on his own Blue Note record date in two weeks' time. Alfred Lion too is keen to get Coltrane on the date. He was impressed when he got him as a sideman on a Paul Chambers led session back in 1956. Now he has him lined up for a fifteenth-of-the-month recording under his own leadership. Sonny's session will give everybody a chance to get to know Coltrane.

Curtis Fuller comes back with the news that John Coltrane is happy to play on Sonny's album. In the studio, next day, they gather for rehearsal. Alfred and Francis have provided beer, sandwiches, burgers and various culinary delicacies, as they do for all their recording sessions. Sonny meets Donald Byrd who will share the front line with Curtis on trombone and Coltrane's tenor sax. At the back, Clark will have Paul Chambers on bass and Art Taylor on drums so he has made sure of a fiery, heavyweight front line and a rock-solid rhythm section. Clark tries to engage Coltrane in conversation but finds that he is even more reserved and quiet-spoken than he is himself. These musicians know just how to express themselves eloquently through their music. Donald Byrd's shining brass trumpet sets the standard 'With a Song in My Heart' off to a flying start. Donald's improvised lines tumble out effortlessly on his solo excursion. Coltrane too is white hot in his follow-on choruses, his tone hard and razor sharp. Sonny comps easily at the fast tempo. Fuller is the last horn, and he too keeps up the momentum staunchly.

Not to be outdone by the tough horns, Sonny's solo glitters with swinging, light-touch elegance before Byrd returns to ride the composition out, aided by the tenor and bone. Sonny has chosen this piece together with two other standards he enjoys playing 'Speak Low' and 'Come Rain Or Come Shine.' Coltrane is bitterly lyrical on 'Speak Low' as he takes the introduction and first solo. Curtis follows with a pretty solo and everybody acquits themselves well. Clark is happy at the keyboard, the one place he feels content as he feeds the soloists with surging chords that defy them not to swing. His piano solo is a nourishing mix of percussive thrust and delicate, light-touch lines.

'Sonny's Crib,' the title track for the album, is a solid B-Flat blues where everybody is wailing purposefully, on good, familiar ground. Sonny knows he has got a really strong record now, as he comps contentedly under Coltrane's blues lines. The recording ends with 'News For Lulu,' an attractive minor theme which Sonny has named after the dog he had in California. It is a bittersweet moment for the pianist as he leads off the solo choruses, reminding him of the animal he was so fond of but painfully failing to avoid memories of the other horrific circumstances that led to him leaving the only brief domestic life he has known since abandoning Pittsburgh all those years ago. His repeated riff sets the piece up before he launches into his glittering solo, at medium tempo. The mood and ambience of the music is bright, optimistic as he fashions an inventive two choruses and pushes all thoughts of those tragic events in his life down and out of mind. As he plays, enjoying his solo and those of his sidemen, he pictures again his dog, Lulu, the part-chow, part-German Shepherd and an animal he thought was wonderful.

As the session ends and the musicians give their approval of the playback, Sonny is more than content. If this isn't his best record to date it is very close. Only the *Blue Serge* recording in

California stands out in his opinion, but that was Serge Chaloff's date, and he was just the pianist. *Sonny's Crib* is all his work, two original compositions and three standards, all played as well as they possibly could be.

Outside of the club gig and the recording studio, however, Sonny's life is threatening to disintegrate. He makes plenty of money, as good as the run-of-the-mill jazz musician fraternity do at any rate. He spends most of it on drugs and tobacco. Lately he has been ensuring that as soon as he is paid, he will buy some clothes. Sharp-patterned shirts, cord or denim trousers. Sweaters. Before the money evaporates into powder or tobacco or booze, he will get something smart. One item at a time. It is good to turn up at gigs and record dates looking smart and well groomed.

Some weeks he is high from getting out of bed until late at night. He will, on occasion, ride the subway all night, unable to sleep or rest properly. He crashes at loft rooms where he knows the other occupants, fellow sufferers and the unemployed, hobos of the streets. Sometimes he will seek and find refuge with a fellow musician who is also addicted. He is barely surviving on his music or the thought of the next gig looming.

He is grateful that the record dates come round frequently. Sometimes within seven days. The recordings with Curtis and Tate Houston were followed swiftly by the John Jenkins/Kenny Burrell date. One week later he was in the studio for another Hank Mobley set and enjoyed playing with the saxophonist and trumpeter Kenny Dorham, another musician he admires. Then his recent *Sonny's Crib* session. It is the days between gigs that are most painful.

Thelonious Monk has kept his promise and is taking him to meet the woman known now as the Jazz Baroness. On the way, Monk explains that Baroness Pannonica de Koenigswarter is an aristocrat of the wealthy Rothschild banking dynasty who has left her husband and children and is living permanently in New York and devoting her life to jazz. She had married Baron Jules de Koenigswarter, a French diplomat in 1935. During World War II, she had fought in the Free French Army under General De Gaulle. Monk goes on to explain to Sonny the unlikely but true story that after the war she had been unable to settle into her usual aristocratic home life and had travelled to the U.S.A. There it was that somebody had played her the recording of Thelonious Monk playing 'Round Midnight,' and she was hooked. She had been determined to trace Monk and indeed had done so. Since then, she had not returned to England but set up home in New York and constantly offered help to all and any jazz musicians in need.

Sonny smiles. Thelonious has a reputation for hardly ever speaking and only uttering two or three words during a two-way conversation. It isn't true. It is true that if you ask Monk the wrong sort of questions, show him little or no respect, or invade his privacy when he does not wish anyone to do so, he then clams up and becomes silent. Conversations between musicians are something else again.

The two men arrive at the large, impressive apartment. Sonny is received by the baroness, a tall, slim, striking looking woman wearing sable, jewels and smoking a cigarette fitted into an extremely long holder. She welcomes him, shakes his hand, beams a big smile at him and ushers him into a large drawing room where the focal point and centre of attention is a big, glossy black, grand piano. Clark, feeling a trifle nervous now, is shown to an armchair, told to make himself at home and handed a large glass of Scotch whisky. With ice. He sips the liquid slowly, carefully.

Monk has not spoken a word since arrival. He has deposited himself in an armchair and sits quietly, smoking a cigarette. Suddenly Monk, silently but with a barely perceptible nod to the baroness, walks over to the piano, sits on the stool and begins to play. Nica, as she has requested Sonny to address her, tells him she is going to the kitchen, and he must yell out if he wants or needs anything.

Sonny takes a cigarette from the box studded with pearls that has been placed strategically on a small table next to his armchair and lights it. He is beginning to overcome his surprise and initial nervousness and is enjoying the good Scotch whisky. Monk is noodling away at a standard tune, beginning to shape it to his own style of playing and transform it. Sonny listens with rapt attention. He marvels at the way Monk alters a song, plays in a percussive, sometimes jagged manner, puts in odd, dissonant notes and somehow manages to make it all sound right. And logical. Sonny believes that Monk's manner of playing, in his usual quartet setting, is the way hard bop should be played, the way it should develop in the future.

The grand piano sounds magnificent. He has never seen or heard such an instrument. Sometimes the club pianos he plays on are barely in tune, often on the edge. Recording studio pianos are much better generally but no match for this fine instrument. Monk finishes his variations on the song and immediately starts to play another piece, toying with it at first, trying out the melody in different ways before settling down to improvise at length on the main theme.

Monk stops playing abruptly, rises from the piano stool and wanders off to another part of the apartment without another word spoken. Sonny raises an eyebrow. Monk can be verbose when in company with fellow musicians or friends but equally, he has his long bouts of silence. Clark puts down his glass and walks tentatively over to the glossy, shining instrument and sits on the piano stool. He holds his hands out flat, just above the surface of the piano keys and keeps them there for a minute. After that, he can resist no longer and launches into a solo version of 'Tadd's Delight,' one of the early bebop tunes he loves, written by the great composer and pianist Tadd Dameron. The notes ring out with startling clarity and a brilliance he has never heard from a keyboard before. He digs into his own variations on this familiar theme, enjoying the wonderful sound that is making his playing so good and pointing up the skill of the composer.

He is so into the music, his improvised choruses and the sound of his favourite music coming across so freshly and vividly, that he does not notice that Nica has returned and is sitting in an armchair facing him. She applauds him as he finishes the piece with a sustained bass note. Sonny looks up, nods nervously in her direction and puts his hands on his lap.

'You play very well indeed,' she informs him. 'As well as any jazz pianist I have heard.'

Sonny smiles, pleased. She goes on to tell him that he is always welcome here, any time, day or night. She is here for him and any jazz musician in need of anything. He can play the piano any time he wants and there is no need to ask permission. If he is in need of money or anything else at any time, he only needs to mention it. She knows how badly treated jazz musicians are, with no respect or consideration from club owners or record companies for the wonderful music they produce.

Thelonious Monk has disappeared, but he is still on the premises. Sonny comes to understand that he is the special musician as far as Nica is concerned and he comes and goes frequently, has the run of the entire apartment, and sometimes just wanders round for hours, rarely speaking but often stopping to play a few pieces on the piano. Nica tells Sonny in conversation that, in her opinion, Monk is a genius. But he is misunderstood and underrated by everybody, bookers, club owners, record companies. She intends to help him, promote him, where possible, finance him when needed. To be, in effect, his patron. Like the dukes and barons of the distant past would be patrons to Mozart, Schubert, and other great musicians of the bygone days.

He tells her he understands. Monk is one of the greatest. Nica smiles. Any friend of Monk's is a friend of hers, so she hopes to see Sonny frequently in future. And to always come to her if he needs anything. Anything at all. She is, he thinks, actively encouraging him to come to her, even repeating herself in her desire to be his friend. Without knowing him. He hears her saying that she recently ordered a brand-new piano for the Five Spot Café because she didn't think the one there was good enough for Monk to play with his quartet. Monk is resident at that club with his combo and has been for a long time.

When Sonny leaves Nica's apartment after being given a good meal and plenty to drink, he is feeling very good. He has made a new friend and one that he is sure will help him in future. If he ever needs help.

Three Wishes - Sight and Sound.
Nica de Koenigswarter - *Heterodox*
Nica de Koenigswarter—Wikipedia entry.

11

MOBLEY, GRIFFIN AND A NIGHT AT THE FIVE SPOT CAFE

SONNY CLARK HAS ANOTHER RECORD DATE. ALFRED LION OFFERED it and asked him what he had in mind for his new recording. He tells his producer that he would love to do a trio set. He has fond memories of a session he did back on the West Coast in 1955 with two local musicians in Oakland, California, and he enjoyed it so much. Most of his music-making since then has been in quintets or sextets, and although he loves a six-piece, the idea of doing a trio with top-ranking eastern musicians appeals greatly. Lion is happy with that and suggests he recruit two of the best in Paul Chambers and Art Blakey. Chambers is a frequent visitor to the Van Gelder studio, and Lion regards Blakey as the greatest, a man he is coming to regard as the house drummer at Blue Note. Clark is happy with that suggestion.

When he meets Paul Chambers two days later, the bassist is keen to be on the recording. He wonders whether Sonny would consider Philly Joe Jones for the drum chair. Chambers agrees that Blakey is great but points out that he has a special affinity with Philly Joe. They have worked for almost five years together in the Miles Davis Quintet and practically breathe together in the rhythm section. Sonny agrees. He loved working with the drummer on Serge Chaloff's West Coast date and would really welcome hitching up with him on his trio record.

On the subject of repertoire, Sonny wants to play some of his favourite bop charts from the first wave of bebop in the 1940s. It will be a statement about where he is coming from musically and where he would like to be associated with. He can play the latest hard bop variation with ease and does so almost every day, but he still connects strongly with the first wave of the music.

In the studio, the trio kick off with 'Bebop,' an early composition by Dizzy Gillespie. Sonny loves playing behind the great horn soloists, feeding them chords and enhancing their improvised choruses, but now he can stretch out acting as the main soloist himself. He plays the original Gillespie introduction to 'Bebop,' putting his own slant on it, altering the melody to make it personal and then swings headlong into a series of explosive choruses. He employs a furious up-tempo, gliding through a plethora of notes with what sounds like relaxed ease. The music charges along effortlessly, the rapid tempo maintained easily by the brisk drive of bass and drums. It is a tribute to Clark's powers of imagination that he plays chorus after chorus, full of inventive lines, using the full range of the keyboard. It is an eight-minute solo of considerable skill. Philly Joe's explosive fills give the performance a special lift. As Sonny ends his marathon workout, Paul Chambers enters playing arco, and then he gives way to a snappy drum solo from Philly. Clark takes it out maintaining the tempo smoothly.

'I Didn't Know What Time It Was' is the first of three solid standards the pianist has chosen which, along with 'I'll Remember April,' are associated with Bird and Diz and early bebop performances. Apart from a short pizzicato bass solo, this one is all Sonny. Gillespie's 'Two Bass Hit' is usually a feature for the bass player, but Clark has arranged his version as a piece spotlighting Philly Joe. Jones responds vigorously.

'Tadd's Delight' is taken at a medium, comfortable tempo with Sonny's chiming notes ringing out melodiously. Good as all three musicians agree it is, the leader asks for a second take just to see if it can be improved. The trio finish with 'I'll Remember April,' a piece of music forever now associated with bop and the early pioneers. The only trouble is, as Clark sees it, everybody in modern jazz plays it fast. 'It's pretty,' he says, 'it's essentially a ballad.' His slow, pensive reading is richly sonorous, flowing gently along as an unaccompanied selection. All of Clark's essential lyrical skill is on display with this solo, his notes played lightly and sensuously. At the end, all three musicians express satisfaction during the playback, and Alfred Lion is especially complimentary. He thinks this is Sonny's best single LP performance, although the pianist just smiles. He likes all of his recent Blue Note discs, but he does admit to himself that this is, maybe, a landmark recording. It is a programme of some of his favourite charts, played to the best of his ability and enhanced by two of the best bass and drum men in the business.

Sonny visits the jazz baroness at her home on a day when he is feeling particularly low. He has had a few days without a gig and no immediate record dates are looming. He has injected a large amount of heroin as his body is now able to absorb the drug. To any new addict, it would have constituted an overdose. It is more than he should have taken, and he knows it. He has dressed tidily in shirt, trousers and sweater and is looking quite smart, but his haggard face and dull, lifeless-looking eyes give him away.

Nica notices his condition as soon as he arrives and is concerned. She invites him to stay at her home and try to get himself cleaned up. She will help and give him all the support he will need to try and get clean. She takes him to visit her doctor who gives him alternative medicine and tablets to help him shake off his addiction. She takes him home with her and gives him food, alcoholic refreshments and cigarettes. In the comfortable, luxurious surroundings of the Baroness' home, he begins to recover.

Slowly, painstakingly, he becomes less reliant on the drug,

taking less and less with every passing day. He relies heavily on alcohol and cigarettes to feed his addictive nature. Nica indulges him. At first, she does not bother him with questions about his addiction and what he intends to do about it but just makes him comfortable. He eats at her home, he sleeps there, he goes out with her to jazz clubs to listen to the music, most frequently to the Five Spot to hear the Thelonious Monk Quartet. Nica can listen to Monk all night and never get enough of his music. Sonny is happy to listen too. He admires Monk and rates him as highly as any jazz pianist he has ever heard.

Nica knows she must do more to help Sonny, but she will not rush it; she will take her own sweet time. For now, coming slowly out of a very bad place, Sonny is content to sit back, relax a little and let his benefactor indulge him. He feels rather guilty and knows he should be standing on his own feet and not taking full advantage of his patron's kindness and hospitality. It is when he goes to bed and his limbs sink into the soft, luxurious mattress and he covers himself with the perfumed sheets that he feels he would just like to spend the rest of his life here.

He gets a gig in downtown New York, and Nica drives him to the club in her large, convertible Bentley. She has to go back home to see to the needs of another young musician who has fallen on hard times and cannot pay his bills. Nica will pay them for him. She promises to came back and collect Sonny as soon as his gig ends and take him back home.

Curtis Fuller has come to the Baroness' home and is talking to Sonny in the kitchen. They are drinking beer and talking about music, gigs, opportunities and, indeed, for some people, the lack of them. Curtis has recently recorded an LP with John Coltrane that he thinks is a great record. A classic of the future if he knows a thing or two. Sonny is sceptical. He has made records he thought were winners all the way and they only sold in moderate numbers. There just isn't enough interest in jazz from the public now. Not like there was in Parker and Gillespie's time. Even his main inspiration, the great Bud Powell, is struggling to make a good living. Curtis shakes his head. He takes his friend's point but says this was an exceptional session. Lee Morgan was on trumpet and he and Trane were onn great form. Sonny's friend Kenny Drew was the pianist and they had Paul Chambers and Philly Joe Jones in the rhythm section. Alfred Lion says they will be calling it *Blue Train* on release. Clark just smiles and says we will wait and see.

Curtis thinks Sonny and Coltrane are very much alike. He tells him that he is hip and a great writer of music. Like Coltrane. 'You and he are alike, dead serious about your music. You are both scholars of music and have great respect for it. You have a different type of creativity, a unique and special touch, and an old-fashioned quality that is also very modern.'

Sonny is flattered and impressed by his friend's words. He and Fuller have been good friends ever since they first met soon after the pianist's arrival in New York. He wants to work with Fuller regularly in future as he rates him highly as a modern trombonist, but he had no idea how highly the man thought about him. It does, though, cause him to focus his mind on the future and ensure that he gets clean again and avoids drugs. He has been in some nasty scrapes in the past three months and been brought down very low by his habit. Now he has someone to actively help him get clean. With Nica's help he can surely rid himself of the evils of heroin addiction and concentrate on a career in music that is looking most promising.

It is looking good again as far as work is concerned. He has another record date with a Hank Mobley session where he is pleased to hear that he will link up again with Paul Chambers and Philly Joe Jones. Art Farmer is booked to play trumpet and Pepper Adams makes it a sextet with his baritone sax. Following his fairly recent trio set with Chambers and Jones, it looks like just the sort of programme he finds ideal. Then, the icing on the cake, another record date with Blue Note on a Johnny Griffin quartet with Chambers once more and Kenny Dennis on drums.

In the Van Gelder studio, Sonny feels he is surrounded by people that are now old friends. Hank leads off the ensemble with 'Poppin,' the composition that will give the record its title when it eventually sees the light of day. It is a bouncy piece which starts off with a now familiar Clark solo, flowing, light of touch, swinging easily. Farmer is in good solo form and Hank fairly steaming along, his lines unorthodox but completely logical to him and working out just fine. The pianist sometimes looks askance at Mobley as the lines the tenor man plays seem to have little musical logic, but he has to admit the solos always appear to come out right at the end. Or give the illusion that they do. The selection ends with some exciting four-bar exchanges featuring Mobley and Philly. Clark plays a delicate, thoughtful introduction to 'Darn That Dream.' Mobley demonstrates what a fine ballad player he is with a richly lyrical solo that has only a tinge of melancholy sadness. Farmer is muted and continues the romantic mood easily, as does Pepper, whose crusty lines offer contrast in tone colour but are just as warm. Sonny's lyricism is right in the mood set by Hank with just a little percussive edge to his notes.

'Tune Up' leads off with a Farmer open horn solo. The trumpeter appears to find the chord changes challenging but winds his way through cheerfully with just a touch of repetition. Pepper follows him, just a little hesitant at times during a pulsating solo. Sonny flows through a charging solo easily, his invention constant, sustained throughout. Hank adapts the chords to suit his delivery and style, as he always does, following a tasty arco expedition from Chambers. He is melodic throughout without losing the thread of the composition in spite of a personalised interpretation that ignores bar lines if they get in his way. Philly Joe takes a swift burst on drums and the ensemble takes it out.

At the conclusion, everybody agrees it is a good session and they are all happy with the result, which makes it all the stranger to Hank when Lion fails to release the record and it does not come out until the Japanese release it some twenty years later. Maybe he forgets it, perhaps he just has too many new releases to put out at the moment, but only Alfred Lion knows the truth. With a cast of top jazz musicians like these and a buoyant, brisk, hard-swinging record, even a few flaws, if there are any, should not have prevented its release.

Three days on and it is back to Van Gelder's studio to record with Johnny Griffin, the Chicago tenor saxophonist. Clark met up with Griffin in Chicago, the man's base, and the two jammed together. The pianist was impressed with Griffin's hard tone and obvious facility on his instrument. He also has a reputation as one of the fastest players alive and can play up-tempo selections at a speed that would make most soloist's toes curl. Sonny has been listening to a recording he made very recently for Blue Note where, in a three-tenor front line, Griffin takes a killing tempo in his stride while, alongside him, even seasoned tenor soloists like John Coltrane and Hank Mobley are struggling to keep up.

So, this will be a straight-ahead, blowing session because Clark knows the way Griffin operates. His last LP, the one with Trane and Hank, was actually titled *A Blowing Session*. To begin, there is a long workout on Griffin's 'The Congregation,' a blues with gospel tinges that will also provide the album's title.

Sonny meets up with a familiar face in the studio, Paul Chambers, rapidly becoming his favourite bass player. Paul is there. Kenny Dennis, a young drummer from Philadelphia is the other man in the rhythm section and this is his first record date.

Griffin floats into 'The Congregation' at a comfortable medium lope. He is soon digging into familiar blues licks in jam session fashion. Honks and cries. Squeals. Sonny backs him joyously. His piano solo keeps up the momentum Griffin has set up, blues chords, spinning lines, mostly upbeat with only the faintest glint of melancholy. Chambers solos pizzicato and even his usually sadness-inflected sound is more cheerful than usual. This is a happy blues. Kenny Dennis keeps a bright, shuffle beat going in sympathetic support of the soloists.

Chicago Alto saxman John Jenkins, an associate of Griffin, contributed 'Latin Quarter.' A typical Latin feel pervades this track which Griffin again takes at a moderate tempo. Griffin's lines are hard and bop-fuelled although Clark and Chambers, again pizzicato, offer sparkling melodic solos. The rest of the session consists of three standards and 'Main Stem,' another funky blues. They finish with 'I Remember You,' a pretty standard where Griffin is at his inventive best on an extended solo followed by Chambers playing arco. Clark sparkles as usual here, referencing the bright melody before improvising freely on the line. Curiously, this track will not be included on the issued LP. Dennis takes his only brisk solo before Griffin wraps it up. Sonny Clark smiles. The session is exactly the way he anticipated it, a good blowing set, no better and no worse than dozens of others he has played on.

The Baroness, Nica de Koenigswarter, has bought a new house in Weehawken, New Jersey. She was asked to leave the Bolivar Hotel in Central Park West by the management following repeated, loud jam sessions in her suite of rooms that often went on into the small hours. The new house will suit her very well now that she has purchased it on the recommendation of Thelonious Monk. Monk told her she should not have to be harassed for having music in her home and should buy her own house and have complete freedom of movement and music.

The house is contemporary and most attractive consisting of two large, joined, square blocks with white facings with a strip of yellow round the flat roof edgings. A garage, built into one block, has a door consisting of twelve square yellow panels, and the entire building is set well back from the road in a pleasant, green field area.

Clark has been dropped off outside her driveway by a musician friend who was going out to New Jersey. He wears good clothes that look as though they could benefit from a brushing. His trousers are somewhat crumpled. Following a four-week spell where he took no toxic substances whatsoever, a brush with a police officer set him back. He was entirely innocent of any misdemeanour but accused of loitering with intent. It happens frequently. No charges were brought, but he found the incident unsettling and visited a musician friend who persuaded him to shoot up heroin. Now, he is feeling low and after a considerable absence has decided to seek sanctuary with Nica.

She welcomes him in and gives him a reviving drink, disturbed at his appearance. He was doing so well, she tells him, last time they met and must try again. If that is what he really wants. She offers to take him back to her doctor who will help him get completely clean. Sonny will go, he says, but not yet. He needs time to rest and recuperate from feeling low and extremely lonely.

Monk is in the house, as he spends much of his time here now. But, as he has been explaining to a close friend, the baroness is his good friend, associate, someone who helps him deal with club owners and people he finds difficult or just plain does not wish to converse with. She is of great help and succour to him in this world of money-grabbing businesspeople who have no understanding of the problems of jazz musicians. She is not his lover. Never was and never will be. Nobody could come between him and his wife, Nellie, the mother of his children. Nellie herself understands that. She refers to Nica as his business manager.

Nica has had an idea. She pours out two glasses of Scotch whisky and hands one to Sonny. She wants to help him beat his drug addiction and knows how difficult it is. She will take him to her doctor later but how about a little practical help in the meantime? She has been thinking of getting a chauffeur to drive her around New York on her many visits. And to clubs in the evenings. How would Sonny like the post? It could work out very well because he could live here, in the new house, legitimately, as her employee. Naturally, he would be free to go to any gigs and record dates whenever, and on those occasions, she would drive herself. She has been doing just that anyway for years.

Sonny nods. If she is sure she wants him in the job, it would be good. And he would feel less guilty about staying in her home for extended periods of time. Lately, he has had nowhere to sleep except for dirty, draughty loft pads or on a friend's floor if they have no spare bed or sofa to offer. It is settled then.

Sonny drives the Bentley down to Cooper Square in Manhattan. He pulls up outside the Five Spot Café in time for Monk's first set with his new quartet. Nica and Monk alight from the car and enter the club. Sonny follows them in. Monk has a brief word with the proprietor and then disappears to the back of the club to meet his musicians. Nica is shown to her favourite table by the manager and she and Sonny take their seats. A waiter approaches and beams a smile as he recognises Clark. His name is Bob Whiteside, a jazz bass player that Clark has seen in clubs a couple of times. He introduces Nica to the man who nods, smiles and tells her he has heard about the good work she is doing for the cats. Nica smiles in return and tells him if he ever needs help, he must call at her house.

Whiteside has been finding it almost impossible to get gigs for some considerable time. He has taken a job as a waiter to earn some bread to keep him going. It is not so bad, he tells Sonny, and at least he gets to hear some good music every night. Nica orders two whiskies and they settle down. She is wearing a white sable, and she lights a cigarette at the end of her long holder. Their table is attracting quite a bit of attention in the tightly packed little club although many of the regular patrons have seen her in here frequently.

Monk comes onto the small stage to loud applause. He has Ahmed Abdul Malik on bass, Roy Haynes at the drums, and Jonny Griffin comes in smiling, holding his shiny tenor saxophone aloft. They begin playing 'Coming On The Hudson,' one of Monk's newer compositions. Griffin is hard-toned, gruff, swinging purposefully as Monk puts jagged but percussive chords under his horn. Malik has a big tone and Roy Haynes' snap, crackle and boom resounds through the small room, his surging drums and cymbals bouncing off the walls excitingly. Clark is enjoying their music and likes the individual contributions very much but has to admit to himself that they are not the fiery, compulsively swinging unit he saw here a few months ago. That was during the wild six months that John Coltrane was the featured tenor player and his wonderful rapport with Monk and the insistent yet controlled swing from Wilbur Ware and shadow Wilson was absolutely electrifying. One night he heard Coltrane blowing, as one critic put it, like a demonic baroque cellist as Monk laid out and Trane brought the house down, causing cheers, applause and foot stomping from the stimulated crowd. Monk knows a good tenor player, Sonny concedes, and Griffin lights up the room with his wild choruses. Monk, not to be outdone by his sideman, plays a fiercely flowing, percussive solo, shadowed faithfully by Malik and Haynes.

As the selection comes to a conclusion and the applause erupts, Monk moves straight into 'Ruby My Dear,' one of his more serene, ballad compositions. Griffin is more subdued here, his tone lighter and greyer, as Monk's colourful chords key in behind him. Malik provides a big bass sound and Haynes' brushes are light as air, discreet. Sonny learns much from Monk just by listening to him. But although he absorbs every note into memory, he knows it will not noticeably affect his own, very personal style of keyboard technique. The influence of the older man on his playing will be subtle, barely audible much of the time, but it will be there, nevertheless. Monk and Bud Powell are his two main inspirations at the present time, to feed into his overall approach.

Tonight, he will sleep well in that luxurious, comfortable bed, as he recuperates slowly and benefits from Nica's close attention. He is happy to function as her chauffeur, at least for the time being, as he finds his feet again and stays away from dirty, uncomfortable loft spaces and the influence of the people he shares spaces with usually. In time he hopes to get his own small but respectable pad, consolidate his already successful live and recording routine. And to get his own working trio that he can take out on the road and work the best clubs like Birdland and the Village Vanguard. He's had one gig with Sam Jones on bass and Art Taylor on drums and that would suit him well if both were available for regular work. Both of them are in great demand, so he might have to settle for slightly less well-known sidemen.

All things are possible now that he is establishing a reputation as one of the better bop pianists in town, but he will have to kick his drug habit and stay off for good. It demands willpower and strength of mind and purpose. As he leaves the club with Nica and holds the door of the Bentley open for her to climb in, he is feeling at his most optimistic.

Nica de Koenigswarter Wikipedia entry.
Sonny Clark Melody and Melancholy—Essay by Sam Stephenson.

12

A BUSY SCHEDULE

AFTER COMPLETING THE JOHNNY GRIFFIN CONGREGATION recording, Sonny does not have long to wait for new recording opportunities to arise. The October recording date was, he thought, perhaps the last of that year, but he was wrong. Cliff Jordan, the young Chicago tenor who knows Griffin well, has contacted him for a November date for Blue Note Records. He will line up with Art Farmer again along with George Tucker, a bass player with a big, fat, blossoming sound and young Louis Hayes from the Horace Silver Quintet.

'Confirmation' has been chosen by Jordan along with 'Anthropology,' both ideal for Clark and his love of Charlie Parker's music. Jordan takes 'Confirmation' at a medium lope after Sonny cues him in with a softly melodic introduction. The tenor man has a pleasing, light bop sound and his solo is interesting. Art Farmer follows with his usual lyrical approach. Clark skips lightly and melodically over the keys in his outing adding fresh melodies to make a personal approach to an old, favourite warhorse. The piece ends with a riff punctuated by Hayes' chirpy drumming.

Sonny stays in rhapsodic mode as he gently plays the introduction to 'Sophisticated Lady' with its shades of Duke Ellington. 'Anthropology' is more to his liking as he chords behind the horns in a blistering, up-tempo workout. Even Art Farmer sounds brassy and right in the bebop frame here. It is, for all concerned, a laid-back, happy session. Nothing spectacular but enjoyable for all the musicians.

Six days later, back in Van Gelder's studio, Sonny finds himself backing the fiery, volatile trumpet sensation, Lee Morgan. After several blast-off sessions, Lee has here assembled a well-chosen quartet for some slow to medium ballads. 'Since I Fell for You' is a melodic item which Lee plays straight apart from a few trademark slurs here and there. Sonny begins his delicate solo with a blues phrase and continues with melodic gems. 'Personality' is slow to medium and still in lyrical, relaxed style. Sonny enjoys working in the section with Doug Watkins, a swinging bass player with very true notes and a glorious tone. Art Taylor is on drums. Only four selections are recorded on this day, so the musicians must return to the studio at a later date to complete the album. Morgan has said that he wants to play a complete programme of soft-focus music to show his versatility and get away from up-tempo burners for a while. Sonny is happy with the programme intention and will make himself available for the return session.

Sonny is pleased when he is invited to play piano on his friend Curtis Fuller's new quintet album for Blue Note. Art Farmer, George Tucker and Louis Hayes are again involved. Fuller demonstrates his inventive prowess on a slow, ballad treatment of 'Too Late Now.' Sonny is pensive, melodic, a wee bit more fragmented on his solo, but it is still a little gem of jazz piano. 'Jeanie' is a Fuller ballad, pretty but sounding a little too much like 'But Not For Me' and 'How About You.' Sonny introduces fresh melodies of his own in an inventively personal solo that carefully avoids comparison with the other songs. Art takes it out after a short bass segment from Tucker. 'Little Messenger' is a bop swinger where Clark plays the opening solo in fierce, hard bop mode.

After the recording is wrapped up and the musicians paid, Clark and Fuller head out for a nearby bar for refreshments and a conversation. Time to catch up after not seeing each other for a while. These two are good friends even though their lifestyles are vastly different. Fuller, like Sonny, is becoming well respected as one of the better young soloists on the scene. Particularly, in his case, because there are very few trombone players who can master the hard bop style and solo effectively. And if he can avoid the self-destructive horrors of heroin addiction, which it appears that he is doing, he should achieve success and a satisfying career as a jazz soloist.

Clark outlines the highs and lows of his progress over the past three months, including the harassment he has received from the police, always without foundation, but plays down his involvement on the drug scene. Fuller's life has been quieter all round although he is pleased with the praise he has been receiving for his contribution to Coltrane's *Blue Train*, an album already highly regarded and looking like a future classic. The two friends then part company in good spirits, both hoping, in their different ways, for a bright and musically satisfying future. They arrange to keep in touch before departing.

As the year 1957 winds down to a close, Sonny Clark receives two more calls to record. He is given another leader date and, with not too much time to organise it, he recruits Cliff Jordan, whose tenor sax playing impressed him on an earlier recording. Kenny Burrell, always reliable and a good blues player, is on guitar. Paul Chambers, now a regular on Sonny's recording dates, is there on bass, and Pete La Roca is on drums. La Roca, whose real surname is Sims, is a promising young percussionist who has already recorded and played in Sonny Rollins' Trio. The quintet play 'Minor Meeting,' an early but sturdy blues written by Sonny a while back. His piano solo follows the ensemble, his notes glancing lightly from the keyboard in glittering fashion. The composer Sonny Clark is beginning to come more and more into focus now that he is getting fairly regular record dates. This composition has been tried out in the clubs and, he recalls, was well received. They maintain a steady, rocking medium pace as first Burrell and then Cliff Jordan take solos.

Next, they tackle 'Eastern Incident,' another Sonny line and follow it with a third, 'Little Sonny.' The playing is completely satisfactory but, unusually, no more music is played on this day. It is most unusual to only record three pieces and not have any other material planned, but it has happened. Clark had in mind three standards, or possibly two and a new piece of his own. But he has not written anything else and can't think of standards that would be suitable for the three tracks already recorded. It is also the case that having put down the three originals satisfactorily, he no longer feels like recording anything else. The sidemen are easy either way, provided they are paid for the music already recorded.

Alfred Lion, who is used to the whims and temperament of musicians, says not to worry. The tracks can be stored and used with a future recording session, when Sonny is ready. Lion already has a backlog of records waiting for release, so he is not going to insist on completion today.

The last session of the year is a Lou Donaldson quintet. Sonny meets Donald Byrd at the studio, along with alto sax leader Donaldson, his good pal Curtis Fuller on trombone and the bass and drum team of George Joyner and Art Taylor. 'Dewey Square' is another piece of music associated with Charlie Parker that sets Sonny off playing with added vigour and enthusiasm. Curtis takes the first solo before the alto sax man begins his blues-based sermon. Clark comps enthusiastically behind him. Donald Byrd is full of fire and brimstone in his trumpet explosion. Sonny flows along lightly but with little skips in his lines that thrust the music comfortably forward. The ensemble is crisply integrated together in a rousing finale.

George Joyner plays a springy, lean bass line introduction to 'Strollin' In,' a medium-tempo, down-home blues. Byrd's solo sketches out brassy blues lines skilfully. Curtis Fuller is also in good form here. Donaldson preaches in typical manner on alto, his sound raw and deep blue, his Parker mannerisms on display as his solo progresses. Joyner keeps up his flowing, springy ideas in a fascinating pizzicato bass solo. Sonny, always more than happy with this type of loping blues, underlines the bass line effectively. His own solo digs into the blues inventively with some melodic interjections. Overall, it is the best and most interesting solo on this track. His counter-lines decorate the closing ensemble.

Sonny leaves the session feeling satisfied with yet another competent performance on a typical, blues-based blowing session. He enjoys this type of assignment without feeling it stretches him in any way.

As he returns home, though, he is thinking about his next date at Blue Note as leader. He wants to do something different but has no clear idea in his mind what to record or how he will go about it. All that comes to mind at the moment is that it will have to be an ideal lineup, carefully selected musicians on each instrument and not just who happens to be available at the time.

This is something to think about tomorrow or the next day or the one after that. For the moment he is absorbed with keeping clean, staying well away from drugs and temptation. And he looks forward to returning to Nica's house and spending time with her and his friend, Thelonious Monk.

13

MASTER WORK 1 - COOL STRUTTIN'

Sonny often noodles away at the grand piano in Nica's drawing room. Sometimes he just plays fragments of music that come to him, embellishes and then drops them. He then moves on to another melody he constructs and plays with it until it develops into something he can use or dies. Occasionally he comes up with a good theme he can develop into a full composition and later use on a gig. Or record it.

Today he is listless, nothing he plays develops the way he would like. When Monk ambles into the room and stands looking down at him, he knows Thelonious is keen to play, so, although no words are spoken, he gets up and lets the big man sit at the piano. He retreats to the nearest armchair and stretches out in it, listening to Monk. The aggravating thing about Monk is that everything he plays sounds fresh, newly minted and complete even if it only lasts two minutes. Amazing, that facility.

He listens carefully to Monk's music, sometimes recognising a familiar theme, often hearing new material. Today he hears Monk play an intriguing piece that even he can't finish satisfactorily. He noodles away at it for some time, tries it several different ways and then abandons it, irritated, in mid-flow.

Obviously, his friend is having difficulty with this tune.

Monk shuffles off to somewhere else in the house, as he often does. Clark returns to the piano and runs through the tune Monk has just been playing, from memory. He alters a note here and there but has no more idea how to resolve it than Thelonious.

He leaves the piano and returns to the armchair. There is something about that melody that sticks in his memory. Monk is his friend. The baroness has told him that the older man likes him and thinks of him almost as a younger brother, one that needs to be looked after and guided. Monk is also concerned, as indeed is Nica, about his frequent use of harmful substances and, in particular, heroin. Not that Monk himself hasn't been known to use illegal substances of one kind or another, but he is not known to be a heroin addict.

Nica wants Sonny to see a man she knows that she thinks could help him considerably. She tells him about Doctor Robert Freymann, a controversial psychiatrist in New York who has helped many artists and musicians over a period of time. Sonny resists at first, but Nica is quite insistent and eventually gets him to agree to a session. She sets it all up and makes an appointment, telling Clark not to worry about his high fees. She will pay the man and will be happy to do so.

Sonny drives to downtown New York in the Bentley with Nica beside him. He parks the vehicle and after expressing doubts about the visit he is assured by the baroness that she will not come in but stay in the waiting room until his session is over. Freymann would not have it any other way, but she does not tell Sonny that. The psychiatrist relaxes Sonny, gives him a cup of coffee and encourages him to talk about himself, his hopes and plans and, eventually, to talk about his addiction and how he feels about it.

The doctor does not make any comments other than to encourage and coax Sonny to talk. What does he feel about his situation and how is it affecting him, does he think? Clark realises, thinking about it as he drives, that he has openly expressed all his fears and horror of heroin, in the one-hour session with the psychiatrist where he himself did ninety-nine percent of the talking. It is a sobering thought. Today, he has talked about things openly that he has never before confronted. Not even to himself.

Nica assures him he does not need to worry. By his third session with Doctor Freymann, he will never want to touch heroin again, as long as he lives. Sonny looks sceptical. Nica pats his hand and tells him to wait and see.

It is quiet in the Blue Note office this morning. Alfred Lion is looking at a recent LP he has released by Cliff Jordan. The cat is still on the windowsill but inside now, the January climate is too severe for an open window. Clark outlines his plan for his new LP. He has Jackie McLean on board and Art Farmer has been approached. Linking up in the rhythm section with Chambers and Jones, as he did on his trio record and Hank Mobley's recent session, he knows they are ideal. He wants to explore in depth two new compositions and two classics from the early bebop phase. Lion reminds him that Blue Note policy is always to have three good-length pieces on each side of a record, and he likes to keep it that way wherever possible. The pianist is planning for just two. Sonny responds that he can't put everything into his two new pieces unless they can play for nine or ten minutes each.

Lion shrugs. Well, Clark knows what he is doing and has been very successful so far. 'As long as it swings,' he says in his heavy German accented English. 'It must swing.' Sonny assures him, smiling, that it will 'sving.'

In the studio, at rehearsal, Sonny tells Nat Hentoff, the author and jazz critic who is writing the sleeve note, how he got the idea for his title tune, 'Cool Struttin.' It was inspired by his wife. It is the only time he has mentioned her since 1955 when he walked out. Hentoff asks if he can elaborate and Sonny changes tack immediately. 'I got the name for it from the way the melody goes,' he replies. It's a feeling of somebody struttin'. I mean the old conception of the word. I guess you could say the tune itself is a funky modern version of an old step. It's a twenty-four-bar blues. Twelve and then twelve.'

He explains to Hentoff that he wanted McLean on alto for his fresh, different sound. He had heard Jackie on a 1953 recording with Miles Davis and had been instantly impressed. 'He was influenced by Bird certainly,' Sonny says, 'but he's one of the very few who has his own way of playing modern alto.' Art Farmer then adds that 'most of the altoists took one primary aspect from Bird – there were so many to the man – and developed that one for their purposes. With Jackie he took that real agonised tone – sometimes it's like a squawk – that Bird would use at times. It's like someone sticks a knife in you; you holler and scream and your voice changes in the pain. So, Jackie developed on that and paid little attention to the more delicate elements of Bird's playing. Jackie has a feeling in his playing that you know immediately is him. He doesn't just copy.'

Sonny nods. Yes, that about sums up why he wanted McLean on the recording, that Parker-like scream. He will ask him to tone it down just a little. He goes over to Mc Lean and explains that he wants a real, down-home, pulsating blues but with a feel-good factor near the surface. Jackie understands.

Sonny tells Hentoff that he wanted Paul Chambers on bass. 'I met Paul,' he says, 'in Detroit in 1954. He was very young and nobody outside the city knew much about him, but I dug him right then. He's very consistent and has superior conception, choice of notes and ability to construct lines. He plays with intelligence, and he always keeps it interesting.' Hentoff nods and makes a note in his notebook.

'Philly Joe Jones?' Hentoff wonders. 'I never heard him until he was with Miles and came out to the coast in 1956,' Sonny tells him. 'Joe,' Sonny goes on, 'has a different way of swinging. He plays all the drums. Usually, when a drummer does that he gets in the way and doesn't make much sense. But Joe's different. He has a very musical conception – and he listens to what you and the other players are doing. Very few drummers really listen. He gets involved in the group effort, and he winds up inspiring you by the different little things he does besides keeping time. Joe really makes it happen. He's always inventing something. I can listen to him develop a rhythmic pattern that I in turn can build on. And always, underneath everything, he's genuinely swinging.'

Hentoff is scribbling away, taking down the leader's words to later construct his sleeve essay. Sonny rounds out his reasons for this quintet by saying that he first met Art Farmer in California in 1952, soon after he arrived on the West Coast. 'I was living in Pasadena, and Art used to come over with Wardell Gray. We'd session all the time. Art, although he was influenced by Miles Davis, had a style of his own even then. In the years since, he's matured a lot and has a more masculine style of playing. Now he's more consistent too and his conception is very impressive.'

Sonny has made his case eloquently. Now, all it remains for him to do is produce the superior hard bop record that he hopes his choice of material and conception will provide. He is certainly optimistic. Although he tends always to feel that each recording, he makes is his best yet, he is aware that this is not always the case. But he has a really good feeling about this one before a single note is taped.

It is time to run down the title tune in rehearsal. *Cool Struttin'* is taken at a brisk, medium tempo with mellow trumpet from Farmer, a cutting, slashing alto by McLean, and Sonny digs into the blues on his two solos, one to begin and one at the end. It is good, not quite there but nearly. He reflects that if this was being recorded by Prestige Records or any of the independents, he would not have had the luxury of a few days paid rehearsal. That is the beauty of Blue Note. The version they have just played would have been the recording. A sobering thought.

He makes a few adjustments. Requests a slightly slower tempo. Asks for slightly less brassiness from Farmer and a fractionally less stark approach from McLean. He will adjust his rhythmic support and Paul and Joe will blend in with him. The musicians trust him because he seems so sure of what he wants,

and they all know what he can do. At the end he says that it was a good rehearsal but could have been better. It is not a problem; tomorrow they record, and it will go as he wants it to.

Sonny kicks off 'Cool Struttin" in the Van Gelder studio. Smooth take off from the horns with rhythm backing spot on. Medium slow blues with a clarion sound. Tempo spot on. The pianist leader goes into his opening solo with a bright flourish of chords and continues with single lines, blues-soaked. The solo flows along like a river on a cool spring morning. No sign of strain. As Art Farmer remarked when talking to annotator Nat Hentoff, 'A primary quality in Sonny's playing is that there's no strain in it. Some people sound like they're trying to swing. Sonny just flows naturally along. Also central to his work is that he has a good, powerful feeling for the blues.' Nowhere are Art's words more appropriate than on this reading of this composition.

Farmer floats into a relaxed and cool-sounding trumpet solo. The tempo remains rock solid as he plays, the trumpet lines fleet, warm and carefully underlined by piano stylings and sturdy yet laid-back bass and drums. McLean piles on the blues choruses, his lines just a fraction less acerbic than his usual sound. Sonny returns to solo mode, spinning long lines melodically with a faint suggestion of percussive accentuation. He closes with delicate chords. Paul Chambers' arco solo is upbeat, smooth. The ensemble plays it out with a singing flourish.

Clark's 'Blue Minor' is another blues, a little faster than medium this time. McLean leads the solos, his sound bop inflected and very blue. Sonny underlines his solo with percussive flourishes. By the time Farmer steps up to blow warm, probing trumpet, the leader is feeling buoyant. This recording session is going just about as he planned and hoped it would. He is soon back in the forefront himself, his lines shimmering and still flowing easily along in natural momentum. So far, so good. Couldn't be better.

Next up is 'Sippin' At Bells.' Sonny told Hentoff yesterday that this Charlie Parker line, was one of the first in his collection. 'I never had the opportunity to play with Bird. I did meet him once in Chicago in 1954 during my first trip there with Buddy De Franco. Bird encouraged me to continue playing. I admire those early Bird tunes. This one for its melody as well as its changes. It's a twelve-bar blues with advanced changes.'

Philly plays a kicking drum introduction as the quintet fly straight into the blues vigorously at a fast tempo. This is the type of bop Sonny Clark came up with and admired since he first acquired a love of jazz at a very early age. Sonny is keen to do justice to Bird's blues. The ensemble plays the opening with brio, similar to the way Parker and Gillespie played it way back in the golden era of early bebop. Sonny's solo flies along seamlessly, not a note wasted or out of place. Mc Lean takes over, throwing in a Bird lick here and there but true overall to his own strident, if restrained style on this occasion. The rhythmic thrust, blues charge and a feeling that this performance is stripping Parker's music down to its essentials, comes through now. Art Farmer is in a brassy mood now although his solo has, as always, that lyrical glow. Chambers takes a very brief arco segment and then the horns combine with Sonny to wrap it up.

Clark told Hentoff that he always liked 'Deep Night,' the Henderson Vallee composition 'for its changes. But until I heard Bud Powell play it in Birdland one night, I'd never heard it played except in a semi-pop way. When I heard Bud play it, I knew I'd have to play it too in my own way.'

Clark's opening solo begins with dramatic chords that soon give way to the familiar, light, flowing sound, his notes chiming as Philly Joe's swinging, sympathetic brushes whisk him along. Full of inventive counter melodies this is very much Clark's interpretation of the song with brief, occasional nods to Bud Powell.

An enormous wave of satisfaction and relief sweeps over Sonny as he finishes playing 'Deep Night.' Alfred Lion signals to him to indicate all is well with the recording and they have enough music for a full LP album. The pianist takes a deep breath and suggests playing one more. The session has gone so well with no hold-ups or second takes, and he still feels fresh, feels like playing. He looks to his sidemen and they all either nod or smile. Sonny calls for 'Royal Flush,' an original of his they ran down at rehearsal. McLean plays an extended, charging solo and is followed by some cool Farmer trumpet. Sonny's piano solo is upbeat, shimmering at times, full of invention. Everybody appears, miraculously, to be as fresh as a daisy even after more than four hours of recording.

Philly Joe provides a high-octane, burgeoning drum solo before the horns, in unison, take it out. Clark, at the piano, calls for 'Lover,' the popular song written by Rogers and Hart. Philly Joe is again prominent, kicking off 'Lover' with a vigorous drum intro and featuring throughout in a frenzied, up-tempo reading. Finally, the session is at an end with more than one and a half albums recorded.

This one, though, is very special to the pianist. He knows he's said it before, but this date, he thinks, really is the best record session he's ever done. By a wide margin. He tells Alfred Lion, who nods and smiles.

'The music was played the way I wanted it and I got the fellows I'd been wanting to record with for some time,' he says.

Lion tells him that everything sounded very good. The two extended tracks at the end were too long to use on the album but no doubt they can be fitted on another Clark session at a later date.

Clark agrees and makes his way off, out of the studio. Later, sitting in a bar with a beer in front of him and a cigarette in one hand, he begins to face reality. He may think the recording he has just made is his best and more than a bit special, but he is sure that when it is released it will just sell the usual number of copies, mainly to the modern jazz faithful and then be forgotten as soon as the next Blue Note, Prestige or Savoy release comes out. The majority of record buyers can enjoy a three-minute Elvis Presley release or a Little Richard disc but their attention span will not stretch to a forty-minute jazz album. That though, he reflects, as he takes a swig of beer, is the way of the music world. In any case, he knows, in his own mind that however good 'Cool Struttin' is, he will record better records in the future.

Fifteen days later he is back in the Van Gelder studio to record with his good friend Curtis Fuller once more. Curtis is teaming up with fellow trombonist Slide Hampton for a two-bone album on Blue Note. George Tucker is on bass and the drummer is Charlie Persip who Sonny knows as a member of one of Dizzy Gillespie's bands, so he must be good. He finds the two-trombone front line interesting and both bone men are good, solid improvisors but he regards the session as just a routine blowing session. Even so he provides his usual sparkling piano solos to the proceedings and is particularly lively on 'Oatmeal Cookie.'

'Mean Jean' is a slow blues which he digs into after Curtis and Slide open proceedings. At the conclusion of the session, he spends some time reminiscing with Fuller about music and current opportunities and then heads off to visit friends in a loft pad and takes a heroin injection. He has been on and off the drug for several weeks now but can't seem to kick the habit completely. Heroin always gives him a special high and restores his waning confidence in his ability and worth as a jazz soloist. It is when the effects of the drug wear off that he hits rock bottom. Then he gets a break. He is offered, unexpectedly, a week at Birdland in NYC leading his own trio. He contacts Sam Jones for the bass chair and Art Taylor who he knows well from record sessions and, fortunately, both can make the gig. He has played with them both before so they will be familiar with his style.

The gig at Birdland goes very well. The pianist strikes a balance between his most recent compositions and good standards for his nightly performances. His most recent trio performance on record was really good. Aided by the considerable skills of Chambers and Jones, he played a sparkling set of bop standards and a couple of popular songs. He will use that familiar formula at Birdland. Much as he wants to get his own compositions out there for all the world to hear, a balance is the best bet for a prestigious gig. The trio proves to be highly successful from the first night. Not really too different from Chambers and Jones. Taylor and Sam Jones support with finesse. Jones' big sound and Taylor's fills, accents and stimulating cymbal beat enhance Clark's melodic, sometimes dazzling, always intriguing piano solos. And he gives them both plenty of solo space.

As the gig winds down towards the end of the week Sonny approaches bass player and drummer about linking up with him in a regular trio. Both, unfortunately, are heavily committed. If he had a strong name outside NYC and the West Coast they might, just might have committed to his trio concept. But could he guarantee a regular number of gigs in NYC and around the country? He can't. Much as he would like to be known all over the country and hailed as a top soloist, he knows this is not the case.

Record sales are steady, according to Alfred Lion. Not in the big league though. Not like the Miles Davis Quintet and Horace Silver's regular combo. Or Art Blakey's Jazz Messengers. Not like the Dave Brubeck Quartet or Jimmy Smith's organ combo. With the record sales these groups achieve and a full gig complement, these bands can afford to tour the country. And overseas.

At the end of the gig in Birdland, Clark is feeling low. It went as well as he could have hoped. But now he has free days that he could do without. The next record date is a week away. Clark goes downtown to meet his connection and seeks out some cats he knows in a loft space. If he feels that he is playing his best and he does, why has he not garnered more recognition. There are no easy answers. Without real recognition from the jazz fraternity, those who buy the records, he feels he is a failure. It is a recurring theme for him.

A swift injection of heroin takes away the pain. He can live with his perceived failure when he feels high. Because it no longer exists. And the drug relaxes him. The cats at the loft space are similarly frustrated. Most are average journeymen. A few are really good jazz musicians. All feel underemployed. And underappreciated. With one, followed by more hits Clark begins to feel a lot less insecure. Beer, cigarettes and heroin are the ingredients for the elimination of insecurity and feelings of failure. Temporarily. There are good nights when all is well. Then there is the cold and sick feeling on the following morning.

Nica is getting used to finding Sonny on her doorstep in crumpled clothes, looking haggard and with his hair unbrushed. She ushers him inside swiftly and brings him fresh black coffee. He can go and take a shower and tidy himself up when he's had some refreshment. She adds two aspirin-based tablets to his coffee. Tomorrow she will make an appointment for him with Doctor Freymann. Sonny does not think it will do much good. She says he is talking nonsense, and he must trust the doctor. Trust her too. She desperately wants to help him kick his habit. For someone so talented he owes it to himself to get clean.

He smiles at her and wanders off into the large drawing room. Monk is there, noodling away at that irritating fragment of song that stuck in Clark's memory. It does not seem to have progressed much. Sonny asks Monk if he is going to finish it. Put a bridge to it and resolve it. Monk shakes his head. 'I don't think so. It's a fascinating few bars, but I don't think it's going anywhere.'

Sonny drives himself and Nica to downtown Manhattan. Nica has another driver on call for when she needs him due to Clark's unreliability. Clark has tidied himself up. Freymann frowns when he sees him and tells him he is going to give him an injection. It contains amphetamines and he will feel great afterwards. He has given these injections to many people in the entertainment business and his wealthy society clients. He won't want to touch heroin again after this. Sonny looks at him in a sceptical manner.

Nica drives back as Sonny is feeling slightly groggy. As the amphetamines take effect, he begins to feel disorientated. It is a strange feeling and not a pleasant one. Later that night it becomes worse, and he begins to feel cut off from reality altogether. If this is a cure for heroin addiction it is not one, he will be able to live with. Nica gets him back home to her place, makes up a bed and tells him to sleep it off; he will feel much better in the morning. If for any reason it does not work, she will book him into the drug programme at Bellevue hospital in town and she will pay the fees if he must stay for a few nights.

The return to Van Gelder's studio is a happy event. If he has felt slightly out of it for several days, at least he has not injected heroin. Meeting up with Lee Morgan, Doug Watkins and Art Taylor is a friendly reunion and they are here to complete the album that they recorded three selections for back in November last year. Four more pieces are required, Alfred Lion tells them, but Sonny protests that it should surely only be three because they already taped three at the last meeting. Not so. Morgan tells him that Lion has rejected one composition, 'Who Do You Love, I Hope,' and they must do it over again. Lion then goes to talk to Rudy Van Gelder about technical matters and the musicians shake their heads in disbelief. They have listened to all the takes recorded in November and are in agreement that everything sounded fine. Someone says, 'Alfred is Alfred. Nothing you can do about it.'

They play the offending popular song once again. Lee Morgan's trumpet is incisive as he fashions an inventive, lyrical solo, the long serpentine lines unlike his usual hard bop, brassy approach. Clark plays a melodic, if choppy solo by his standards and if he could, he would have reproduced an identical solo to the rejected one which he thought was fine. His imaginative facility however won't allow this; every solo is fresh, new and does not sound like anything else he has ever done.

Art Taylor kicks off 'Candy,' and Morgan is once more relaxed, playing super cool trumpet. It is such a departure for him that the sidemen are in a state of disbelief. Clark's dancing lines are so laid back and effectively swinging the entire rhythm section that he inspires Morgan to return and play out some of the best improvised lines he has ever recorded. At the end of the session, Alfred Lion is at last completely satisfied as they all listen to the playback. It is Morgan's first quartet record and will be his only one.

The musicians congratulate each other, convinced that they have just recorded a winning disc. Sonny is happy that it is as good as it is, following on from his successful *Cool Struttin'* session. It shows consistency in the quality of his playing. He thinks his best solo on the record, and one of his best ever, was on 'Since I Fell for You,' where he began with a quote from a Charlie Parker blues that blossomed out into a flowing stream of invention played with glittering single notes.

He returns to Nica, satisfied with the music but still feeling somewhat disorientated due to the lingering effects of Doctor Freymann's injection.

Sonny Clark *Melody & Melancholy* **Sam Stephenson**. *The Paris Review*
Sonny Clark - *Cool Struttin'* Blue note 1588. Nat Hentoff's liner note.

14

TINA BROOKS MAKES A MINOR MOVE

On a cold winter afternoon, Sonny calls in at the Blue Note office to find Lion and Wolff struggling with a pile of LP records and reams of paperwork. Lion tells Sonny it's not recording the music that is the pain, it is getting the records out onto the market and arranging distribution. Sometimes it is all too much. He welcomes the pianist in and invites him to take a seat. Lion and his partner have been working flat out for days on paperwork and calling people on the telephone. And generally trying to sell the discs. Francis Wolff goes out to make coffee and brings back three mugs of the beverage.

Alfred Lion smiles and says it is time he took a break anyway. Working until he drops won't help his state of health. He has just had Hank Mobley in complaining that his last album, the one with Sonny, Art Farmer and baritone man Pepper Adams has not been released. It isn't that he does not intend to put it out, it is just that he hasn't had time to arrange for cover artwork and liner notes yet. Hank never seems to understand the pressure they are under at Blue Note. He will get round to it, but Mobley should be patient. He sips some coffee and asks Sonny what he thinks of Mobley. He has, after all, been on quite a few sessions with him.

'I never heard Mobley until I came to New York,' Sonny says. 'But I listened to his records with the Jazz Messengers and dug him very much. He plays in my style, and I was very happy working with him and very satisfied with the results.'

He tells Lion that he thinks Mobley is a very soulful player. Lion looks pensive, repeats the word 'soulful,' and asks Clark what he thinks soul in jazz means. 'I take it to mean your growing up to the capacities of the instrument,' Sonny responds. 'Your soul is your conception, and you begin to have it in your playing when the way you strike a note, the sound you get, and your phrasing come out of you yourself and no one else. That's what jazz is, after all, self-expression.'

Lion nods and smiles. Can't argue with that really. He is thinking that this young man is very deep, bright, intelligent. He has the talent to make a big impression in music too. It is a pity he is gaining a reputation in jazz as a shambolic young fellow, often sleeping rough and going on benders. Heavily into heroin addiction too, which is terrible, although so many of the musicians are in the same situation. He knows that from the dreadful state of the bathroom at Van Gelder's studio after a recording has taken place. Blood everywhere and used injection equipment abandoned. What a dreadful mess that must be cleaned up. Although Van Gelder guards his grand piano fastidiously, not allowing even a cigarette in an ashtray to be put upon it.

Lion promises that all the records made that pass his rigorous tests of quality will be released, if he and Wolff have their way. The odd one or two may slip the net. Inevitably perhaps. When you consider the pressure, they are working under. And he has good news for Sonny. *Cool Struttin'* Clark's latest has now got a catalogue number and will be in the record shops and major stores soon. As for those two additional tracks recorded that day, 'Lover' and 'Royal Flush,' they were excellent and will make up one side of an LP he intends to call *Cool Struttin' Volume 2*. He intends to make up the second side with the three selections Sonny made late last year with Kenny Burrell, Clifford Jordan and Pete La Roca. Does he remember 'Eastern Incident,' 'Little Sonny,' and 'Minor Meeting'? He has a catalogue number ready for it, Blue Note 1592, and will use the same cover picture with different colour lettering. This is good news for Clark whose only reservation is that the three earlier tracks are good enough. He thinks on balance that they are.

Paul Chambers on bass is the only holdover from the first session to the second. Sonny nods. He reminds Lion that he has used Chambers on every leader date he has had on Blue Note apart from his very first when Paul was out of town, and he had Wilbur Ware. Paul's conception, note choice and ability to play imaginatively both arco and pizzicato make him the ideal bassist as far as Sonny is concerned. He does not add that the two of them share another preference. For shooting up heroin and drinking heavily. Many a session has ended with a get-together.

Lion has another recording date coming up for the pianist. He is giving a first leader date to a young tenor saxophonist he thinks will be a big name in due course. Tina Brooks from Fayetteville NC. He has already used him as a sideman on a couple of records but is very impressed with his blues-based, sanctified style of blowing. Because he is relatively unknown, he is putting him in the studio with some top-class sidemen. Lee Morgan will be on trumpet, Doug Watkins, who is a Lion favourite on bass and his idea of the ideal drummer, Art Blakey. Sonny will be the other top dog, on piano.

Sonny thinks that such a lineup of heavy-duty sidemen may well frighten the young tenor sax man out of his wits. But he says nothing. He has heard about Brooks and his ability to blow up a storm on the blues and thinks the session will be right up his street. He says he will look forward to it.

The rehearsal for Tina Brooks' first Blue Note album is like a friendly reunion. Clark is welcomed by Lee Morgan who promises he is going to be more fiery on this taping. He enjoyed going for a sweet, honeyed approach on his last quartet outing, but this looks more like his usual music. Solid hard bop. Doug

Watkins remembers working with Sonny a short time ago, and they exchange notes on rhythm section playing. Then Sonny meets Brooks, a shy young man who Clark has heard on somebody else's record and was impressed.

Art Blakey is last to arrive. He is late but Art has a reputation for arriving late at recording sessions and rehearsals. Unless it is to record his Jazz Messengers. Then he is first there before the studio doors are open, ready and waiting. When they get started, playing a rundown of 'Minor Move,' a Brook's original, Sonny is impressed by the tenor man's intense, blues-soaked almost preaching style. It is similar to his own.

There is much discussion and suggestions about how the music should be played, but Brooks, to his credit, stands firm in the way he wants it performed. He is looking, he says, to get a personal sound from ensembles that will be, in time, recognisable as a Tina Brooks trademark. Judging by the sceptical looks all round, the cats all think that is an unlikely outcome. Sonny keeps silent.

In the studio, the quintet play 'Minor Move,' one of two originals by Brooks he has chosen to record. Clark plays enhancing lines behind Tina's opening solo, a blues-soaked exercise in good hard bop. Morgan's solo is explosive, clearly designed to outshine the new young tenor player. He succeeds partially, due to his experience and inventiveness on this kind of material. Clark keeps the good blues mood going with a free-flowing solo where he easily matches the preceding solos. A new take of 'Minor Move' follows. Brooks is a little less intense here. Sonny supports him with as much sturdy accompaniment as he put into the first take. Morgan is less fiery but just as inventive as before. The piano solo is different from take one but as energetic in the lines Clark supplies; he rarely, if ever, repeats himself. Clearly, the first take is the superior one.

'Nutville' is a slow, stomping blues, and Sonny Clark opens the solo sequence with deep blue lines, carefully constructed and setting a good, groovy mood immediately. Morgan follows on his best blues behaviour. Slurs and half-valve effects are used effectively at first and he doubles the time after a while. Blakey cues in Brooks with a drum roll. It is an exceptionally good tenor solo, carefully and sympathetically orchestrated by Blakey from his drum stool. Sonny introduces 'The Way You Look Tonight' as Brooks plays a short opening solo followed by Morgan's effort. Brooks then moves into a long solo sequence, the tempo brisk, his lines full of bluesy invention. He never falters as Clark, Watkins and Blakey shadow him skilfully. Morgan is fleet, finely tuned in a unique solo that only he could have come up with.

Sonny thinks this is a very good session and he is more than impressed by young Brooks, but he does sense a certain amount of tension in the studio as they play. Lion is looking on with a slight frown on his face. Not a good omen. His own solo skips through with a solid swing that bass and drums support staunchly. The final four-bar exchanges between Brooks, Blakey and Morgan are fierce and exciting.

The well-known popular standard 'Star Eyes' is a more relaxed performance. Brooks puts his own stamp on it; the tenor player is obviously working out his own sound that he wants the entire combo to conform to. On the playback, at the end, the musicians smile and nod approval, but Lion is muttering about the ensembles sounding a little untidy. And Rudy Van Gelder is saying that there is an odd, slurred sound on Blakey's cymbals on some of the tracks.

Lion is not happy, and he has heard, or thinks he has, a sloppy sound on some of the ensembles. He is very fussy about clean ensembles. The music is some of the very best hard bop recorded in 1958, but Alfred Lion will not be releasing the record and it will remain in the vaults for many years before coming on the market.

The amphetamine injections are not working. Sometimes the unpleasant side effects are worse than shaking off a bad heroin reaction. Sonny has told Nica that he can't take any more of Freymann's vitamin treatment, as he calls it. She promises to have a word with the doctor and come up with a solution. An entirely different treatment perhaps? Sonny is sceptical.

That evening, he does not return to her home. He will often wander off, disappear for days, weeks even and then re-appear just as if he'd never been away. Or he'll have a record or afternoon gig and say he will see her in the evening but not return. Nica is used to dealing with the dozens of musicians she welcomes to her home on a casual basis. She knows their ways and never questions their reasons.

He has not ventured far this time. A couple of bars and then he bumps into Thelonious. The older man asks how he is doing, and Sonny tells him his outlook is bleak. He is having treatment now, but prior to that he had spent all his money on heroin and is now in dire straits. Monk, who looks on him very much as a younger colleague, perhaps even a wayward younger brother, gives him some money. Has he got anywhere to stay though? He has not. Monk insists he come back home with him to his little apartment where his faithful wife, Nellie, will feed him and provide a bed for the night.

Clark stays three days and three nights. He can see, watching them closely, that Monk is devoted to Nellie and she to him. The recent tales he has heard from cats about Monk and Nica must be untrue. The baroness is a patron to Monk and their friendship is purely platonic. How could he have doubted it? Somehow the rumours keep surfacing, again and again. He has found out that Nica regards Monk as a genius and will do anything to promote him and proclaim that genius to the world. Or anyone who will listen. How could anyone doubt it?

Sonny leaves Monk's pad and wanders off into the night. Nobody knows where he goes, but he does show up at Nica's house the following morning. She has been awaiting his arrival as she wants him to see Doctor Freymann. Urgently. Nica takes Sonny, almost kicking and screaming, to the doctor's offices and waits for him to go in before returning to her car. Clark tells the doctor he won't accept another injection, under any circumstances.

Freymann tells him he is putting him on a course of methadone treatment. He needn't look worried this is a synthetic opiate and has proved highly successful in recent times at curing heroin addiction. It's taken in pill form or liquid orally, so no injections involved. It is addictive, however, but the doctor is sure that Sonny will find it considerably easier to live with than heroin addiction. And, in the fullness of time, he will be completely cured. At that point all Freymann will have to do is gently ween Clark off the methadone pills. It all sounds too easy and unlikely to Sonny. He's heard similar optimistic stories before.

Out on the sidewalk, it is a bright, cloudless day. Just a light, cool breeze. Sitting in the Bentley, across the street, Nica is beaming a smile at him and holding a thumbs-up sign.

Sonny Clark - *Dial S For Sonny*. Blue Note 1570. Robert Levin's sleeve note.

15

TWO RECORD DATES THEN INTO THE WILDERNESS

LOUIS SMITH IS ANOTHER OF THOSE BRIGHT YOUNG TRUMPET PLAYERS that Alfred Lion claims to have discovered, and the Blue Note boss is anxious to record him. He had gone into the studio with a top combo including Cannonball Adderley, masquerading as 'Buckshot La Funke,' and Duke Jordan on piano in February 1958. That record was actually recorded by Tom Wilson of Transition Records, Boston, but the company is going out of business, unfortunately, and Wilson has sent the tapes to Alfred Lion. Lion sends test pressings to jazz authority Leonard Feather to ask him what he thinks of Smith. Feather is just as enthusiastic as Alfred.

The album, *Here Comes Louis Smith*,' is well-received critically although sales are not brilliant. Lion brings the young trumpeter back as leader at the end of March and assigns Charlie Rouse on tenor sax along with Paul Chambers and Art Taylor. And Sonny Clark at the piano. This time it will be a Blue Note recording set up and recorded by the company.

At rehearsal, Sonny meets the cats he doesn't know and shakes hands with Smith and Charlie Rouse. He knows nothing about Louis Smith but is aware that Alfred Lion is renowned as a good spotter of talent, particularly trumpet players. Alfred has been known to boast that he was the first to discover the talents of Clifford Brown and Lee Morgan. And quick to record them both. That should be all right then. He will be interested to hear the new man playing. And Charlie Rouse, who he has met at Nica's house. Charlie has been around for some time now and is well-regarded by jazz musicians in the city.

With Doug Watkins and Art Taylor, it is a meeting of friends now. They run down a slow, down-home blues, the type that Sonny loves to play. There are two good standards as well. He is not too enamoured of the originals on offer to play but thinks that they will suffice, and, in any event, you can't have everything.

The recording session goes well. Sonny can't remember enjoying a session as much as this one with the notable exception of Tina Brooks' record which was a real goodie in his opinion. 'Smithville' is slow, funky and gives musicians like these a feel-good factor. Chambers introduces it with a slow, pulsing line. Smith's sound is relaxed, cool, blue-tinted, as are the fills Clark plays behind him. Sonny's blues lines are prominent as Smith traces a blue-streaked path. Rouse is warm, laid back, sensuous. Clark is really into this blues, his accents urging the horns on constantly. The leader comes back for some further, more exploratory solo lines. Sonny digs into his solo enthusiastically, bending blue notes effectively as he slips into yet another free-flowing solo that causes the three-man rhythm section to purr like a well-oiled machine. He introduces melodic variations to the theme without losing sight of the original line. As he gives way to Paul's pizzicato bass, the track is really cooking, a slow burn but solid. Clark controls and guides the down-home ending.

Sonny, enjoying himself, introduces 'Embraceable You.' His notes lead Smith into a heartfelt ballad reading. Although the trumpeter indulges in a double-time phrase, he keeps it slow and romantic throughout. Sonny keeps the mood beautifully, mixing soft-focus single lines with juicy chords. He and Smith are the only soloists here and they keep it warm and tasty. Rouse cooks effectively, his own personal sound prominent on the up-tempo pieces impressing Clark. He makes a note to keep watch on Rouse and perhaps play with him again in future if the opportunity presents itself.

Outside the recording studio, he is not feeling good. He thoroughly enjoyed playing with the cats, but he experiences that sinking feeling as soon as it is over. He convinces himself that he is unsettled because of lack of recognition from the jazz enthusiasts who seem oblivious to his music. Monk, his friend, has a long-running residency at the Five Spot that has gone on for months. Why can't he get more than a week, two weeks exceptionally? Why can't he sell records in the numbers achieved by Miles Davis, John Coltrane and Dave Brubeck? Sonny Rollins. Even Monk is beginning to make good money from recordings and is under exclusive contract with Riverside.

He hates the methadone programme. It makes him feel sick and lifeless most of the time. The side effects are, to his troubled mind, as bad and sometimes worse than heroin. His skin is dry and grey, his hair lifeless. His face is bleak and looks drawn. His clothing is getting shabby again. Monk has advised him to stick with the methadone. It will benefit him in the long run. What does Monk know? The man treats him like a father at times, or the way he imagines a father treats his son. His own father died just after he was born, so he never knew him. He needs to get clean and warm. Spring is coming and the weather will improve but sleeping rough is unpleasant. He decides to return to the Baroness' house and find some comfort and a welcome. He does not want to take advantage of her considerable generosity or be seen to be taking her kindness for granted. At this moment though, he has no choice.

Nica welcomes him in as usual, smiling but unable to suppress the shock of his appearance as the smile fades. He has never appeared looking this dishevelled before. Nica moves forward to take Sonny by his shoulders, but he pulls away. He needs a shower and says he is not fit to talk to her or anybody else until he has had one. She makes a smooth gesture with her right hand, indicating he is free to go to the bathroom.

Later, in the comfort of her sitting room and two large goblets of Cognac, she asks him how he is getting on with the methadone treatment. He responds by telling her it is agony, and he feels sick most of the time. Nica offers to make an appointment for him to see Doctor Freymann and see if he can come up with another solution. Sonny refuses, tells her he is going to continue with the methadone, however miserable it makes him. At least it is keeping him off heroin. For now.

His next recording with Blue Note looks promising. Bennie Green, the trombone player is the leader, and Sonny has admired his playing on various records. Gene Ammons, known as Jug to the cats, is on tenor sax, along with Billy Root. Two tenors should make it interesting. Elvin Jones, who Sonny has heard about as the younger brother of Hank and Thad, is on drums. Particularly intriguing is the inclusion of bop vocalist Babs Gonzales. The title track, 'Soul Stirrin',' is also the title planned for the LP when released.

Sonny digs into the slow, earthy blues of 'Soul Stirrin','along with the funky frontline horns. Gonzales is famous for his vocal interpretations of horn lines, which he contributes effectively here as an opening solo effort. The chunky front line traces the melody leading into Green's trombone foray. Deep blue lines flood the studio as Green warms to his improvisation, and Clark feeds him nourishing fills and blues lines. Ammons follows with a fervent tenor blast. Sonny's lines are melodic and drenched in the blues. This is one more session where he can lose himself in the music and enjoy the general style and format chosen by the leader. 'We Wanna Cook' suits the pianist just as well, a fast blues where he backs Gonzales' vocal interpretation of the theme followed by a wild trombone excursion from Green. Sonny could play music like this all day and never tire, even if he had no solo. He has often told interviewers that he enjoys comping in a section almost as much as playing solos. This is one such occasion as he lays sympathetic blues chords, fills and percussive prompts under Green, Ammons, Root and Gonzales' voice, in turn.

He turns in a gem of a rhapsodic piano introduction to the ballad 'That's All,' then applies lush comping to Green's ultra-slow, sensuous trombone solo that follows. It occurs to him, as he leads the rhythm section through the various tracks that he is only really happy and fulfilled when he is playing piano in situations like this. His short jewel of melodic improvisation on 'That's All' is one of his best, brief, concise and very much to the point in this reading of the ballad.

'Lullaby of the Doomed' is unusual, sombre, brooding. It brings out some of the most challenging, melancholy solo work from the horns and Clark. It is not really Sonny's type of music, this track, but he is happy because it is so different and therefore challenging. He has no piano solo on this piece, but he underlines effectively everything the horns play. 'B. G. Mambo' seems almost corny after such a challenge as the preceding music, but Sonny treats it as though engaged in an important piano concerto. His solo is 'swinging the mambo' all the way.

'Black Pearl' wraps up the recording neatly, medium tempo. This is one where the pianist can return to straightforward propulsive swinging, light touch, lyrical, as he does on his opening short solo.

So much music and yet he would like more. He would be more than content to stay on this piano stool, playing music endlessly. Pausing only to take a drink and eat but playing almost without end. In such a situation he would not need heroin or methadone or anything else. But Sonny Clark has just played his last record session for a very long time.

It has been four weeks since Clark was last in the studio recording with Benny Green. No real work of any kind either. It only took three days of loneliness. Suddenly the methadone programme he had promised Nica and himself he would stick with, was forgotten. Hanging out with a couple of musicians he had visited in their loft space, led on, invariably, to seeking and making a connection. In an instant, he was hooked again. Now he feels the effects of four weeks of scuffling, meetings with old friends and shooting up.

Meeting up with fellow pianists has been frequent. Bill Evans, the studious-looking white boy who has recently been signed by Riverside Records. Sonny and Evans get high together. When his friend tells him about the Riverside contract and the fact that he has actually told Orrin Keepnews of that company not to hurry and record him as he hasn't enough material ready yet, Clark bursts out laughing. Can Evans really afford to do that? He can but it turns out he has received a good number of sideman dates for record companies recently and been busy in clubs.

Evans, with his fair hair and glasses looks more like a student than a jazz musician. Sonny eyes his smart appearance enviously and thinks it will be easier for him. Everything will fall into line. He will get work in the best clubs, record for the big record companies and become famous. All these thoughts flood in but he says nothing. At this moment, Evans is just a friend he is hanging out with. Getting high.

In the evenings Sonny does not get much sleep. Up to all hours with cats in similar situations to himself, they drink beer, shoot heroin, talk about injustice. Sleep is rare. Spasmodic.

The other regular friend in his life now is Hampton Hawes. He met Hawes in L.A. Sonny recalls enjoyable jam session nights at the Lighthouse in Hermosa Beach where he and Hampton often linked up. In more ways than one. Playing piano sets, one pianist following another and playing up a storm. Drinking up a storm as well. And disappearing into the night to seek the inevitable connection.

Now, they have met up in New York. One night they move

into a cheap, scruffy, none-too-clean hotel room after a night of drinking and shooting up. Work is thin on the ground for both of them at the moment but perhaps not surprising given their general appearance. They descend into a pattern of hustling. Out on the sidewalk and down to East Village, in the clubs. Mostly in the clubs, in fact. Well-respected band leaders will do anything to get rid of them including giving them money. With money, they can buy drugs. And get high. When their connection comes to do business, he is so shocked at the state and smell of their hotel room that he refuses to come inside. Purchasing drugs is done out in the corridor.

Sonny is shocked, horrified almost at his own state. He decides he must pull himself out of his present state and clean himself up. Physically and mentally.

He goes to see Alfred Lion at Blue Note once he gets himself tidy. Alfred has nothing to offer at this moment. The pianist asks if the record he made for Tina Brooks is coming out, but Alfred tells him it won't be. Sonny thinks it was a great record, but Lion refuses to put out an LP where the ensembles are ragged, in his opinion. Clark regrets the loss of royalties that sales from extra records would bring. He asks about the Hank Mobley set he recorded back in '57 with Donald Byrd and Pepper Adams. Lion can't remember.

He doesn't think that one has been released but, the thing is, there are so many at this moment. He and Wolff just have too much to do and really, they are recording more than they can put out on the market. Sonny wonders what's the point of recording music if you are not going to release it but he says nothing. Alfred and Francis are busy as usual, so he doesn't stay.

Another four weeks have passed and there is little improvement. Two brief gigs that were not particularly well paid and no recording work for more than two months. Sonny is reaching an all-time low. He feels worthless, even questioning his ability and the only way he can feel at all at ease with himself and the world is to take more and more heroin. It lifts him temporarily. When the effects wear off though, he is desolate.

He meets up again with Hawes and they get high together. As always. He knows he is taking bigger shots of the drug than are good for his body, but he has had lots of practice and built up considerable resistance to ill effects. He goes to a club and listens to Hank Mobley in good form. Hank, as usual, is not in sociable mood between sets so he hardly gets to talk to him. He is becoming desperately short of money. He gets one more, short gig and enough money to keep the wolf from the door. Feeling almost suicidal, he takes two more hefty injections of the drug over a short period of time. He wanders around in crumpled clothes, visits other addicts and finally finishes up passing out in a shop doorway and is moved on the next morning by the agitated proprietor.

It is time to seek help. He doesn't want charity and is reluctant to take further advantage of Nicas' kindness and generosity. He can see no other option though.

Nica welcomes him in, sits him down and brings him black coffee with cakes. He attacks the food wolfishly, drinks the coffee and begins to feel a little more human than he has for months. Nica shakes her head. He is not in a good place, she tells him, but she is not judging him. He needs help and she is prepared to provide it. She can see the drugs doing him permanent harm, physically and mentally. If he doesn't give up. She can get him further appointments with Doctor Freymann, but he shakes his head vigorously. No more from that man. In that case Nica can get him into Bellevue hospital, where they have a drug programme. He is still shaking his head negatively. Nica assures him that they can help him there to get off heroin for good. She will book him in and pay all his hospital fees; he does not need to worry about that.

He is still in negative mode, so Nica goes to get him more black coffee. She suggests that he drink up, go and take a long bath and then go and sleep for the rest of the day and night.

There is no rush, he needs to recover and rest here, and they will decide, together, what do over the next few days.

Nica breathes a sigh of relief as Sonny agrees and walks off to the bathroom. She wants to help him but, really, he needs to help himself too. She has so many people to worry about. On a recent trip to an out-of-town gig, when she was driving Monk, they stopped at a motel to use the bathroom. A police officer approached before they could set off again and an altercation ensued. The officer, suspicious of a white woman and a black man in a car together, announced that he was going to search the car. He found packets of marijuana. Nica, fearful of the extreme harm a prison sentence could do to Monk, told the officer the drugs were her property. Now she faces a short prison sentence herself when the case comes to court.

Nica sighs. Monk is a musical genius, as she has always maintained, and she will do what it takes to protect him. Even going to jail. The granddaughter of the 1st Baron Rothschild may have left a life of gentle, sophisticated privilege in England, but after distinguishing herself in the Free French Army during World War Two, she is now fighting another bitter battle, to establish jazz musicians as true creators, deserving of respect and recognition of their art. Nearly all the main jazz soloists of the day have visited her home over the years, many in need of help or funds and she has never refused a request.

When Sonny Clark, cleaned up and rested, requests money, to help get himself straight, she complies. Even though she knows well enough where the money will go. She practically begs him to book into the Belleview hospital to clear his drug dependence but leaves the final decision to him. He is not ready to go into hospital yet and he tells her so. When and if he needs to, he will go. For now, he has got himself into a dreadful state and intends to work hard getting himself out of it. Nica shakes her head wearily and tells him she is always there for him.

Clark must go out into the outside world, pursue his craft playing music and attempt to get himself clean. He has done it many times before and will do it again. Nica thinks it is too late now, but she keeps the opinion to herself. So, Sonny wants to rest up at Weehawken and that is fine.

Little changes at Nica's house. Musicians wander in and out at all hours. The whole house is full of cats, literally hundreds of them, for the eccentric lady is a keen animal rights activist. She has been known to trawl the slum areas slowly in her Bentley and scoop up bedraggled, feeble-looking cats into her car and take them home. There she will feed and nurture them. Thelonious Monk has named her home 'The Cat House.' She is also a keen photographer and will take pictures at random, often catching her subject unawares.

Sonny, cleaned up and spruce in good quality casual clothing, picks up a cat casually and begins to stroke it gently. Nica spots him, comes up quietly in front of him and snaps him holding the cat almost before he realises what is happening. He smiles. She is pleased because not too many of the musicians like cats and many are irritated by them. It tells her he is capable of warmth and gentleness even though his outer demeanour is often bleak, sometimes even surly. The drugs have hardened him, given him a dark outlook on the world but perhaps, she muses, it is not quite too late.

Nica tells Sonny about her picture postcards. She photographs a musician and asks him to tell her what he would like if he were granted three wishes. Then she puts picture and words together on a postcard and adds it to a scrapbook she is keeping. Sonny grins and says he has no idea. Nica presses him. To encourage him, she tells him that Charles Mingus said he'd like enough money to pay his bills. That was all he said, but Wes Montgomery wanted 'happiness,' then 'no discrimination, ever,' and finally, 'peace.'

'Cannonball Adderley also wishes for an end to racial discrimination everywhere,' Nica says wistfully. 'And others said the same.'

Sonny is shaking his head as though he is tiring of this game. 'What about Thelonious?' he asks. 'What did he wish for?'

'His first wish was to be successful musically. Second, to have a happy family, and his third wish was "to have a crazy friend like you."'

Sonny laughs. Just what he might have expected from the Monk. Nica is murmuring about Elvin Jones wishing for peace on earth and Ornette Coleman wishing for eternal life. She shakes her head. Sadly, both will be disappointed, for different reasons. She wants to hear Sonny's wishes now.

'Money,' he replies. 'My second wish would be for all the bitches in the world and my third for all the Steinways in the world.'

Nica muses that Hank Mobley, Philly Joe Jones and others wished for money. Then she tells him she doubts if he could manage all the world's bitches. And all those Steinways? Sonny, in brighter mood now than at any time since he arrived back at Nica's home, says that he would play every Steinway in the world, one after the other and never tire. Music forever. Nica laughs.

Then she says that Miles Davis was most revealing in his wish. 'To be white.'

She tells Sonny that when Monk told her his three wishes she told him that he had all those things now. Clark gets up from his seat and walks over to the window. He gazes out over the Hudson River to the far shores. He has rested well and now it is time to move on, out into the big world.

Nica sees him standing by the window in almost the identical position that Monk occupies frequently. She feels confident that she can protect Thelonious and promote his music, but she is not so sure about Sonny.

It really hasn't worked out well for Sonny Clark. Since leaving Nica's house he has spent two months scuffling around town, spending what little money he had from her on heroin. He has not worked in a club or been on a record date now for almost four months. His only chances to play the piano have been when he returned to Weehawken. He played on a couple of jam sessions at the house with well-known musicians and enjoyed it, but it was not the same as being paid. And having an audience. He spent two days at Nica's where he played the piano all day and well into the night with barely a word to anybody.

He has visited Monk when he was back in his home. Thelonious introduced him to his young son, and Sonny taught him how to make a sling from roadside and hedgerow rushes. A trick he learned living in the country at Herminie years ago. Sadly though, he nearly always finishes up crashing in another junkie's loft space, high on heroin and feeling sick, weary and disgusted with his situation.

He feels he has reached the end of the road. Nothing is working out as he planned or hoped. Bill Evans is busy working and planning a new LP. Hampton Hawes is nowhere to be seen; perhaps he has gone back to Texas. Or California. In a state of grim lethargy, he watches the guy he has moved in on trying to find a clear space on his arm to inject into. One without pock marks or sores. He looks at the man's face, his skin grey and pinched, his hair lank and his dead, lifeless eyes. It occurs to him that this is the way he himself must look at times. It is time to get some help; he has postponed it long enough.

Nica is relived when he agrees to go into the hospital. She will arrange it, drive him there and pay all the hospital bills. He tells her he is grateful, and she is great. And he is very grateful. She is always there for him and for all the cats who are struggling. No recriminations, just a desire to help in any way she can. The baroness is truly one in a million. He determines in his mind to repay her for all she has done. When he finally gains acceptance as a major jazz pianist. When his records sell in their thousands, and he has gigs in the best clubs and records for the big companies. Like Columbia and RCA. Like Miles and Coltrane do. Mingus and Rollins. He can do it, he knows he is good enough as a jazz pianist and soloist. Bandleader in the future possibly.

He must get clean, though, and stay that way. Miles did it and Coltrane quite recently, so he has heard

on the grapevine. Rollins kicked his habit years ago. Mingus appears clean, and even Monk is said to avoid the hard

stuff. He will avoid Lee Morgan and Hank Mobley except on record dates. Although if he can't find a bass

player who suits him as well as Paul Chambers, well, he does not have to socialize with the guy.

Nica wants to get him straight into the hospital, but he asks for two days of peace and quiet here, in her house. Well, alright, she will go along with that even if she thinks he should not really delay any further. What does he want to do on his two days anyway? Sonny says he doesn't want to do anything. Just chill out. He does just that, lounging around, playing the piano in an abstract manner, playing fragmented passages as though searching for a theme or melodic phrase that is alluding him.

On the second day, he links up with Thelonious Monk and does even less. The two men retreat to a quiet room and settle in armchairs with drinks and cigarettes. Behind Monk's chair is an entire wall of glass panels. The two do not speak and have not said anything for hours. Sometimes it is good to just rest in silence and listen to the sounds all around you.

Nica drives Sonny to the hospital. He is feeling raw and not wanting to go, but she assures him the treatment will set him up. He finds the routine intrusive and boring. He is given all manner of tests and asked endless questions by various doctors and experts. The tablets he receives and must take regularly do diminish the craving for heroin. He can't wait for release from hospital. It has been more than six months since he last made a recording and almost as long since he played a club date. He will be, he thinks, a forgotten man.

When he finally gets his release, he sets about making contact with the people he knew in music. Surely somebody will help him get back into working, recording, playing the music he loves?

Three Wishes. An Intimate Look at the Jazz Greats - Nica de Koenigswarter
Raise Up Off Me: A Portrait of Hampton Hawes – Hampton Hawes and Don Asher.

16

MASTER WORK 2 - MY CONCEPTION

SONNY MEETS UP WITH OLD FRIENDS CURTIS FULLER AND HANK Mobley. Both are surprised that he hasn't been seen for so long and wondered what had happened to him. He tells them he has been unwell, which is true, in a sense, but not as they meant. Hank keeps very much to himself and is not one to hang out with other cats. He does not seek out Lee Morgan or Paul Chambers, thinking that it might lead to get-togethers that he might regret later.

Alfred Lion at Blue Note accepts the being ill explanation, but Clark detects a knowing look in his expression. When cats like him are away for six months, he knows what they get up to. Lee Morgan is frequently off the scene. Lion canthough arrange a trio date for Sonny if he will be patient for a few days.

In the Van Gelder studio, it is quiet and not at all like a typical Blue Note date. Sonny wants no fireworks or exhibitions of virtuosity either from himself or anybody else. He would like a reflective session where the focus is fully on pretty piano playing and highly skilled, sensitive support from bass and drums. He has, he feels sure, got the right men. Jymie Merritt is on bass, naturally. Merritt gives him exactly what he wants, every time. He only has to ask. He has provided foundation for

Art Blakey's Jazz Messengers but is relaxed and reliable against Blakey's explosions. The man is one of his favourite bass players. On drums he has Wes Landers, a good time-keeper and steady musician who is unspectacular in style and approach but thoroughly dependable. He met Wes in California when they were both in the Buddy De Franco band for a short time.

'Black Velvet' is a pretty melody. Clark plays it straight to start off then begins delivering those cascades of jewel like notes and enhances the line. It is a relaxed performance ending with Sonny rephrasing the melody softly. Much the same treatment is given to 'I'm Just a Lucky So and So.' The Ellington-associated ballad is ideal for some tinkling, bright gems from the pianist along with some smooth variations. Merritt and Landers are lightness and shade. Just the sort of backing he wanted. 'The Breeze And I' is a solid, high-quality standard and one Clark loves. This one is taken at a much brisker tempi, but the same lyrical format is retained. Sonny's lines flow in streamlined fashion, prettily but swinging naturally and the bass and drums are, again, supportive, unselfishly drawing attention to the piano music.

'Ain't No Use' is a slight departure being a slow, earthy blues but the treatment is the same. This is Clark playing hearty blues lines but in a cleaner than usual, melodic fashion. The blue notes shine through though, vividly, in this reading. A similar lighter than usual approach is applied to 'Gee Baby Ain't I Good To You.' Lion suggests an alternate take on this one, so the trio play it again with little variation.

'I Can't Give You Anything but Love,' is often played up-tempo, but Sonny's reading is slowly pulsing along, the brittle, shimmering piano lines pointed up by the cruising brushes from Landers and that rock-solid bass line by Merritt. The pianist smiles as he plays. This is coming out just as he planned and hoped. In every way. He knows Jymie was disappointed when he told him there would be no bass solos. No drum solos either. He just wanted a tranquil set emphasizing the music of jazz piano and heightened in warmth and intensity by just that solid bass and drums marking his lines. Merritt is a thorough musician and professional though, he understood. So did Landers who is currently excelling with just a minimum of fills and cymbal splashes. Just enough to make it all unique.

After six full months of deprivation with no music and stress and trauma all down the line, he might have been expected to come back to the recording studio anxious to play up a storm, tear up on the up-tempo material and have Art Blakey or Philly Joe behind him with Chambers, fiery and explosive. This gentle, ultra-reflective set is just what he required to readjust to becoming, once again a challenging piano soloist. Time for the fireworks later. And they will come, that is for sure.

At the end of the session, all the musicians admit it went well, better than the bassist and drummer expected. Lion is pleased. It was melodic, warm, refreshing and, his one real unshakable requirement for all Blue note albums, it was swinging. Or 'svinging,' in Alfred's German accented voice. Lion is so pleased with what he has just heard that he voices the opinion that it might be good to return to the studio in a couple of days and record a few more selections. Merritt smiles, Landers nods enthusiastically; all three are up for it.

It turns out to be rather longer than days before Lion provides another recording date. He does offer Sonny another date in the studio with Benny Green, similar to the earlier set because Alfred has been pleased by the results of the earlier LP. He is bringing back the popular bop vocalist Babs Gonzales for two tracks to try and bolster sales. He plans to issue a 45rpm single as well as an LP. Eddy Williams is on tenor sax next to the trombonist leader, Jerry Segal is on drums, and Clark is pleased to note Paul Chambers is the bassist.

When they meet up in the recording studio, Clark mentions the upcoming trio session to Chambers. He explains his idea of a record highlighting the swing, melody and harmonic scope of a piano focussed set and Paul says he is happy to go along with that. He loves to play bass solos but is always willing to try something new and different. His job is to provide whatever rhythmic support the leaders want. Sonny smiles. He was more than happy with Merritt's contribution last time but thinks that Paul's bass will give the new sessions that extra dimension. And Chambers is, after all, his favourite.

A slow 'Why Do I Love You' and some vocal blues gymnastics from Gonzales make Green's recording interesting. It is a good blues-based album, and Clark always enjoys playing the blues. He leaves the session early, as soon as they have listened to the playback and not noticed any blips in the playing or recording.

It is three weeks after the first trio tapes that Clark returns to the Van Gelder studio with Landers in attendance. Chambers arrives next and they commence to add six additional pieces. Sonny produces a straight-ahead version of 'Blues in the Night,' swiftly moving to a set of variations on the familiar melody. Taken at a slow ballad tempo, he is able to bring out the delicate counter melodies he had in mind. His light touch on the keyboard delivers a sweet and sour sound as his improvised choruses are laced with melancholy and a touch of the true blues. As he suspected, Chambers fits in perfectly in this situation, enhancing the lines but discreet and tasteful in his choice of notes. This is probably the most exhaustive, thorough exploration of this tune. 'All Of You' is a popular song that has been covered well by many popular and jazz groups and singers. It is transformed in this reading by Clark's persuasive investigation of the chord changes as he glides along, riding on a smooth, propulsive carpet of rhythm. Sonny, seeking perfection or something close, calls for another version of 'Blues in the Night.' At the end, listening to the playback, Sonny decides that the second take is just better by a small margin and asks Lion to select that one as the master take.

He leaves the studio with another six tracks of piano-focussed music with no bass or drum solos. It is an experiment he wanted to get out of his system although, he concedes, he is unlikely to repeat it.

Winding down after a recording session is always a strain, he finds. It is a time when, unless he has taken an injection of heroin, he feels low, questions his worth and ability to play and frequently broods on why the jazz record buying public do not take more interest in his albums. There are plenty of them out there. None are selling brilliantly. He has had enthusiastic reviews for *Cool Struttin'* That was certainly his most successful LP to date, and it forms in his mind that perhaps the quintet format, with the very best sidemen he can muster, is the way to go for his next recording date. After all, it was the one that Charlie Parker used frequently. Mostly, in fact. Choice of sidemen will be crucial if he is to match and build on that album's success.

It will be more than five weeks before his next recording date. He should get a gig or perhaps even two in clubs before that, but he can't be sure of course. A long period without useful, paid work is always a worry. He has a strong temptation to buy a bag of heroin from his connection but resists. He will survive, somehow on methadone and alcohol which is a lethal enough combination anyway. he does not wish to undo the good work achieved by his hospital course of treatment and the generosity and concern shown by the jazz baroness. Tonight, he will crash out on the floor of a loft space in town, being careful to pick a friend who, like him, is working desperately hard to kick the heroin habit.

The news is out on the street that Hampton Hawes has been arrested. The word is that the police have been out to get him for some time, and now they have, it will be tough on Hamp. A long prison sentence is predicted by all. Sonny gets the news in a downtown bar where he is having a couple of beers and thinking about the next gig. The news hits him like a sledgehammer. If Hawes is in police custody, he could be next.

He goes back on heroin, as he always does at times of real or perceived crisis. Just a modest injection that makes him feel warm and confident of his abilities. He is no longer worried. He has been contacted by Jackie McLean, who tells him he enjoyed the *Cool Struttin'* session very much and thought it was an ideal lineup. Jackie has a record date early next year in January and would like Sonny on piano. He has a promise from Paul Chambers and Philly Joe Jones that they will make it although he has in mind Donald Byrd for the trumpet spot. Clark says he is more than happy with that. He has worked with Donald and loves his open, brassy sound. He will likely use him himself before long.

The recording session starts off well. Jackie says he wants to tackle 'Quadrangle,' a composition he wrote out some years ago, without piano. To get it, he says, in free-flowing mode without chords leading the horns anywhere. Sonny nods and sits back to listen. Byrd, Jackie, himself, and the ebullient Philly Joe Jones are all in great form. Experimental it may be, but it comes across as a very contemporary piece.

'Blues Inn' by Jackie is right up Clark's street. He digs into the blues with his usual enthusiastic invention. His joyous comping behind McLean proves the truth of his statement that he enjoys comping as much as playing solos. This is swinging, hard bop stuff, and Sonny is back in clover. Donald Byrd's trumpet solo is top drawer. Sonny's cruising piano solo is given added momentum by Philly's little fillips behind him, just the sort that spur him on and add to his invention.

All is going so well that Sonny is convinced that he is on yet another strong bop record. 'Fidel' is the next track, introduced by some snappy Philly Joe Jones drums. Both horn soloists shine in their solo outings. Sonny practically reinvents the melody with a pulsating piano segment that jumps all over the place, his single-note lines resembling a horn solo more than a keyboard effort. This is one of the qualities in his playing that distinguishes him from other modern jazz piano players. The song glides to a satisfactory conclusion and Jackie calls for another blues.

Nothing goes right with this selection. There are clinkers in two of the opening solos, and it appears to unsettle the rhythm section as they work desperately to rescue the music. Finally, it grinds to a ragged conclusion, and all agree that it must be rejected. An attempt at a fifth tune becomes messy almost from the start, and Jackie calls a halt before it is half-way through. Sometimes, this is the way things go. After three tracks have been recorded, the session starts to disintegrate for no apparent or obvious reason.

Jackie spreads his hands and raises his eyebrows. Do the guys want to try again? There is no enthusiasm from anybody. Lion has rejected the last two attempts and says that they have three really good tunes, enough for one side of an LP. He will set them on one side and will set up another session for Jackie very soon to record three additional tracks to make up an album.

It is disappointing, but Sonny shrugs as he returns to New York City. It has happened before and will happen again. If Jackie wants him for the second session, he will be there. If not, it is onward and upward to his next gig. He is reflecting on the good sounds he heard from Byrd, McLean, Chambers and Jones and resolves to make sure he recruits some, if not all, these cats for his next album recording.

He is called for another record session with trombonist Benny Green. It will feature Benny Green and Jimmy Forrest on tenor sax. George Tucker is on bass, and he is always there with a big, fat sound. It is for a record label called Enrica, not known to Sonny, but a gig is a gig he says. Sonny greets them all, and the leader introduces him to drummer Paul Gusman, a new name to the pianist.

Benny wants to call his album 'Benny Green Swings the Blues,' and that sounds like a good omen to Clark, always up for the format. They kick off with 'Been Walkin,' where the pianist plays the introduction, quotes a nursery rhyme theme before digging into the blues. 'Blue Mambo' is started by Sonny with a medium-tempo blast of Latin chords before the trombone comes in. 'Penthouse Blues' is a basic, medium-tempo workout with cheerful solo work from Green and Forrest before Sonny takes over and swings it along gracefully. He leaves the studio feeling content with another good blowing session completed, but his mind is already on his upcoming Blue Note date. There are five weeks to go first, and he has upcoming gigs in clubs to keep him going.

As the recording date approaches, Sonny makes plans in his head to try and ensure that this next record will be a real goodie. Unlike *Cool Struttin'*, there will be no bop standards. He plans a programme of Sonny Clark originals, compositions he has been working on in his more lucid, sober moments. He will ensure that they are his best work with catchy, melodic themes, and the personnel must be the very best available. At first, he thinks of Art Farmer on trumpet but then decides that he wants a more robust, brassy horn man. Donald Byrd would be ideal. Paul Chambers can make it, but Philly Joe is unavailable.

Alfred Lion suggest Art Blakey, if Art is free on the day. Sonny nods. He regards Art as one of the great drummers currently on the scene, along with Philly Joe, Max Roach and Roy Haynes. Jackie McLean is busy on the day, so Sonny recruits Hank Mobley, someone he knows will bring that little bit extra to the date, if only because his lines are unorthodox, and he always plays solos to fit with his idea and not necessarily where the harmonic pattern should end. And he always swings, naturally, easily and often unconventionally, just as Clark does himself. With this cast of sidemen, the pianist goes into two days of paid rehearsal cheerfully, confident of a good result on the day. He drives the horns hard in rehearsal, sure in his mind that the rhythm section will play forcefully with his percussive lines and Blakey taking charge of the rhythm and pushing the soloists, as he always does.

Clark explains to the sidemen what he hopes to do on this

recording. The way he would like the horns voiced. The rhythmic thrust and the overall sparkle he would like to create. They all nod. Then Art Blakey says that in his opinion every tub must stand on its own bottom. Sonny knows that means everybody doing their own thing to achieve best results. He is not concerned. He knows that although he can be forceful, overbearing even at times, Art is there to do a good job. How many times has he heard Art saying, let me know if I can do any little thing that will help you in your solo? I'm there to help and make you sound good. He will be dominant, but Sonny expects that.

Clark has chosen six of his own originals for the recording. Four are almost new pieces he has recently composed. 'Minor Meeting' is a particular favourite which he recalls contributing to the Lawrence Marable, James Clay session back in California in 1956. He intends to record a fresher, more spontaneous version here. 'Royal Flush' was one of the last tracks to be recorded at the *Cool Struttin'* date, which, to Clark's irritation, has not been issued as Volume 2, as Alfred Lion promised he would do. Well, it will be done again here and done well.

In the Van Gelder studio Sonny poses for Francis Wolff's publicity photograph. He is in Rudy Van Gelder's recording studio at Hackensack, New Jersey, perhaps for the last time. Rudy is building a new custom-made studio at Englewood Cliffs, just down the road from here. The building is big, airy and has a high ceiling, vee shaped and rather like a big church. It has wooden beams, high ceiling and is very modern, with an ideal acoustic for sound recordings. He sits on the piano stool, wearing his striped, dark jersey and with his fingers poised over the keyboard, two of them actually pushing down keys as though he is playing. Blakey sits smiling brightly behind his drums, sticks in hand. Byrd and Mobley are photographed holding their instruments looking cheerful enough. Only Paul Chambers looks positively grim and depressed, his eyes appearing lifeless. Sonny is not unduly concerned. He knows Paul is often seen looking sad or miserable, and he puts it down to the effects of addiction on the young bass player. He himself knows better than anybody how that can make you feel. But Paul always does a first-class job in the section and as soloist. He will today.

Two minutes into playing 'Junka,' Sonny is convinced that this will be a special recording. The ensemble floats out, cruising easily until Hank launches his solo. Clark spurs him on with neatly played fills as Art Blakey begins to take charge of the rhythmic thrust. It is exhilarating to Sonny to play in such a free-wheeling ensemble where the rhythm just floats naturally, and the solos emerge out of the thrust forward. His own melodic solo turns the heat down just a fraction and Blakey eases back very slightly before pacing Paul's arco bass solo. Then Art is back in control but in a good way, conducting ferocious four bar exchanges between Donald, Hank and himself.

A grooving, slow to medium 'Blues Blue' follows, Hank garrulous in his hearty solo. Donald's trumpet notes spill out excitingly. Sonny just floats, his ripe notes following each other in an insistent, logical flow. This is just what he hoped would happen on this session and here it is, happening joyously. It is at times like this that he experiences the full joy and satisfaction of jazz performance. Nothing else matters at these times; pain, addiction, frustration all fade to insignificance as the music unfolds creatively. On the spot creation, the magic of improvisation by masters of the format.

This reading of 'Minor Meeting' is twice as effective and inventive as the 1956 *Tenorman* recording was, as he had hoped it would be. Blakey is now in complete control, virtually conducting the ebb and flow of the music from his drum stool. With such a solid, thrusting beat and prodding accents, everybody's solos come to life brilliantly. His own solo roars down the track with Art egging him on all the while. Much the same happens with the second version of 'Royal Flush,' the track pulsating happily along even more together than the last session played in 1958.

It occurs to Sonny that it is probable that only Blakey could have made this recording the success it undoubtedly will be. He looks forward to Alfred issuing the LP swiftly and anticipates that sales will be the best yet. Everybody who bought *Cool Struttin'* will surely want this one. Along with thousands of other enthusiasts. Well, he can hope, can't he? Sadly, for reasons unknown, it will be twenty years before this great record sees the light of release and initially only in Japan.

The session ends with sparkling versions of 'A Few Clark Bars,' a bright swinger and one of Sonny's latest compositions along with the pretty ballad 'My Conception.' At the playback, everybody is happy with the final results. Listening to the warm lyricism of Hank's solo on 'My Conception,' the rhythm players praise the tenor player's creative input. The horn players point out that it was the thrusting, supporting rhythm section, as a whole, that made this date special.

On this occasion, Clark goes back to New York City experiencing exhilaration and a feeling that the recording went as well as could possibly be expected. Everybody played their part to perfection. As indeed the men on *Cool Struttin'* had. Some recording sessions just sizzle, and these two did. The immediate concern is that this album comes out early. It has six Clark originals, and he wants that music out in the public domain, being played and heard frequently. As the composer, he hopes for more royalties in due course. He is feeling upbeat and content with no immediate worries or concerns. How long can it last though?

17

NEW YORK CITY BLUES

AFTER THE FEELING OF EUPHORIA COMES DEPRESSION. THE HIGH comes from a successful performance and, depending upon how good it was, can last a day or two, maybe three. After the *My Conception* recording, Sonny is fine for four days, but that is unusual. The future looks bleak. No gigs or record dates on the horizon. With the insecurity that lack of continuous work can bring, Clark goes into a spiral of self-doubt, self-loathing and debilitating insecurity. His heroin use has been kept to an absolute minimum up to the record taping, but after the period of rejuvenation, he has stepped it up.

He goes on a round of scuffling not matched since the last time he spent with Hampton Hawes. Money that he has earned from recent club gigs and recordings has been stashed away in hiding places only he knows about. It is there for when he needs it, and he knows the time will come when he needs it. He spends days with musicians he knows who share his habit. One of them will always give him a place to crash and sleep at night even if it is a bleak, two-room apartment with blocked up sink, blood splattered bathroom and dirt everywhere.

Some of these people he hangs out with are on the fringe of jazz, rarely playing. Most have other jobs outside music or, more likely, no work at all. Sometimes he meets up with Bob Whiteside, the bass player who does not play much but does work as a waiter and bartender at the Five Spot. They go around together, cruising the dingy streets, when Bob is not working, going into dingy clubs in Harlem to hear jazz combos that are often very good, their music unknown to the outside world. Here it is, in a dingy Bronx club that he listens to Tina Brooks playing, a great tenor saxophonist who is still unrecognised by most of society. His *Minor Move* disc, with Lee Morgan, Art Blakey and Sonny, has never been released. Brooks tells him that he has never had a gig at Birdland or the Village Vanguard or any of the recognised jazz clubs in NYC.

Such a waste of a great jazz talent, Sonny thinks, but then his own situation is not much better. He does get to play the good clubs occasionally but is still unknown to most of the jazz audience. *Cool Struttin'* was Sonny's last leader album, more than a year ago. When he talks to Alfred Lion, he is told he has no idea when *My Conception* will be released. If ever. It does not have its title yet or a catalogue number. Lion is busy scheduling new records by Jimmy Smith, Jackie McLean and The Jazz Messengers. Horace Silver's Quintet. Albums that he knows will sell in reasonable numbers. He and Francis Wolff are extremely busy, and Sonny must leave them to get on with it. He fully intends to put everything out, if possible.

After spending many bleak weeks scuffling around, drinking, shooting up heroin, looking unsuccessfully for gigs and becoming more and more depressed, Sonny makes a sudden, spur-of-the-moment visit to Nica. She gives him money, provides a good meal and stiff drinks. She tells him that Monk is doing well; he has a prestigious gig at New York Town Hall with a ten-piecemini orchestra featuring Donald Byrd, altoist Phil Woods, Art Taylor on drums and others. He has worked hard arranging it over the past months with assistance from Hall Overton, a good arranger. Riverside Records is recording the music. It is something of a departure for Monk and he is, in his own way, quite excited about it. Nica says he has five albums on Riverside completed now, most of them already selling steadily, and he is pleased with his Riverside contract. Nica is pleased for him. Sonny says that he too is pleased for his friend's success but can't avoid feeling a little envious.

Sonny has been told by a musician friend in the same condition as himself about a loft at 821 Sixth Avenue. Many musicians and other junkies meet up, stay there and hustle generally. It is where Clark believes Monk and Overton met up to work up their arrangements for the Town Hall concert. Sonny becomes involved with a crowd of people there who have hustling for drug money down to a fine art. A group take him out as an observer to show him how to play 'Murphy.' The junkie poses as a pimp to approach one of the many men from out of town who are looking for a hooker. He takes his girlfriend with him, posing as a prostitute and offers the victim a chance to go with her. They persuade him to meet in a very remote spot, away from other people and once there, attack and rob him.

Sonny watches horrified but does not get involved. Later, with the stolen money, a large amount of heroin is purchased and shared with all the junkies back at the loft. He is unable to resist accepting some of the heroin and shooting up with the rest of them. The next day, after the effects of the drug have worn off, he feels remorse. It is too late now though. He is in a drug-fuelled environment, sleeping at the loft and a part of the scene. As the weeks pass by, he gradually begins taking more and more heroin, sinks lower into the abyss and, on one occasion takes an overdose. The group rally round, and one man, pushing air desperately into his lungs, breathing into his mouth, pressing on his chest heavily, brings him back to normal state before he begins croaking and moaning pitifully. Sonny Clark has reached a new depth of heroin-induced horror. He is in a mess, unkempt in appearance with his clothes crumpled and dirty.

Baroness Kathleen Annie Pannonica de Koenigswarter cruises slowly through the dark New York night in her pale blue Bentley Cabriolet. The big car glides through the mean streets of Harlem almost silently on the lookout for those in distress. She may, on any given night, pick up a stray, emaciated cat and take it back to Weehawken to give it food and shelter. On this night, however, she picks up a man and woman, ragged-looking, sitting on the kerbside and clinging together desperately. She gets out of her car, inspects the couple, who can barely speak, and then helps both into the back of her vehicle. She takes them home with her. She gives them food and shelter for the night.

The next morning, she drives back to Harlem and leaves them on the street where she found them. Both are back to some semblance of normality. They thank her profusely for her hospitality and the night of food and shelter. She cannot help them any more for the time being, but she has left two struggling people feeling refreshed and nourished. At least for now. This is Nica. It is what she does. Far, far away are the wealthy relatives who will have nothing to do with her and the grand house with extensive grounds just outside London, England.

Sonny is struggling. He is scoring for heroin every day the best way he can. He has begged for and received money from a prominent bandleader who tells him that from now on they are strangers to each other. It is five months now since he worked and recorded what he believes is one of his very best albums. He is at the lowest point in his life to date. He sleeps nights in the loft at 821 Sixth Avenue or in a number of cold-water apartments with disgusting plumbing and blocked sinks with failed or failing jazz musicians and other junkies who share his desperate condition. He has grown to know these people very well. If he scores, he shares the heroin he buys. If they score, they share with him. Two men he hangs out with persuade their girlfriends to act as hookers in town to raise drug money. When he meets and hooks up with a woman, he conducts his association with her in clandestine hotel rooms that are seedy and grimy in the extreme. He knows that he cannot go on like this. He must clean

DEREK ANSELL

himself up and get back to playing music or his great talent will be wasted.

He goes into the grubby bathroom at the loft and prepares. He takes a grimy bag of items out from behind the toilet tank. He takes out a spoon, a spike, an eyedropper, cotton, matches and a long strip of fabric to tie off his arm. He takes the spoon and puts a little powder in it with water. He lights a match and puts the flame under the spoon to warm the mixture. Next, he draws it through the cotton into the syringe through the needle and ties off his arm. He seeks a patch of his arm that is free from scars and lines. This is not easy as there are hardly any clean patches left. At last, he locates a tiny patch of clear flesh and injects the heroin into it. His troubles and all his sadness melts away as the drugs take effect and he feels a warm glow all over. He goes out into the corridor.

He does not get far along the corridor. He begins to feel hazy and even a little short of breath. He sinks down to the floor and leans back against the wall of the corridor. A couple walk past slowly but do not take any undue notice of his condition; they have seen it duplicated many times before. He experiences a brief moment of panic which disappears almost as soon as it comes due to the calming, euphoric effects of the heroin. His last thought as he slips quietly into unconsciousness is that he might have taken too much on this occasion.

In the big, long room at the loft, they are having an impromptu jam session. Piano, bass and drums are carving out a heavy, loud beat and a succession of tenor and alto players are taking turns to come forward and take a solo. A couple of well-known jazz musicians are present, but they are nodding out in a corner and neither seems interested in playing. Sonny Clark wanders into the room and sits close to the piano. He does not know any of the rhythm section and does not think any of them are particularly good, but perhaps this is just one of those nights. Any other night and it might be Thelonious Monk on the piano stool or Red Garland. Wynton Kelly maybe. Zoot Sims is often around and his pal Al Cohn.

When the pianist takes a break, Sonny goes forward to take his place at the piano. The drummer nods to him, smiles briefly. He can play well, and these two know he can even if they can't. Clark is happy enough to play with anybody, anywhere, but it has been such a long time since he played. Now he needs to get back into serious practice and find some work. He plays a couple of standard songs at medium pace. A competent but not particularly impressive tenor sax player steps up and begins to solo. Sonny finds it relatively easy to accompany him, spur him on indeed, but when it is time for him to solo, he does feel a stiffness in his fingers.

He struggles a little to get his solo flowing, and it does, eventually but without the easy fleetness he is usually capable of. It is at this point that he realises that nearly six months off the scene have taken a toll. He has sat in at Harlem clubs occasionally, but the last of those gigs was two months ago. He must practice regularly from now on and somehow find a way back to regular gigs and recording.

Sonny embarks on a programme of serious cutting down on his intake of heroin. He struggles with it desperately for some days but realises he is not really winning. What to do? He must give up this life of scuffling and scoring and get back to regular playing. Music is his whole life, and without it, he is lost. He can't believe he has let himself fall into this endless round of degradation. He telephones Nica and tells her he needs to book himself into a drug rehabilitation programme at the hospital but is worried because he has no funds. Nica tells him he is doing the right thing and promises to pay any bills for him. He checks himself into the hospital.

It is difficult to survive without drugs now that he is fully addicted. He has tablets though to keep him going, and he feels sure that he can cut down the drug use to almost negligible proportions. He leaves the hospital after three weeks of intensive help and encouragement.

On a chance meeting in the street with Philly Joe Jones, he receives an unexpected boost. Philly has been recording for Riverside as leader of a combo to be titled 'Philly Joe Jones Showcase.' The band has some top musicians on board including trumpeter Blue Mitchell and Bill Barron on tenor sax. The piano player is Charles Coker, but he is not available for the next session to complete the album. Philly needs to record two more selections, perhaps three to finish it off. If Sonny would like it, the gig is his.

Sonny would like it very much.

1961 *In the Loft* – Virginia Wald.

18

WILD NIGHTS AT THE JAZZ LOFT

THE SMART YOUNG MAN EMERGING FROM THE SUBWAY WALKS swiftly. He's been away for far too long now and is anxious to get back to his old, professional musician life. It has been a fascinating if harrowing seven months. In the wilderness. In and out of the jazz loft and other places where addicted jazz musicians congregate, a lot of lows but no real highs. And reaching a state of appalling degradation towards the end that will take forever to live down.

Now, he is on his way to Philly Joe's record date. Having left the hospital, cleaned himself up and, most important of all, kept off the heroin. He hasn't kicked his addiction completely, not yet, but he is working hard on it and keeping it down to manageable proportions. In any event, he has tablets to take that will keep the craving at bay.

Philly Joe greets him at the studio and introduces the boys in the band. Sonny has heard Blue Mitchell in the clubs around New York and he thinks he's seen Bill Barron somewhere. He nods to trombonist Julian Priester and then shakes his hand. He does not know Jimmy Garrison, the lean young bassist, but Philly explains that he has been working with him for a while now, and Joe forecasts a big future for him. Joe also tells him that he is breaking out on this record. He has recorded a track playing piano, just him and Garrison's bass. Then he recorded a drum track so he will be heard accompanying himself on the LP when it comes out. Sonny smiles.

It all seems as if the last seven months never existed as Sonny sits at the piano and producer Orrin Keepnews tells them that they are now going to roll. As they begin to play 'Minor Mode,' a Bill Barron line, Sonny picks up the comping behind solos by Barron and Mitchell, easily and naturally, with no sign of strain or stiffness in his fingers. His own solo flows along gracefully, bright, melodic, short and to the point.

Joe seems happy with the take, and they move on to 'Interpretation,' again by Bill Barron who takes a steady, relaxed first solo ahead of Blue Mitchell on trumpet. Sonny follows, piano in full melodic flow. And that is it, two selections to round out Philly Joe's album. On the playback, Sonny is surprised to hear how gentle and lyrical Philly Joe's piano solos are. Compared to his explosive bop drumming, this is quite a revelation.

Orrin Keepnews, the enthusiastic Riverside producer, thanks Sonny for filling in on piano and chats amiably to him. He remembers the pianist on Sonny Rollins' album when Clark first recorded in New York. Unlike some of the record producers and company executives Sonny has approached in the past two weeks, Orrin is friendly, helpful, encouraging. He has heard that the pianist has been off the scene for a long period and has had a bad time. Keepnews tells people that one of the first musicians he recorded, alto player Ernie Henry, died from an overdose of heroin in 1957 and he was truly shocked. Apart from recording him, Henry had been a personal friend. He is always sympathetic to people in Sonny's situation.

Clark resists the temptation to accept Philly Joe's invitation to hang out together after the session. He invents a previous engagement and says they should catch up later. He knows that getting together with Philly after recording would lead to a riot of heroin intake and heavy drinking. Philly Joe has a reputation, and indeed, Sonny is swiftly gaining one himself.

He is trying hard to keep intake down though and convinces himself that he will eventually kick the habit for good. He's been told frequently that addicts are notorious for self-deception but is convinced that he is different. He is truly getting back on track.

The building at 821 Sixth Avenue is not a pretty sight. Built back in Victorian times it has nearly a hundred years of dirt, grime and petrol fumes added to its structure. In daytime there is at least the odour of fresh flowers wafting through the street from the nearby flower market. At night-time, no such luxury. The occupant is W. Eugene Smith, a noted photojournalist who moved into the building in 1954 and opened it up to anybody who cares to walk through the front door. He takes photographs endlessly, catching jazz musicians practising or jamming, alone or in a group. One room in the loft is covered wall to wall in a wallpaper of photographs.

He intends to document everything that goes on in the building and has begun the task of rigging up microphones all over the loft building. On every floor. In all the rooms, in the corridors, on the landings, even in the bathroom. Sounds of music, conversations, arguments, disputes, cries and laughter, all is documented.

During the daytime the people coming in and out are assorted, but most are in trouble or on the fringes of society. Prostitutes, pimps, drug dealers and users make up much of the visitors. At night the jazz musicians begin to drift in, one by one but these are the unemployed, a few are unemployable. It is late at night, after midnight that the regular musicians come in, after their gigs finish, seeking a suitable after-hours joint to play or practice. They are looking for a place just like this, the Jazz Loft.

There are two pianos at the loft, one an upright, the other a battered Steinway Grand. Both are tuned. There are double basses placed on the floors and complete drum kits set up. It may be dirty, funky as hell, and it may have mice, cockroaches and even rats, resident but for jazz musicians seeking after-hours places to play, it is ideal. On any given night, visitors may see Zoot Sims, Art Blakey, Elvin Jones, Miles Davis, Doug Watkins, Louis Hayes or a dozen other well-known names. And Sonny Clark.

Sonny was a fairly casual visitor during the early part of 1959, but now, as the year winds down, he spends much of his time here. Today he meets up with Ronnie Free, a drummer he has jammed with frequently at the loft. The place is ideal for Free who, unlike most of his fellow percussionists, suffers from stage fright. Appearing in public is something of a nightmare for him, so to jam in comfort, at the loft where there is no audience and nobody bothers you, is perfect.

Bass player Bill Takas is a regular here. Almost always available, Sonny has hitched up with him and Ronnie to form a rhythm section and they make themselves available for anybody who wants to jam. On this relatively quiet night, there are no saxophonists, guitarists or trumpet players on the prowl, so the three musicians begin a late-night trio set that will, with suitable breaks for cigarettes, beer and other substances, both mild and toxic, go on into the early hours and the dawn. They set up in the big, long room close to Eugene Smith's quarters. There are packets of cigarettes placed under the piano stool. For easy access. Takas picks up the double bass, which is lying on its side, next to the piano. In doing so, he disturbs the cat. Tabun is Smith's black cat with a white mouth and nose, and she is always around. Somewhere in the building. Or chasing rats and mice.

Sonny sits at the piano and strikes a few random chords. Free has joined them at last and they are ready to play. Sonny begins playing a standard tune without a word to anybody. Bass and drums pick up what he is playing and join in. You can do this sort of thing in this type of situation. It is such a pleasure to wind down after a gig by playing just what you want, for yourself and no audience to worry about. They play for an hour, oblivious of time or anybody else coming in or out of the room. Smith will be recording this trio recital, as he records all music in the building. Sonny knows this as he can see the strategically placed microphones, but it does not bother him. In this place, you do as you like anytime, anywhere.

Sonny has just finished a gig at Birdland a short time ago, so he is feeling in good shape, and he knows he is playing well. He shoots up heroin when he needs it. You can do that here and nobody will bother you. Precautions are taken, of course. Use of the bathroom is recognised as the place for such activity. They have also gone to the trouble of obtaining large plywood boxes to cover up the mattresses so that passing police officers, should they wander in, will not be concerned. If they thought considerable numbers of people were sleeping in the loft, there might be trouble. Arrests could be made.

After an hour of jamming, playing standards and Clark originals, the trio need a break. They all light up cigarettes and Free goes to collect beer bottles. Sonny will drink his beer and then walk along to the bathroom before they start playing again. He will only take a small injection of heroin because he is still actively cutting down his usage to less than half his normal intake. He thinks it is going well and he will be off the stuff in a month or so. On his way to the bathroom, the cat passes him going in the other direction. Smith's cat walks around as if she owns the place.

Another night another session. Takas and Free have been limbering up playing bass and drum duets as they wait. Sonny arrives and the three start to play a standard. They are only three-quarters through their interpretation when a tenor saxophonist comes into the room, takes the horn out of its case and starts blowing a chorus before he even reaches the piano. Some nights it just happens. The rhythm section begins as a trio but ends up in the small hours as a septet. Or more, sometimes nine or ten musicians. On this occasion, Sonny is in great form and appears to inspire two tenors, an alto and a baritone sax man to raise their game. Some of this crazy solo work would likely drive an audience into a state of appreciative euphoria. If there had been an audience. Only the cat is in attendance. Finally, late on, a guitar player plugs in his amplifier and joins in for the last two tunes.

It is a wild night on New Year's Eve, 1959. Doug Watkins, the bassist best known for his work with the original Jazz Messengers and Horace Silver's Quintet, has just walked in. With him is Louis Hayes, Silver's current drummer. They have both been playing at gigs all evening and are now looking for some after-hours action. Sonny is at the piano already and he rises to greet the new arrivals. Hayes and particularly Watkins are like old friends. He has played with the bassist frequently. Are they looking to play? They are. Free and Takas are hovering, but they are happy to give up bass and drums to the illustrious pair of rhythm players. There is nobody else in the big room, but this is New Year's Eve and that will likely change as the night wears on.

In less than half an hour, saxophonist Sam Parkin has arrived, and he starts to blow with the trio almost immediately. A little later still, Zoot Sims comes in and begins blowing relaxed, refined tenor sax. After two more selections, they are joined by Jimmy Raney on guitar. It is a light, swinging session, everybody in laid-back mood, blowing almost quietly but comfortably. Sonny's solos ebb and flow smoothly and when one of the soloists takes over, he provides the little spurs and percussive fills to ease them on their way. The six-piece unit could carry on like this for an hour, maybe more but this is the last night of the year, and anything can happen at the jazz loft. Suddenly everything changes.

The door opens and in comes Lee Morgan brandishing his trumpet and grinning broadly. He is followed by Yusef Lateef with his tenor sax. Pepper Adams, the studious-looking baritone sax player is the last arrival, holding his horn ready. The new arrivals position themselves round the piano and commence playing with the combo. The music takes off like a jet plane with Morgan blowing in brassy, wild format, his trademark trills and half-note effects incorporated. Lateef's tenor is bright, burnished, and he blows a chorus of high-octane, blues-based lines as Pepper adds ballast to the bass lines before commencing with an intense solo segment. Swept up by the full power and energy of the new people, the rhythm section tightens up, offering a charging, swinging backdrop. Clark plays with loud, percussive fire as Raney adds guitar chords and bass, and drums drive the rhythm forward relentlessly.

It is one of those nights when the music is inspired, reaching out to new levels of inventive improvisation and finding them. One by one the band musicians drop out to drink in the New Year with a bottle in one hand and a cigarette in the other. As one player returns to re-commence blowing, another comes out and drinks, then returns. The playing goes on for more than ten minutes; it has turned into a stomping blues. When it ends, they begin a new selection, up-tempo all the way.

All that is missing is a wildly appreciative audience, but not by these musicians. On this night, in this place, they are playing for themselves and their own enjoyment. One or two players retreat to the bathroom but return as soon as they feel the adrenalin flowing and join in the music-making. How to end this spontaneous jam as dawn breaks and light seeps in slowly through the windows? A full-blown raucous blues is the answer, up-tempo, pulsating, robust, long solos all round and tumultuous four-bar exchanges with all the horns and Louis Hayes at the drums which seem as if they will go on forever.

So much has happened to Sonny Clark since he arrived in New York in 1957. Two short years in total but a lifetime of music and a feeling that he is now where he should be and will stay for the rest of his life. Much of his time now is spent at the Jazz Loft even if it is just chilling out when he has no gigs and little chance of getting one. Sitting talking about music with drummers Frank Amoss and Ronnie Free. Hanging out with Bill Evans who is becoming a good friend. Listening to Roland Kirk play two or more saxophones simultaneously. Chilling with Stan Getz and Zoot Sims. Mostly playing piano of course, in a trio, a combo or just on his own at the instrument. The only thing that disturbs him is his full integration now with the drug culture. So many of the dozens of people who come and go at the loft are on heroin and even when they are not injecting, they are passing around various other oral substances. Saxophones, cymbals from drum kits and other items are regularly stolen to be hocked for instant cash. Sonny is glad he plays piano, and the instrument is too big to be stolen.

Occasionally the ambience in the loft is different. In the silence, at dead of night, when no music is heard, Sonny experiences a deep loneliness that is felt even with a considerable number of people in close proximity. At other times, a lone baritone sax, wailing mournfully, can be the saddest sound in the world.

He has known the bad times in New York like being busted for heroin possession. A spell at Rikers Island which was hard. He has known good times, most of them with Nica at her house, and her generosity has got him out of many a bad scrape. If he feels guilty, it is because he knows he has let her down. Nobody has tried harder or spent more money trying to help him give up his debilitating habit.

Now he must make yet one more attempt to get clean and find regular work.

Sample text for Library of Congress Control Number 2009020875
Author's telephone conversation with Orrin Keepnews in 2002

19

TIME RECORDS

It is a bright, fresh day in New York City. Cold, though, very cold. Sonny is out there, spruced up in his best casual attire, washed and clean-shaven. He is making his way to number 2, West 45th Street, the offices of Time Records. It looks like an interesting gig, but at this particular time, any gig of any kind is a good one for him. He has left the loft for now, been on the move, but has cut down his intake of heroin to a fraction of his usual dosage. He looks, as many observers have noted, like a smart young man about town.

The opinion of many people in New York is just that; Sonny is well dressed, polite and never in any way offensive towards anybody. It is not an acquired look but rather his natural state. Even those few people who have seen his haggard and strung-out appearance know that when he needs to clean up, get smart in both dress and state of mind, he can do it.

He has not seen much of Nica. He knows she is currently waiting for the court case concerning her owning up to being the possessor of marijuana found in her car to protect the vulnerable Thelonious Monk. Her lawyers are dealing with it still and have tried to assure her that all will be well. With that on her mind,

Sonny has kept away, apart from a brief social call to advise her that he was in good shape.

Time Records are a small independent label, but they are seeking to make their presence felt on the jazz scene. The recording date in progress features tenor saxist Stanley Turrentine. He is an interesting, up-and-coming soloist on the scene and known to be a swinger with a healthy appreciation of the blues. Sonny is intrigued. He is told that he would be filling in on piano for Tommy Flanagan who has already taped half of the album. Somebody suggested Sonny as he is gaining a reputation for being a hard-swinging, lyrical soloist admired by many reed- and brass-playing leaders. Clark is up for it.

Of specific interest to the pianist is the rest of the rhythm section he will be working with. George Duvivier on bass is highly regarded in practically all jazz circles as a steady, swing-oriented bass player with a big, full sound. Max Roach is considered by many to be the master drummer in bop and hard bop. He is someone that Clark would love to play with, as he represents the best of first-generation bebop, the drummer of choice by Charlie Parker and Dizzy Gillespie. For Sonny, there is no finer jazz to be had than the music those two giants have played and put on record.

In the studio, Sonny is met and greeted by master percussionist Max Roach. The drummer is polite, friendly and welcoming. If he has heard of Clark's reputation, he mentions only the good and says nothing of the bad. They commence the session with 'Sheri,' a smooth blues written by Turrentine. Max sets the groove, and the sax man comes straight in, his sound rich and warm. Sonny provides supporting lines and goes into a down-home solo, full of blues phrases and clean, shimmering single-note lines. When the tenor man returns Sonny is right with him, spurring him on together with tasteful, unobtrusive rhythm from bass and drums. There are smiles all round at the conclusion.

'My Girl Is Just Enough Woman for Me' is taken at a medium-tempo lope. Turrentine has a robust but rich tenor sound. Clark is as happy accompanying him here as he is soloing. His own solo clips along briskly, swinging with ease, as always. The ultra-crisp, restrained rhythm works well here. Sonny is dominating the rhythm in a tasteful manner as the leader takes the piece out. Roach is aware of what is happening but gives the young pianist his moment.

Roach and Duvivier are in charge all through 'Mild Is the Mood,' an up-tempo swinger kickstarted by the drummer. Clark has to be on his toes all through this one, but he holds his own and offers a chiming, fast-paced solo of his own, full of inventive, melodic lines. It is a very good feeling for Sonny to be in such august company and he realizes, with a sudden pang of regret how much he has missed playing with musicians of this calibre for so long now.

On completion of the third track, the album is finished, and all four musicians can relax and listen to the playback. Max is impressed with Sonny's solo work throughout and tells him so. He asks the pianist if he would like to do a piano trio record. Clark says that would be an ideal recording situation. He did one a year or so back with Paul Chambers and Philly Joe Jones which he enjoyed very much, although it was all standard tunes. Today he would love to do a piano, bass, drums set of all originals he has written in the past five years.

Max asks him to leave it with him. He will make a few enquiries. Sonny is ecstatic at just the thought of recording his own music with Roach and Duvivier. The bassist worked with Bud Powell in his trio way back in the early fifties. Sonny's main inspiration. Max was with Parker and many of the early beboppers. Working with those two would be a dream assignment and allow him to put his own spin on early bebop. His music in the style he loves. With just the modern, personal touch of his own style to make it near perfect.

He dares not think too much about it, in case it falls through. Or Max doesn't have the influence he thinks he has. It turns out, though, that Max does have the influence he may think he has, and Sonny learns that Time Records are up for a trio album, and he can have full choice of material.

In the studio, there are just the three of them, the producer, the sound engineer and Nat Hentoff, the jazz critic and author who is writing the sleeve notes. After a discussion about his material with Max and George and a quick run-down of three of the titles, they are ready to commence recording.

Clark kicks off with 'Minor Meeting,' his oldest composition, one that he remembers playing on the Marable/Clay album in California that was issued with the title *Tenorman*. He also recalls how successful it was when he recorded it for Blue Note on his *My Conception* LP. Blue Note has not yet indicated when, or if, they are planning to release that favourite disc of Sonny's, a sore point at the moment.

The pianist plays 'Minor Meeting' at a comfortable up-tempo, his notes spinning out in Bud Powell mode, either consciously or subconsciously, although his own, personal drive and melodic note production are much in evidence. The accuracy of his beat is another feature. Playing four-bar exchanges with Roach is exhilarating. Sonny Clark is grooving contentedly.

'Nica' is dedicated to his lovely friend and benefactor, the Jazz Baroness. After Sonny plays the introduction and embellishes the melody, Duvivier takes a solo, his fat, juicy notes prominent. Although it is swinging crisply, the pianist is, perhaps, a little restrained in this, his homage to classic bebop. His lines have a smooth flow, and his choice of every note is judicious. Even so, the producer calls for another take and then more after that. The chosen take is good, although Sonny likes take four where he considers he sounds more relaxed, and the music has a much more refined, natural flow. He likes Duvivier's extended bass solo too. George Duvivier introduces 'Sonny's Crib' with a short, snappy bass line that leads Clark in. The pianist rolls out more glittering lines as bass and drums shadow him accurately. They are spot on with the accompaniment, and there is not even any need to take charge of the rhythm as Max did on the earlier

Turrentine recording. All three musicians are as one in harmony, melody and rhythm. More exchanges with Max's drums are played with precision before Sonny glides his composition to a close.

Next up is 'Blues Mambo,' which is precisely that. Sonny is cruising now; he feels as though he could fly through this recording session without concentrating, it is going so smoothly. He will shortly be playing new, trio interpretations of 'Junka,' 'Blues Blue,' and 'My Conception,' all material that was on the Blue Note album, but he has no great confidence that LP will ever be released. This way he can ensure that the tunes will be out there and heard. Only Blue Note appears to have such a casual attitude towards issuing what they have recorded, but he knows there is nothing he can do about it.

As Sonny digs happily into the blues on 'Blues Blue' and 'Junka,' his troubles evaporate, at least for the next few hours. Music like this is the antidote for all his ills. Sitting in the passageway of the Jazz Loft last week, too strung out and sick to raise himself up and go to the nearest piano. Drinking in a downtown bar with a musician who was in a worse state than he and becoming more and more depressed as the night wore on. Now he just feels joyous as his flying notes key in with Duvivier's bass line and Max's spurring percussion. He will finish this sterling session with an unaccompanied piano solo. Sonny feels that this session is refined bebop, a new slant on the crazy music of the 1940s. With these two musicians and their wide experience, all is possible. On his composition, 'My Conception,' a mixture of warm ballad and fast runs up the keyboard, the ultimate self-expression even without the excellent support of his two colleagues. They do try it with bass and drums, but all three are in agreement that this composition works best as a piano solo. The way he plays it. The final track is 'Sonia,' an up-tempo swinger where all three players swing naturally.

Nat Hentoff says that he thinks this is by far Sonny's best album. 'Because you've never had rhythm support so apt for your style.' Sonny smiles. Hentoff says the set indicates a marked growth in Sonny's development. He adds that he plays with a much more personal style than on any of his other recordings. And he cannot remember Sonny ever having improvised before with so relaxed and self-confident a beat.

Sonny nods. He may not agree with the critic that this is his most relaxed and confident recording, but he does acknowledge that it was very special. 'This rhythm section,' he says, 'has had so much experience that they're immediately able to get down to what you want to do.'

Hentoff speaks about bassist Duvivier, praising him and saying that he had the most challenging kind of trio experience working with Bud Powell. Clark agrees readily. 'He has a real good beat, a real sound, and his notes are always choice. And Max, aside from his ability to swing always plays so cleanly. He helps make a trio full. These are two dream cats for a pianist.'

Sonny goes off after the recording feeling satisfied with his and his sidemen's performances but unconvinced that the album, when it is released, will cause any kind of stir in the jazz world. It will be released, no doubt, and be bought by a small group of dedicated fans and a trickle of enthusiasts up and down the country. He will, though, still be wondering why he is not better known and respected by jazz folks everywhere as late as nineteen sixty.

Reading the jazz press and listening to the radio, he can answer his own question. Almost all coverage by the critics is of the music of the new thing. Freeform Jazz, or whatever they call it. Articles and record reviews are all about Ornette Coleman, Don Cherry and his quartet. Eric Dolphy, the multi-reed player, and a piano player called Cecil Taylor. Sonny has heard Coleman's quartet and was impressed that their music was so fresh and original, but it surely shouldn't overshadow the current jazz style, which is hard bop?

A few have established themselves and are doing very well commercially and musically. Clark understands that and admires the playing of most of them. Sonny Rollins, Miles Davis, John Coltrane, Bill Evans, Thelonious Monk. Maybe it really was that they all played in famous bands or were pioneers of bop like Monk. If he, Sonny Clark, had been recruited into the Davis combo, or Blakey's Messengers five years ago would he now be well known, respected in the entire jazz world, revered? He doesn't know but suspects it would have helped considerably. The trouble is, he knows, he has always been a lone wolf, seeking his own musical path, working in any combo that wanted him and willing to work anywhere, with anybody, provided he had the freedom to always express himself musically, in his own way. He will continue to play the way he plays now, safe in the knowledge that he is developing his own style fully, based on the tradition of early bebop and today's hard bop. The difference is only that hard bop is bebop stripped down to its essentials in terms of swing and has a healthy injection of modern blues.

Today he is feeling low because he has run out of money. He's been paid for recordings up to date but has spent every dime on drugs and food. There are no immediate gigs or record dates in sight. His best hope is the usual method of addicted musicians, to borrow money against royalties from the record companies he has recorded with recently. To do so, his immediate task is to get money for a ride uptown as it is too far to walk. He reluctantly decides to visit old friend, the bass player Bob Whiteside who lives off Second Avenue with his girlfriend Jackie. It is well known that Jackie is sympathetic towards jazz musicians who are in trouble. When he arrives and talks to Whiteside, he is looking way past his best, not too well dressed on this occasion, haggard and in need of a fix. He notes that Whiteside, wearing a short-sleeved tee-shirt, has needle marks all along his arms and is obviously strung out. Whiteside grins, as Sonny, showing solidarity with his friend's situation, rolls up his sleeve and shows a similar pattern of needle marks decorating his own arm. Both smile in recognition but no words are spoken.

Jackie gives him money and he thanks her and Bob and departs, slightly embarrassed but knowing that Jack has been in a similar position himself on more than one occasion and both he and Jackie understand that. In any event it is better than stealing money, something he wants to avoid at all costs and even if the horn players can do it and frequently do, he cannot pawn a piano. Not that he's ever owned one. Clark proceeds on his mission, knowing that he will be able to borrow some money from one or more record companies. Naturally, he will have to have it deducted from future payments when he next records but in his situation, you have to live for the moment and your present needs. And his needs, at this moment, are pressing hard.

Sonny Clark Trio Time Records 70010 Nat Hentoff's sleeve note.
Melody and Melancholy – Sam Stephenson in *The Paris Review*.

20

BACK TO THE WILDERNESS

IT IS A TIME OF LIMBO FOR CLARK AS HE BORROWS MONEY FROM record companies and anyone else who is close to him. Blue Note appears to have abandoned him. It is nearly two years since he last recorded for them and there is still no sign that *My Conception* will ever be released. He feels let down and abandoned and fearful for the future. On his last visit to the Blue Note office, he was told by Francis Wolff that Alfred was out. Sonny doubts that he was. Most likely hiding in the next room to avoid meeting him.

He has regular small injections of heroin now but still convinces himself that he is cutting down intake, step by step, and will soon be off the drug. Clean as a whistle. Even if he should fail, he holds on to the thought that he can keep it under control if he takes small amounts. A cat once told him about a famous jazz drummer who is an addict, but you would never know it. Because he keeps it so well under control. Clark can do that, can't he? Of course, he can.

The association with Time Records is not finished yet. He gets the call to play on Bennie Green's new LP for them. As he arrives at the studio, he feels a brief wave of euphoria. The trio record made so recently turned out extremely well and now he is back recording for the same company. Surely the future is not really looking so bleak. Is it?

Bennie Green greets him like an old, long-lost friend. The two musicians have worked together frequently on records and in clubs although usually at long intervals. Green tells Sonny that he is going to record two of his friend's compositions. Sonny is pleased, not least because he is the composer and will get credit and maybe a few extra royalties. In due course.

It feels strange playing 'Cool Struttin'' now, two years after his classic Blue Note version. Bennie plays a neat, cruising trombone solo, but to Sonny, it lacks the blues-drenched passion that Jackie McLean, Art Farmer and he put into the original. Jimmy Forrest is up next on tenor sax. Clark's crisp, melodic solo is delicate and free-flowing enough, but he does not think he has done very well on it.

They play 'Sometimes I'm Happy' with the addition of Joe Gorgas on conga drum. Al Dreares is the drummer, and Sonny's old companion George Tucker is the bassist. Clark's solo on this one is intense, striking through the rather thick rhythm at the slow to medium tempo that feels unusual on this piece.

Clark's composition, 'Sonny's Crib,' takes him back to early days in New York. Forrest takes the first solo and builds a good, steady, medium-tempo groove for the follow-on soloists. Sonny's own solo is fresh, skipping lightly and differently to any way he has played it previously. It is his best solo of the date and a candidate for best of the session. A few sweet notes on the piano introduce 'Solitude,' played slowly and with a warm approach by everybody. Green is rich in lyricism on this selection, one of his most effective solos today. An ensemble flourish introduces Forrest who is robust and exploratory on his segment. Sonny sounds more reflective as he solos briefly and concentrates on comping thereafter.

Leaving the studio, Clark feels that it is another successful recording but nothing really special. It was good to link up again with Bennie and George Tucker.

Sometimes Clark's intentions are good, but when reality kicks in, he goes in a different direction. He is back on the street, strung out after taking a heavy hit of heroin, much more than he should and dangerously close to an overdose. He pulls through but suffers the pain and discomfort that follows. He has been on the loose in New York City for two months and hasn't been near a recording studio. He makes his way to the Jazz Loft where he knows the door is always open. The usual junkies and pimps are littered around the stairwell and on the various floors of the six-storey building. Smoking pot or drinking beer, at least those that have it; others, with nothing, gaze into space.

He passes the open door of Eugene Smith's space and sees him in there, staring out of the window at the street below. Smith spends long periods just staring down. Soon he will return to his photographs, many of them spread out on the crowded table just inside the room. His tape machine is running. It runs permanently, picking up the sounds of the building from every corner. Voices, fragments of conversations, arguments, music from the room upstairs filtering down now to the present level. The cat walks by, silently at first, but as Sonny moves as if towards her, she mews loudly and continues on her way.

Smith moves away from the window and back into the main area of his room. He notices Clark standing there but they do not speak. Smith seldom speaks to anybody. If you want conversation, you need to ask him a question or initiate an exchange of words. He never will. Sonny feels lethargic, unwilling to do anything at this moment. Not even play the piano. Eventually he turns away sluggishly and walks slowly up the stairs to the next floor.

He goes into the room where the piano is playing. The usual bass player and drummer are backing him. Their playing appears to key in with the bleak, sombre atmosphere on this evening. Dark, chunky blue chords from the pianist. The bass player supplies low notes, deep, resonating sounds at the bottom of each chord. The drummer swishes away moodily with wire brushes. Sonny sinks to the ground and rests against the back wall, smoking a cigarette and listening. When the pianist gets up to take a break and smoke a cigarette, Sonny considers getting up and taking his place on the piano stool. The bassist plays a scale. The drummer begins trying out some rhythmic patterns as the bass falls silent and the player departs.

Sonny nods off and eventually drifts into a long and troubled sleep. He will not move far from this spot tonight and will remain in the building for two more days. The next night finds him in the mood to play. He is swinging through Miles Davis's 'The Theme' with a baritone player and trumpeter he does not know very well. Sonny's invention is in full swing over a long solo as he takes over from the baritone and trumpet segments and becomes so involved, he could go on playing all night long. Only the sound of an out-of-tune piano causes him to frown.

He has returned to Weehawken in bad shape. He is still at a very low ebb. Nica frowns involuntarily as she notes his appearance and ushers him into her drawing room. She gives him Scotch whisky and he sinks into an armchair to consume it and smoke a cigarette. She encourages him to go and take a leisurely bath. He does so, and when he returns, she prepares a meal for him.

Coming back here always rejuvenates him to some extent, no matter how low he has sunk. He feels guilty at having let her down so many times. She has done all in her power to help him get off drugs. But even when he has been booked into the hospital and cleaned himself up it never takes long before he is back on the drugs. Shooting up. Even so, she never condemns him. Never criticizes. Such a good friend.

In conversation, she tells him about Thelonious Monk. Her star pupil is doing very well currently. He will be back before too long but is currently spending time with his wife, Nellie, and his son, who hopes to be a jazz drummer one day. Nica's close attention to Monk's needs and her efforts to promote him and secure profitable gigs has paid off. She tells Sonny that Monk has been signed up by Columbia Records, just about the biggest of them all. There his music will be marketed properly, promoted and sold into stores everywhere in the land. Overseas too. 'It's Monk's Time,' Nica says, 'and he deserves it.' She does not give any indication of the part she has played in his latest success, but Sonny is aware of the work she has put in. The people she has spoken to.

He tells her he is very pleased that Monk has found success at last after twenty years of being misunderstood and neglected. He himself would love a contract with Columbia, but he knows he will never get one. Monk will be touring round, in this country and overseas too, promoting his records.

When Clark asks Nica about her own troubles, the suspended court case where she has already been convicted and is likely to spend three years in prison, she perks up. It now looks likely that she will not go to jail. Her lawyers have established that the police did not seek Nica's permission to search her car. They found marijuana, but her lawyer is convinced he can get her off. It's a technicality, of course, but any port in a storm. He is pleased for her

Sonny spends some time at Weehawken. His moods hover between elation and despair. In conversations with Nica, he is always upbeat, the jokes he tells her and her loud, tinkling laugh. Moments to savour. It is when she is not around and at night when he is alone. Sometimes the place is full, and he gets into conversation with other cats, prior to an evening jam session where he sits at the piano and supports anybody who gets up to solo. When somebody else is ready to play piano, he always gives way gracefully and is happy to sit listening to them.

The afternoons chilling out in the living room, staring out of the window at the Hudson River, are his favourites. Talking to Nica. Pouring out drinks at her invitation. Sometimes she tries gentle persuasion to get him back in the hospital for further drug treatment. When he tells her he will but not just now, she does not press him. He needs to get his head round it he says and now it isn't.

Now she is sitting there calmly, drinking her Scotch whisky and asking him about his recent music. When he tells her about the session with Max Roach and Duvivier, she is impressed. He must have enjoyed that. He did, but it was months ago, and he has done virtually nothing since. Well then, he must be patient, he is too good a pianist to be left out and good offers will come along. In the fullness of time. Clark likes her cheerful optimism and refusal to look at the dark side. He knows that unless he can control his drug habit and get himself cleaned up in every sense, further good gigs are unlikely. Perhaps he will never work professionally again.

Monk has left a sheet of music paper on the piano. Sonny reads the notes and recognises the basic tune that Thelonious had been tinkering with months ago. He appears to have resolved it at last into a complete song. He plays a few bars and smiles. Yes, it makes sense now where before neither Monk nor he could resolve it. Idly, he picks it up and puts it in his pocket. Monk will not miss it, he feels sure. He noodles away at things but often forgets them and moves on swiftly to something else. In any case, he has probably just abandoned it now it is finished. Sonny tries to persuade himself that he has only taken something Monk had finished with. And he had contributed to.

He glances over at Nica, settled in her armchair reading a book, glass on the occasional table by her side. He still can't fathom out the relationship between her and Monk. He is the one. The musician she has devoted her life to. To making a success of his. Nica loves the music, Sonny thinks, not the man. But then the man and the music are inextricably linked. Then again, she is genuinely supportive of all jazz musicians and will help each and every one of them when they are in trouble. He should know, she has stood by him and gone to great lengths to help him clean up his act.

Which is why he cannot intrude and take advantage of her hospitality any longer. He has to get himself together and seek work. He leaves her promising that he will not forget his promise to go back to the hospital very soon. Back on the streets, good intentions fade as he meets up with fellow musicians who share the same habit. Inevitably, it seems to him, he can't avoid getting high every night and being unfit to work. If he had any work. Alcohol, heroin, tobacco and a little food when he can remember to buy items or when he realises, he must eat something to live.

It is a long dark road with no turning when you hit the depths of addiction pain. He has been there before, briefly and somehow, through sheer force of will and ambition, crawled upwards and out. Now he is feeling helpless. It is a year since he saw the inside of a recording studio and he feels abandoned. It hurts that nobody has contacted him or offered him anything, but then he realises that he has been almost invisible to record company executives. And to many fellow musicians. In and out of dilapidated lofts, in musician's grubby apartments. Mainly, though, to people on the fringes of jazz and not very well known.

Living just for the next fix and finding money to pay for it. Sometimes he gets lucky and is offered a fix by someone he helped out years ago. Or two weeks back. Borrowing money against royalties from record companies has drained dry. Offers to record for them have not materialised. Time is running out.

In the clubs he has played in, he has listed his address as Weehawken, New Jersey, Nica's pad. Well, they know how to get hold of him. As long as Nica can track him down, but she knows all the regular cats he knows, and they would flush him out if she asked. For a musician who desperately needs to be playing to convince himself he has some worth, it is becoming a bleak outlook indeed.

Sonny is in and out of the Jazz Loft. There is always somebody there that he can tap for a loan. And music with the chance to play. When he feels capable and wants to play. This is the third day he has been in and out himself. The place has been exceptionally busy with Charles Mingus, the virtuosi bass player there along with Bill Evans, Stan Getz, Bob Brookmeyer, the trombonist and countless others. Art Blakey is in today and playing with a pickup group. Clark wanders into the room where they are playing and listens for an hour. Blakey is on great form, spurring on recalcitrant horn soloists and beginners who are not used to this sort of ferocious, make or break accompaniment. Many fall by the wayside to be replaced, immediately, by the next hopeful. Sonny could wait for a break and take over on piano, but he does not feel he is at his best in his present condition. With Blakey, you just have to give everything. He knows he needs practice badly so decides to take the plunge. But then Blakey gets up and leaves the room abruptly, heading no doubt for an evening gig downtown.

He goes out of the room and to another part of the building. There he encounters Alfred Lion talking earnestly to a jazz organist. Alfred nods, to acknowledge him, and as the organist bids farewell and departs, Sonny finds himself asking Alfred if there are any record dates coming up that he could be considered for. Lion is quite polite but brusque and tells Sonny he will need to get himself sorted out. But he will see what he can do. The pianist knows well enough that he is a favourite of Alfred, and he will use him if he can, if he is clean, tidy and fit to play.

Sonny returns to Nica and tells her he is going to make a colossal effort to get clean and find work. She arranges for him to have vitamin injections and methadone prescribed by Doctor Freymann. He will spend the next weeks getting the treatment and somehow, anyhow, staying off the heroin. Nica is happy to pay for his treatment but is disappointed that he will not book himself into the drug programme at the hospital. He tells her he will definitely go but not until he has got his career back on track. A few weeks of vitamins and methadone will help him secure record dates and club work, and once he is re-established, he will go for the longer option.

The next weeks are crucial. It will be difficult, painful, almost unbearable at times, but worthwhile in the long haul. He is absolutely desperate to get back on the scene and playing again, regularly. He has done it before so many times and is convinced he can pull it off once more.

Sonny Clark, inconsistent as ever, abandons the methadone treatment after just one week and injects heroin into his arm.

The Jazz Loft Project—Sam Stephenson

21

THE SUMMER OF '61

It can be hot and humid in New York in the summer. Relatively quiet even, as so many people evacuate the city on their annual holidays. Sonny Clark walks the hot streets endlessly wearing just casual clothes and soft shoes. He is going to a bar or meeting up with musicians he knows who have similar lifestyles. Or he is making a connection with his heroin supplier. If this is his way of life now it is one, he has been building up to for some considerable time. In his sometimes-befuddled mind, it now starts to occur to him that this way of life will never change. When he is able to think clearly that is.

Much of the time he doesn't think at all. He just goes from day to day. There comes a time in an addict's life when it dawns on him that this is his life and he had better begin living with it rather than trying endlessly to change it. Then again, he may feel differently next week. Or tomorrow. At the moment, on this day, he lives for a fix. He goes to his connection and buys some heroin. Next, he meets up with a fellow addict who is also a musician and the two go down the street to a seedy apartment where other junkies hang out.

The place is not a good place to be. Everywhere is dirty,

unkempt. There is grime all over the uncleaned windows. On the table a bottle of milk and half a loaf of stale bread are slowly rotting. The kitchen sink, near where they sit, is blocked up. None of this matters to Sonny or his companion or the three other men in the room. Now that the heroin has taken effect in his system, he is feeling a warm glow and can relax and chill out. This is the good feeling all over that the addict lives for, the sense of pleasure and freedom from worry, guilt or anything else. They can sit here for two or three hours and are doing just that. They have not spoken a word to each other for half an hour and will not do so for their remaining time in the room.

Sonny walks slowly to 821 Sixth Avenue to the loft. It is cooler in the building as he enters and makes for the creaking wooden staircase. The squireling graffiti is all over the walls as he mounts the stairs, ugly patterns of ill-considered shapes with little or no artistic merit. The Jazz Loft has become something like home to Sonny over this spring and summer. Whether playing piano on one of the three instruments available, alone or with a makeshift combo, or just chilling out. Sitting in the hallway sometimes. Sharing space with people in a similar state to himself. Sometimes getting into conversations, other times sitting silently with silent people all around.

He needs to work.though. In his more lucid moments, he knows he must hustle for gigs because he can't live without playing jazz piano. In public. In front of an audience and lapping up the applause. This he will do, and he will make some effort to clean himself up and appear at the clubs, dressed neatly. Having shaved. After all, he reasons to himself, he is not the only jazz musician with a drug habit. Far from it indeed. Most of them secure regular work even if they suffer in their private lives.

Today though he is sitting in a large space in the loft with a fellow musician, drinking beer. It is a hot day so he will not move far and will not hustle for anything. His companion shares his idea of lethargy.

At the same time a young man named Chase Chaffer, a

Harvard graduate, is driving his ex-girlfriend Virginia McEwan and her current lover, the tenor saxophonist Lin Halliday, to New York. Chaffer is a wealthy young man who has friends in New York to visit and is happy to act as chauffer to Virginia. Driving from Cincinnati, Ohio, they reach the Pennsylvania Turnpike. Virginia, or Gin, as Halliday calls her, asks if they can go to Wilmington to visit her grandparents. Chase raises his eyebrow but dutifully drives to Wilmington. They find the house and park up outside. After sitting there for a few minutes, Halliday asks if Gin wants to go in and visit her grandparents. She doesn't. She just wants to sit there looking at the house she grew up in.

The aim is to get to Maryland where Lin and Gin can get married. It is late now, though, and too far to drive. It is even later in the evening when Chase's car finally pulls up outside 821 Sixth Avenue in New York. A jazz musician he played a gig with recently told Lin that if he was ever in need of a place to crash in New York, make for the Jazz Loft. Chase waits as Lin goes in, up the rickety staircase to ask if he and Gin can stay. He is directed to Eugene Smith's space and is told that he can come in, stay the night, stay for a year if he'd like to. 'Anybody can come in,' Smith says.' Door always open.'

Lin and Virginia make their way up the dim, gloomy staircase, carrying their few possessions, gazing at the graffiti on the walls, barely visible in the gloom. All mattresses were occupied hours ago and there are people stretched out in the hallways and stairwells. A solitary tenor saxophone is heard playing mournfully somewhere in the building. Gin is tired from hours of travelling and Lin, although he would like to go out and score some heroin, is also weary. They flop down onto the hard floorboards and slowly drift off to sleep. Close by, a drug addled Sonny Clark has also just slipped into troubled sleep.

Lin Halliday and Sonny get talking the next day. Neither is sure how they came to discover each other, but it soon emerges that both are jazz musicians. Lin tells Sonny that he plays tenor saxophone and Sonny nods. He takes an immediate liking to this well-dressed young man and his girlfriend. Gin, he speculates, can't be much more than sixteen or seventeen. She is attractive. He likes her long dark hair and tall, slim frame. He does, though, soon notice the way she looks at Lin and realises quickly that she is in love with her saxophone player. Best not to make a pass.

Lin and Sonny go to the fourth floor to play. Sonny introduces a standard tune and Lin picks it up immediately, blowing wispy threads of tenor sax notes at first. Then he tightens up. As the music progresses, Clark hears a bop tenor, a burnished, warm sound with a touch of Lester Young in his phrasing. The pianist nods approvingly at his partner who continues with a long solo. Sonny then plays one of his own full flowing, melodic solos. The two men are impressed with each other. They continue blowing for some time, first as a duo and then a quartet as a bass player and then Ronnie Free on drums, join in.

Sonny and Lin talk music for an hour, joined shortly after they finish playing by Gin, who joins in the conversation from time to time but is soon out of her depth on the technical aspects.

The days and nights continue. Playing on the fourth-floor space, eating, sleeping and the two musicians going out to score heroin and shooting up. Gin is not an addict. She appears to take Lin's addiction in her stride however, sitting with him contentedly as he nods off, alongside Sonny.

The three friends go down to Birdland to hear the music currently on offer. Unfortunately for her, Gin cannot go in with them. Birdland is one of the few jazz clubs that insist on age identification. She says she will wait in the Ham and Egg Café across the road from Birdland. She is busily doing a correspondence course to complete her education. Tonight, she will continue with her studies and drink coffee.

Gin walks down to Penn Station to mail in her schoolwork and collect mail for her next study. She goes down every morning without fail. Her aim is to graduate without actually being in school or college and she will, over this summer, succeed. If there is pressure to lure her into drug taking or prostitution, and there is, she will resist firmly. A determined young woman living in a dangerous environment.

Sonny and Lin get a gig at The Fat Black Pussycat, a Bohemian spot where jazz enthusiasts rub shoulders with folkies, beatniks and other assorted customers. Gin can come in and listen to them playing here; the place has a free and easy attitude to everybody. Sonny and Lin adapt easily to the location and enjoy feeding off each other as the music proceeds. Lin smoothly picks up chords supplied to him by Sonny and sails into inventive solos. Often, he will provide wispy filigrees of sound on tenor behind Sonny's more complex piano solos. The music gives them both a positive high. At other times they receive a debilitating high from heroin injection.

Even so, life is beginning to assume a pattern that is acceptable to Sonny and Lin. For the present moment at least. With such a rich assortment of people coming into and out of the loft in Sixth Avenue, you just never know who is wandering around. And listening. It may be Roland Kirk practising circular breathing on one of his many saxophones. The manzello or the stritch. Or a more conventional tenor. It may be Sonny playing piano into the early morning hours when the rest of the pick-up band have drifted off to sleep or into town. Eugene Smith, who oversees the entire building, never seems to sleep. If he does nobody notices. This morning, in the early hours, he is listening to one of his constantly running tapes. Sonny Clark is improvising at length on 'My Funny Valentine.' He gets into some complex harmony, his touch feather-light on the keyboard. Other early risers or late-night refuge seekers are also listening in. They may be regulars or casual visitors. They may be other musicians, homeless wanderers or even agents from the club scene, listening out for something special. Word has gotten out about the jazz loft.

It can and occasionally does lead to gigs for Lin and Sonny and some of the best musicians. This keeps them going and provides money for the drugs they crave. This may be one of those moments.

When Lin and Sonny venture out into the city, they usually carry their drugs in Gin's bag. She looks so young and innocent no police officer is likely to ever stop her. This morning they are careless though. Gin is studying alone, and the two men are heading for a shop that sells pills containing drug substances. A cop stops them, and they are found to be in possession of heroin. They are arrested, and Sonny uses the one telephone call he is given to call Nica. She sends a lawyer to defend him, and he is let off with a caution. Halliday is found guilty and serves a short but harrowing prison sentence.

Back at the loft, Sonny tries to explain that the two of them were separated at the police station and there was nothing he could do to help Lin. Gin looks unhappy and glares at him, but he is unable to defend himself further. He keeps his distance from her while Lin is away. On his own more, Sonny tends to drift into the company of the more hardened drug addicts, some are musicians, some not. He scores with them, hangs out with them and returns to the Jazz Loft to nod out alone.

Sonny and Lin have a gig at Birdland. They walk down briskly with Gin and leave her by the Ham And Egg Café. It will be a long night as she is still too young to be admitted alone. She tells them not to worry about her, she has a bag full of books and her notes and intends to spend the next few hours studying for her graduation.

Over at Birdland, the musicians get ready for the first set. Sonny is happy playing this famous club although he dislikes the Master of Ceremonies intensely. Pee Wee Marquette is a diminutive man with a high voice who asks all musicians who play Birdland to tip him. If they refuse, he mispronounces their names from the bandstand to the amusement of the audience. Clark has heard a report that pianist Horace Silver once refused to tip and was announced by Marquette as 'Whore's Ass Sibler.'

He enjoys playing in the same combo as Lin Halliday. Halliday's lines are lean and in the hard bop style, but there is also that smooth sound he gets on ballads. Sonny's lines are open, bright, scintillating. It always surprises him how easily he can adapt to being on stage, in the spotlight, playing with warmth and sometimes abandon just twelve hours after taking a large dose of heroin into his system. This is a good night; the audience is more responsive than most and the music is flowing effortlessly.

It is not such a good night for Gin McEwan. Three girls she has seen in the café before are talking to her about becoming one of their 'family.' They have a pimp who looks after them, makes sure they are well paid and taken care of generally. They are trying to persuade Gin to join them as she is trying to concentrate on her school studies. She tells them she is married but they seem to know that Lin is a junkie, and this just increases their attempts at persuasion. If she turns tricks with them, she can look after her man even better than she does now.

Gin is quite strong though. She knows her own mind and she certainly does not want to get involved with prostitution. She is not an addict herself and never will be. She explains all this to the girls who gradually come to realise they are wasting their time. Gin can now return to the more pressing matter of studying Shakespeare's *Othello* and posting her lesson back tomorrow morning from the mailbox she has rented at Penn station.

Sonny Clark, meanwhile, is constructing intricate lines on 'My Funny Valentine,' which he has worked on quite a lot in the past few weeks. Slowing it down. Bringing out blues and deep sadness in a slow ballad reading that follows a good few up-tempo burners the group have been playing. He is back in his element on this gig.

These are the good times. Playing jazz in The Fat Black Pussy Cat and at Birdland. Playing creative jazz night after night, two of them on stage one listening, whenever she can. The good times are mixed with the bad and the terrible. Shooting up heroin is debilitating, often sordid and can even be life threatening. On two occasions, Sonny has come close to death through taking overdoses. He knows his body is primed to withstand large quantities, but occasionally he underestimates the effects of overindulgence. Taking a large dose one night, he sinks into semi-consciousness, only alleviated by the swift reaction of Gin, who is with him, by her pummelling of his chest to revive him. And talking to him continuously. Clark survives.

The fortunes of the three friends have moved up and down this summer in the Jazz Loft but at least work has been plentiful for the two musicians. Sonny has got a gig at The White Whale, a coffee house in the East Village. It is the type of gig he likes best where he finds he can play the type of hard bop and blues he really enjoys. And with ideal sidemen. Along with Lin on tenor sax, he has Butch Warren, one of the new young bass players currently making names for themselves and Billy Higgins on drums. It is an impressive, swinging line up. Sonny knows Higgins' work from hearing him play with Ornette Coleman two years ago and with other combos since. His clear, swirling accompaniment is much in demand. Warren is new to him, but together with the drummer, Sonny finds these two make an ideal trio.

The gig is going well, the music sounds great every night. Occasionally the combo is augmented by Tommy Turrentine, the trumpet player brother of tenor sax man Stanley. Clark loves his sound. There are some sterling sessions, enjoyed by audience and musicians alike.

It is late night. Another great gig at the White Whale has finished and the musicians are winding down. After a few drinks at the bar, Sonny and Lin take their leave and make their way back to the Jazz Loft. They both feel in need of a fix to bolster up and retain their good spirits. The door to Eugene Smith's loft space is open, and Sonny steps inside. The place is a mess. Items of photographic equipment, plates and boxes are strewn across the floor and the table is plastered with photos, overflowing onto the floor. Sonny grins and says to Smith, 'There's a lot of shit in here.'

'I've been shitting a long time,' Smith responds, grinning back. Clark raises an eyebrow and then he joins Halliday and the two go along the landing to the bathroom. They shoot up heroin, which usually works out fine for them both but on this occasion, Sonny overdoes it. He injects a large amount of heroin into his arm which constitutes an overdose. Then mist begins to swim in front of his eyes, and he feels sick suddenly. Sitting stretched out on the bathroom floor with Lin, he is conscious that all is not well.

Sonny begins moaning, a long, agitated gurgle of sound from deep in his throat. He is slipping slowly into unconsciousness. Lin looks at his friend, alarmed. He starts to shake Sonny and begins talking to him, keeping up a constant flow of words. Then he starts to sing to him. But Halliday does not know what to do, he is alarmed by Clark's appearance and the groans that subside as he loses consciousness again.

Halliday shakes him vigorously. Sonny comes round and begins groaning, a sound that is being captured on tape as it happens for future generations to hear. Smith's tapes roll on regardless.

Halliday remembers that Sonny overdosed a short time ago and Gin pummelled his chest to get him breathing and keep him awake. Lin is panicking now. He calls out loudly to Gin, but there is no response. He begins hitting Sonny's chest not knowing how or what he should do. He calls out again urgently.

'Gin, Gin, Gin.'

Where is the girl? he wonders, feeling agitated. She must have gone off down into the murky depths of the building. He is on his own so he can't stop but continues to prod and push

Sonny's chest vigorously. His friend is awake now but looking grey, his face a mask of frightened misery. Slowly, painfully, Clark begins to breathe more easily and naturally. Halliday realises with immense relief that his friend is over the worst and starting to recover. He leans back against the murky bathroom wall and breathes easier himself.

The two men nod off in due course and spend more than an hour slipping in and out of consciousness. When both men come out of their drowsy state, the effects of the heroin in their bodies gives them an aura of slowly permeating exhilaration. They lurch out of the bathroom and decide to go downtown to buy milk and cheeseburgers. They collect dozens of empty bottles which Smith has given them to redeem for cash at the grocery store. Working a club currently means they are not short of money, but they keep it in reserve to feed their habits. Food can be bought on the proceeds of bottles returned. They pack the bottles into bags and set off.

It is pitch black in the streets. The cold night air helps to resuscitate them both and they are soon eating burgers and drinking refreshing milk. It has been a long day and even longer night. As Dawn's greyish white light filters slowly through the darkness the two musicians breathe easily at last. Clark has had a bad scare. So has Halliday for a different reason, but he begins to realise how much worse Sonny's addiction is and think about his own situation. If they carry on as they have been doing, it can only get worse. As most of the citizens of New York City are getting up and ready to face a new day, two jazz musicians are finally about to go back to the loft and take a long sleep.

If the trauma endured by Sonny's overdose was a warning, the pianist does not heed it. He is soon out on the streets looking for a connection as there is a shortage of heroin. An Air Stewardess was caught bringing in a huge supply from abroad and now there is little to be found. Sonny, Lin and Gin are cruising through Harlem looking for someone selling. A fellow addict is driving. It may be a stolen car, but nobody is asking any questions.

They park the car, and the two men go searching. Gin crouches down on the back seat of the car waiting. If anybody comes into view, she ducks down below the level of the window. Gin does not wish to be seen. Not here, not anywhere close. She is beginning to wonder if she should be in New York at all. Sonny and Lin return, but they have been unsuccessful. This will make them both edgy, awkward and unpleasant to be with.

Suddenly heroin is available again on the street. Lin and Sonny breathe sighs of relief as they can now go out and score.

Baroness Nica has tracked Sonny down. He is sitting in the front passenger seat of her Bentley in a quiet street. Lin and Gin, who were with Sonny, are invited to sit on the back seat. Nica wants to know all about Clark's recent activities, his gigs and how he has been getting along generally. They all smoke cigarettes and talk animatedly for over three hours. Nica opens the car windows and clouds of smoke swirl out. Sonny is carefully editing his recent activities for the baroness. If he places great emphasis on his recent gigs at Birdland and The White Whale, who can blame him? Nica is pleased to hear he has been working, but is he alright generally? He is, he tells her. Nica expands the conversation to bring in Lin and Gin. She has met them before when she picked them up in her car and took them home to give them dinner and temporary shelter. The conversations, all around, are amiable but Nica is aware that she is not hearing the full story.

When the time for the clubs to close arrives, Nica says she must go and collect Thelonious Monk from his current gig. He will be expecting her. They go with her to collect Monk who is waiting. Nica, Monk, Sonny, Lin and Gin leave the car and go on to the musician's apartment where they are expected and where there will be heroin and beer. Monk does not talk at all and very soon he and Nica leave the apartment. It is the familiar pattern that has become constant in Sonny's life during this hot, humid summer of 1961. They meet up in a grimy, unkempt apartment, they talk, drink beer and shoot up heroin. Then they nod out and those that have injected lean back against a wall, or a battered sofa if they are lucky, and cool it. With contented looks on their faces, drug-induced.

Sonny has become used to it more than ever this summer. As has Lin. The odd one out is Gin, who sits loyally with her man, bored, often tired and frustrated, waiting for him and Sonny to come out of their self-inflicted semi-coma. For how long can it continue though?

Clark has been invited to go round to Thelonious Monk's apartment. He goes with some trepidation wondering why Monk would summon him. It is most unusual. He expects to see Monk, Nellie and possibly their son, known as Toot. The family are not there. Monk and Sonny Rollins face him, and both are looking serious. They are there to try and persuade him to go into the hospital and kick his drug habit. He is told that Nica is most concerned about his current state. Although he is working occasionally, in the clubs, his life is unravelling in a frightening manner. Rollins tells him how he himself suffered as an addict and how he kicked it at a resource for drug dependency and can now live a full and normal life, drug-free. Monk agrees and backs up his statements.

The pianist listens carefully to the good advice of his friends. He tells them that he will take action very soon. They must leave it with him. He has promised Nica and knows he can count on her for help and support. He will set things in motion within the week.

Sonny goes back to the Jazz Loft and resumes life with Lin, Gin and the rest of the itinerant people there. He makes no effort to change anything. But the long summer is winding down slowly, and change is in the air. Lin, desperately short of funds, has attacked and robbed a man for money to buy food for Gin, who is now pregnant. She is horrified, appalled. He has done bad things in the past year but never sunk to this level. She is now thinking that she cannot continue this life of scuffling even if she does still love Lin. She fell for him as any young girl might fall for a talented jazz musician, and she has been loyal and loving towards him, all the time resisting the ever-present temptation and pressure to become an addict herself.

On the fourth floor, they hear the sounds of music wafting through the corridors of the loft building. They sit on the floor of the crowded loft space and listen to the sounds of tenor saxophone, piano, bass and drums. It has been quite a day for music. Zoot Sims, Stan Getz and two relatively unknown pianists have been in and out. Roy Haynes has been in, borrowed Ron Free's sticks, and played up a rhythmic storm behind a scratch combo. Lin, Sonny and Gin are listening to the latest combo, nodding and tapping their feet as usual. It is not quite the same though. There is an atmosphere that Sonny, for one, is unable to pinpoint.

When Gin tells Halliday she is leaving and going back to Cincinnati, he does not argue or press her to stay. He knows she is thinking about the forthcoming baby and her life from now on. As an addict, he cannot promise her a stable life. Like Sonny, he is caught up in his present existence and cannot change.

Gin McEwan is sitting by the window on the fifth floor of the loft. She is gazing out hopefully. She has telephoned her good friend Chase and told him she wants to return to Cincinnati. She hopes he will not let her down although she realizes she is asking a lot of him. Her ex-boyfriend. The drummer Frank Amoss is sitting with her, talking to her about her plans. She tells Frank that when Lin attacked and robbed someone, he crossed a line. It was too much. She could never condone that although she does realise the depths to which addicts will sometimes descend. She has kept up her studies and will graduate.

She breathes a sigh of relief as Chase's car draws up outside. She bids a swift farewell to Lin, Sonny and Frank. Then she is gone. Clark and Halliday return to the room they were playing in and continue practising. Their lives continue. Such are the lives of committed addicts who know of no other remedy for sadness and loss than the next gig and the next fix.

1961-In The Loft by Virginia Wald. *The Jazz Loft Project*.
Pannonica, Lin And Gin. *The Jazz Loft Project*.

22

FIVE WILL GET YOU TEN

IT IS A TIME FOR WAITING. WAITING AND WONDERING. CAN SONNY Clark come back from obscurity? It has now been thirteen months since he was last in a recording studio and some time since his last good club gig. He has spent the last year back in that wilderness he was in before. Scuffling for the most part. Playing very occasionally. A few good gigs and some not-so-good, only in the less salubrious environment of the Jazz Loft or on occasional visits to Nica's house. For the rest, it has been months of hustling, scoring loans from musicians that are never going to be repaid, begging, borrowing, lying, cheating. No action taken to be proud of. The good nights in the Jazz Loft and playing with musicians of equal ability have been few and very far between recently.

Hanging about in the jazz clubs, hustling between listening to the music, has made him unpopular with the owners and managers. Joe Termini, owner of the Five Spot, has asked him to leave on more than one occasion. His reputation is now as bad as it can be. He has sunk lower than ever before. He desperately wants to climb up, but for once, his usually unshakable belief in his own ability has been tested.

He has bathed and tidied himself up, aware that first impressions are important. He's had his clothes cleaned and pressed. All he can do at the moment is sit tight and wait and keep calm. Even though he hates it. And feels constantly sick.

It is just at the point when he feels most hopeless and extremely vulnerable that he gets the call. Jackie McLean wants him as pianist on his new Blue Note album. Alfred Lion has been talking to Jackie and it has been agreed, even if Lion has expressed reservations. Sonny's conduct over the past twelve months has not gone unnoticed. Even though, to many people, he has appeared to vanish from the face of the earth, a few have been aware. And people talk.

Sonny arrives for rehearsal and is greeted warmly by Jackie McLean. The alto man has had his own problems with heroin addiction and does not judge. On the contrary, he seeks to help. Jackie tells him it is a strong lineup with Tommy Turrentine on trumpet, tenorist Stanley's brother. The rhythm section includes one of the new boys, Butch Warren, an up-and-coming young bassist who is rapidly making a name for himself in New York, and Billy Higgins, the lively, sensitive drummer who Sonny heard as part of the Ornette Coleman Quartet. He remembers fondly the gig at the White Whale and how he enjoyed playing with Warren, Higgins and Turrentine. The pianist was impressed hearing Turrentine in 1959. And again in 1960 and particularly that recent gig. When they discuss repertoire Jackie says he has material of his own but could do with another composition. Clark does not hesitate. He shows Jackie the tune he has taken from Thelonious and tells him it is a new piece of his own, which he is calling 'Five Will Get You Ten.'

They run the new selection through, and it sounds good. Everybody is happy and Jackie says they will play it on the album. Sonny is just beginning to grow in confidence even though he has been away for a very long time. He does not wish to return to that wilderness. He gives only a cursory thought to his theft of the Monk piece, convinced in his mind that Monk will not miss it. In any case, he has tinkered with it himself and can easily convince himself that it is, at least partially, a Clark original.

The quintet rehearses Jackie's material and breaks for the drinks and snacks that Lion and Wolff always provide for musicians. Clark likes the sound of the rhythm section; they are relaxed and flow along freely without any sign of strain. Turrentine, too, is heard to favourable advantage. He has a warm, burnished sound, brassy but not too harsh, cooler than most. Sonny is feeling more optimistic than he has for the past year and ready for action.

It is recording day. The band play 'Five Will Get You Ten.' The well-structured composition grooves along at a comfortable medium tempo. Jackie's bluesy solo fills the studio as Sonny places sustaining chords underneath him. The pianist is feeling exhilaration as he comps cheerfully. It is almost as if he has never been away, and if his lines are not quite as spontaneous as when he is on top of his game, he is not far short. Now it is complete, the tune does not feel at all difficult and he wonders why he struggled with it back at Nica's house. Jackie gives way to Turrentine whose trumpet floats out inventively. His long lines are logical, melodic, highly suitable for this music. Sonny takes over the solo spot and is flying. Complex lines mix with fast melodic runs. He is enjoying playing, aware that his invention and natural, easy swing have not deserted him in a long absence.

Sonny's lyrical piano introduces 'Subdued,' a slow, melancholy ballad with a blues flavour. Jackie's solo catches the sombre mood, and it is continued by Tommy's fleet, muted trumpet. Pain and sorrow can be heard in Clark's blues-tinged piano interlude. He sustains the atmospheric hue of the performance all through his solo before handing over to Jackie to take it out.

'Sundu,' next up, continues the melancholic mood as Clark gets fully engaged in the music, pleased that it is taking on this melancholy hue as it fits in perfectly with his own changeable state. It both rejuvenates and steadies him as he immerses himself fully in the creation of improvised lines and contributes fully to the overall structure of the session. This will be an extremely good album; he senses it all through the recording and does not fail to notice that Lion is looking very contented. As indeed is Francis Wolff when he comes to take the musician's photographs for the LP liner.

For Sonny and the rest of the musicians present, this music is very special when a session goes as well as this one has. Hard bop at this time is part of a culture, a continuation of bebop, hipness, dress and drugs. The music has a tension in it, derived from a combination of musicality, energy, creativity and the enforced cool resulting from heroin addiction. As writer Ben Sidran put it, the music had a tenseness in it that was almost a signature of life in New York City. The enforced cool, produced, he suggested, an attitude of 'furious, passionate indifference.' As the music proceeds towards the mid-sixties – 'when players let go and the individual was free, jazz then was about the rhythm section, the group feel, the common conception.'

No time to reflect or think even. Sonny is booked into the Englewood Cliffs studio on the very next day to record a new young guitarist that Alfred Lion is very excited about. He has lined up Grant Green who he is anxious to record extensively with Butch Warren on bass and Billy Higgins on drums. Listening to the Clark, Warren, Higgins unit on McLean's recording, Lion was convinced it was the ideal rhythm section. Sonny is there in good time, smartly dressed and ready to play. With a successful gig and a good record session behind him, he shares Lion's enthusiasm. The three mesh together ideally.

Green is Clark's type of guitarist. He sounds like a modern version of Charlie Christian. His single-note lines, clear, bright and fresh as a spring morning shine out. Sonny comps happily behind him on 'Woody 'N' You,' and then takes a springy, gliding solo himself. Warren adds a brisk bass segment, and the guitarist takes it out. It is the beginning of a long series of recordings for Blue Note, but on this first day, they only manage to record this one selection. They play a version of Damerons' 'Lady Bird,' but get hung up on the chord changes and Alfred calls a halt. They play more than seven takes on 'Woody,' and that does not go too smoothly either. Lion seems unperturbed. He says they will come back to it again at a later date and record a full album. Before the date breaks up Lion tells Sonny he would like to offer him a leader date in about a fortnight.

He exchanges a few friendly words with Warren and Higgins. They talk about getting together again soon as they appear to have hit a very happy groove as a rhythm section. Sonny goes off feeling content, temporarily rejuvenated. He has managed to come back from the wilderness yet again and his music prospects look great. He goes on a drinking spree and ends up shooting heroin, anxious to preserve his happy mood.

It is two fifteen am. A warm, clear night as Clark returns to the Jazz Loft, virtually his home at present. He walks into the loft from the clear night air and immediately breathes in the rank, foul air of the building. Nothing is different. The only variation to the vile odour of the loft is when something unusual adds to it. Like the time when Tabun, Smith's cat, gave birth to a whole litter of kittens in his space. Now there are many cats on the prowl. Sonny mounts the rickety stairs to the fourth floor. Smith's door is open, but he is not there. He is in Japan on one of his photography expeditions. There is a jam session still going, and Clark thinks he can pick out the sounds of baritone saxist Pepper Adams blowing a long solo. It sounds like Horace Silver on piano, but he can't be sure. So many hard-bop pianists sound similar. He is sure it is Ronnie Free playing drums. Most of the jam sessions have Ronnie on, he is always there, always happy to play and is adaptable enough to perform in any style. Even Charles Mingus, a hard taskmaster when it comes to sidemen, is happy to play with Ronnie. In the loft anyway. And Ronnie is free as a bird to experiment, accompany briskly and not have to worry about his nervousness. There is no audience here to trouble him.

He is still here when almost everybody else has departed to sleep or disappeared into the remnants of the night. Sonny though is playing here still. He hunches over the piano working out fresh variations on a couple of standard tunes before segueing into one of his own sparkling compositions. He is still high and still ready to play until morning arrives. As dawn breaks only Zoot Sims is still playing. And Zoot started before Sonny.

Jackie McLean HIPNOSIS BN LA483-J2 Ben Sidran's sleeve note.

23

MASTER WORK 3 - LEAPIN' AND LOPIN'

SONNY CLARK IS THINKING ABOUT HIS FORTHCOMING RECORD DATE. He has recorded as a leader now on five albums for Blue Note and one for Time Records. He is reasonably happy with all of them but likes to think each session he plays on is slightly better than the last. It isn't easy though, he must acknowledge to himself and having reached peaks of creativity on *Cool Struttin'* and *My Conception*, where else is there to go?

In conversation with Jackie McLean at his recent recording session, Sonny was surprised to hear the altoist say that he was feeling inspired by the New Wave. The music of Ornette Coleman was making him think about heading in a new direction. Playing free jazz. Clark told him he was not ready for that and would pursue the path of bop and hard bop he had grown to love.

He wants to find new expression on an old format. He has listened closely to Coleman and admired his adventurous spirit. The man certainly has something fresh, different, and highly original to offer but Sonny wonders if it has the substance and staying power of bop. He thinks not. His idea is that he will continue along the hard bop lines he has always followed and try to find something fresh and previously undiscovered there. Unlike McLean and several other musicians who are saying they are inspired by Coleman, pianist Cecil Taylor and reed player Eric Dolphy, Clark will continue to try and expand the world of bop.

The personnel for his next recording will give him pause for thought. He may be sitting here in the squalor of the rat-infested loft, alongside alcoholics, other junkies and down and outs but he is still respected by the best jazz musicians because they know what he is capable of. It should be easy enough to get either Don Byrd or Art Farmer for the trumpet chair. Paul Chambers has always been his favourite bass player and until the date with Roach and Duvivier, was always his first choice and first call. Philly Joe Jones is Sonny's idea of a near-perfect bop drummer. As are Max Roach and Art Blakey.

Great as those players are though, would it amount to more than a good, typical hard-bop album? From Blue Note who specialize in such sessions. It occurs to Clark that he finds such mutual understanding in the Butch Warren, Billy Higgins combination that it would be ideal, if not logical, to continue that association with his new record. And how refreshing would a totally different and lively front line be?

Sonny has washed, shaved and generally tidied himself up today. He has grown a droopy, Mexican-style moustache and he is inspecting it in the rust and slime-decorated mirror in the bathroom. He was growing tired of people saying he looked far too young to be a professional musician. An experienced jazz pianist? Never. Now it is fully grown he feels comfortable with it. He feels older and looks more experienced.

In Alfred Lion's Blue Note office, he is greeted by the two principals. Lion has a third man to introduce, tenor saxophonist Ike Quebec. Does Sonny know him? Sonny knows of him, by reputation of course, and he has heard him on record. He shakes hands with Ike.

Ike Quebec has a special relationship with Alfred and Blue Note Records. When he was a big name in jazz back in the nineteen forties, Lion recorded him. More recently he has acted as a scout for Alfred, recommending musicians to him, and although he has been out of favour on the jazz scene in recent years, he has recorded some 45rpm records for Blue Note. Even more recently he has played at jazz clubs with a more modern sound and approach. He is making a comeback. A jazz critic recently heard him at a club playing in what he described as a Sonny Rollins style. He has not kept to that approach though.

Alfred explains that he is seeking to ease Ike back gently onto the scene. He plans a full LP for Quebec and wants to test the water first. He wonders if Sonny would be prepared to feature him on one selection on his forthcoming album. Sonny would be pleased to oblige. On the question of personnel for the new record, Lion says he has been giving it a lot of thought. It is well known that Lion always chooses the personnel for Blue Note records. Sonny says that he has too. He would like to record with the rhythm section he has been working so successfully with recently. And have Charlie Rouse, Monk's tenor player and trumpeter Tommy Turrentine in the front line.

Alfred Lion smiles broadly. That is precisely what he has been thinking would be good. And as to the proposal of Rouse and Turrentine, he sees no problem in that selection.

Sonny hangs out with Butch Warren and Billy Higgins. He has become very friendly with the bass player since the White Whale engagement. Sometimes the three get high together although Warren is not happy in such situations. 'That heroin is very hard,' is a phrase he uses, and he has frequently complained about feeling sick and most ill at ease after coming back from an injection. Clark should not encourage him, and he knows it. He likes companionship though with friends or fellow musicians to hang out with and he misses Lin Halliday. The saxophonist has gone off somewhere, Sonny does not know where,

Billy Higgins is a genial companion and easy to get along with. Warren is quiet but friendly although he has, unfortunately, had distressing mental problems and received treatment. With a forthcoming record date though, all three are in good spirits and ready to go. When they get to the rehearsal and meet up with the frontline players, Clark has a good feeling once again.

Sonny discusses the ballad 'Deep in a Dream' that they are going to play with Ike. The pianist would like to play a strong, rather long introduction and ease Ike in to play one of his warm, sensuous solos. Quebec is happy with this arrangement. Sonny tells Ike and Warren that he wants to create a mood on this track and, in fact, throughout the record. When asked what sort of mood Sonny shakes his head vaguely. Pressed further he says merely, 'Dark.'

In the studio for the recording, Clark is not free of heroin, but he has certainly not overindulged. His mood is sombre, but he is in complete control and anxious to produce a particularly good album. With Rouse and Turrentine sitting out, he begins the planned ballad feature for Ike Quebec. Delicate, sad piano chords are underlined by deep blue bowed bass from Warren. The pianist has only asked Butch to play arco lines behind him, but the effect is just what he wanted. If the mood is dark and despairing, it is maintained by Quebec's almost heartbreaking tenor solo. Full of intense lyric pain, the selection is a combination of Clark's mounting despair and Ike's painful condition. Quebec is dying of lung cancer but only he knows it. Sonny plays a brief melodic solo and then leaves it to Ike to take it out.

'Something Special' is a minor-keyed blues, the first of three compositions Clark has written for the date. Despite, the minor key the piece is an infectious swinger, played by the horns in unison leading to Rouse's charging tenor sax solo. Sonny supports him joyfully, his mood changing backwards and forwards as the session proceeds. Turrentine has that light and floating quality to his trumpet solo, his lines dancing merrily on this selection. The piano solo glides along crisply as Warren and Higgins swing easily alongside.

'Melody For C' is a modal tune, melodious but with just the hint of gloom creeping in as the solos develop. Rouse is exploratory digging deeply into the melody to extract his own variations. Turrentine maintains the searching, seeking feel in his crackling lines. Clark is especially inventive here, but the undercurrent of a secret sadness is present. Even in the flashing, incandescent single lines he plays. Warren's bass solo keys in with the rest of the soloist's contributions. This version is done early in the recording and chosen for the LP. Towards the end of the date, another version is played, and Sonny thinks this is the best. It is immediately chosen, and the first taping becomes an unissued alternate take. There is, though, very little to choose between the takes.

'Zellmar's Delight' is a straight-ahead bop line, a bright and breezy enough piece, but it does not really fit the mood and ambience of the session. Good, sturdy bebop solos all round. It will not be included in the album issue.

'Eric Walks' is Butch Warren's contribution, requested by Clark. It swings smoothly decorated with bright, upbeat trumpet, buoyant tenor sax and Sonny at his most lyrical.

Warren's dark bass and Clark's ominous chords introduce the moody 'Voodoo.' It floats out slowly, slow to medium tempo, Rouse probing, Sonny's chords melancholy. This piece swings the pendulum of the music into dark, treacherous territory, filled with gloom and foreboding. Sonny's grim solo, full of pain, joy, despair, all mixed up together, shines a musical light on his state of mind. The music glides slowly and inevitably through nightmare territory before Sonny's tinkling, down beat notes, bring the track to its conclusion.

'Midnight Mambo' wraps up the main thrust of the recording

session. Clark loves Turrentine's cool, floating trumpet lines that have just enough brassiness to keep them solidly in the tradition and the little twist at the end of his solo that both concludes it and leaves the listener waiting for more. Latin grooves are highlighted by Sonny's mambo-styled solo and Billy's polyrhythmic drum solo.

It is finished. Sonny has put everything into this latest record, perhaps more than even he realises. The choice of material, the musicians to play it, the darkness in the attractive ballad 'Deep In A Dream,' the ethereal atmosphere created on 'Voodoo,' and 'Midnight Mambo,' all have gone towards the fashioning of a superior hard bop jazz session. Deeper and darker than *Cool Struttin'* more sophisticated and hard-swinging than *My Conception*, this session is a masterwork in contemporary jazz.

Every recording he makes under his own name continues to seem to Clark to be better than the one that preceded it. It may well be the case as his music improves gradually with experience and maturity. It looks as though this time he is right, and *Leapin' And Lopin*, as it will be called on release, will stand as his best record of all time and the album will go down in history as a superb example of recorded hard bop.

After the recording session and the musicians have listened to the playback and voiced their approval, it is time to go. Sonny goes off with bassist Warren and the two hang out together. They have become good friends after the gigs and recordings. With Halliday away, Sonny has sought a new companion. He has frequently been alone in the past, a solitary lone wolf, with only his own thoughts and troubles to deal with alone. Now he and Warren have started to hang out regularly, he gets to know the bassist better. Warren tells him his father was a pianist and he sent Butch to be trained by a classical bass player. He played around Washington, where he is from, as a teenager until he had a gig with trumpeter Kenny Dorham. When Dorham told him he was good enough to make it in New York, he decided to go for it. He arrived in New York at age 19.

Warren tells Sonny that he has been signed up by Alfred Lion at Blue Note to be available for a multitude of recordings. He is pleased and flattered. He tells Sonny he is virtually the house bass player at the label and Billy Higgins the drummer of choice. If Sonny were to be the house pianist, they would have an ideal rhythm trio that would only become better and better with time. Sonny would be up for that, but it is, of course, up to Alfred Lion. These two musicians, though, are in accord. Both are rather quiet and get on with playing music in clubs and recordings with little or no fuss. Sonny is now an exceptionally gifted and original piano soloist and can take charge when he is the leader of a group or a recording session. It is just a matter of regret that he is still not recognised as a leader in spite of his excellent LPs and has never achieved his goal of putting together a regular working trio.

Warren is, if anything, even less self-assured. He just wants to play bass. He has moments of schizophrenia and depression but keeps his mind on his music and virtually nothing else. Both of them are heroin addicts though and their time together usually ends up with injecting the drug and nodding off.

Nothing has really changed for Clark since the Summer of 1961. Now in mid-November he continues to live in the same way. He has not seen anything of Nica or Thelonious Monk lately as he feels he has not kept his word to either of them. He has no desire to go to hospital for treatment now as he thinks he is past any cure of his addiction. He's had short spells in prison and been pulled up by police officers when he has done nothing wrong. His overall feeling, when and if he stops to think, are that nothing will ever change or improve. It is the way of the world. His world.

He lives as he lived through the summer months, in and out of grim, filthy apartments where he scrounges the use of a couch for a night's sleep. Always in the company of other addicts because they are the only people, apart from Nica, that he knows and can communicate with. He has no regular home to call his own apart from the Jazz Loft. It is here that he goes to practice, to jam with others occasionally and to chill out. Sometimes to sleep. It is here that he returns to now, tired and sick, sick and tired.

Butch Warren- To Hell And Back - *Jazz Times*.
Conversations with Butch Warren- YouTube videos.

24

JAMMING WITH GRANT GREEN

USING THE UTMOST TACT AND NEVER ACTUALLY SPELLING THE WORDS out, Alfred Lion informs Clark that he will always support him and offer him recording dates. Provided, he hints, he keeps out of trouble and out of prison. He is highly regarded by Lion. Alfred thinks of him as the premier hard-bop pianist on the scene today. Only Bud Powell and Thelonious Monk outshine him, but they are both historical figures in terms of today's music. They have been on the scene causing mayhem and controversy since the late nineteen thirties. They are charismatic figures if for different reasons. Bud is also looking more like a tragic figure these days.

Sonny can hold his own with the very best in Alfred's opinion. None outshine him. As to his lack of recognition and the appreciation of the jazz public at large, Alfred has no explanation. It will come in due course. Another player Alfred is anxious to promote and record frequently is guitarist Grant Green. He has an almost equal belief in the ability and potential of the guitarist as he has in Sonny. He is putting Clark into a recording session led by Green two days before Christmas. The two of them will lock together just about perfectly, in Alfred's opinion.

Sonny would love to team up again with Green as the last

short session did not quite jell, but he has a good feeling about the combination. And with Warren and Higgins. He feels the three of them make an ideal contemporary rhythm section. Lion informs him that this will not be the case, he is putting in Sam Jones and Louis Hayes from Cannonball Adderley's band. He wants to present Green as a modern jazz soloist with a melodic style that will appeal to jazz enthusiasts of all persuasions and, he hopes, some folks who are not really into jazz. With Clark and Green linking up with smooth, melodic lines and an adaptable, restrained rhythm team, the music should flow easily. A great but slightly less edgy rhythm section is what is needed for these tracks.

Grant Green shakes hands with Sonny as they arrive at Van Gelder's church-like studio. Playing 'Moon River,' a currently popular song, the pianist begins to see what Lion had in mind. Green's floating single lines, smooth as silk are riding on a gentle, refined rhythmic backdrop. His own gentle piano introduction sets the music in motion. Bass and drums are discreet, swinging, never intrusive. The popular song, pretty but undistinguished, is transformed into a jazz staple. The pianist's delicate petals of sound on his own solo consolidate the mood. The swing is laid back but insistent. Comfortably so.

'Gooden's Corner' is relaxed blues. Sonny's piano chords are softly provocative. Green's ceaseless invention is never strained or forced. Sonny's syncopated solo lines breathe easily as he picks up the momentum crisply. He matches the leader for spontaneous invention throughout his solo. For variety, he adds percussive blues chords to Green's final burst.

Lion has asked for one track to feature tenor sax man Ike Quebec. Another favourite he is promoting in different ways. 'Count Every Star' is a catchy melody. A 1950 popular song that few people now play. Sonny plays a very pretty piano introduction. It is mostly Green, persuasively lyrical, and Quebec takes a ripe chorus. Clark does not solo. Lion will release this one track on an Ike Quebec LP later.

'Shadrack' is up-tempo all the way. Green's guitar flies along with a precise lightness. It contains its own relentless but relaxed flow. Sonny picks up the mood in his own free-wheeling solo spot. Singing lines all through. The other selected titles are played in the same manner whether up, medium, or slow. At the end, Lion is pleased with the result and says so. It is just what he wanted. Strange then that except for 'Count Every Star,' which comes out on Quebec's *Blue and Sentimental*, he does not catalogue, number or issue this music. It will have to wait a good twenty years to become available to the jazz public. Maybe he is too busy, maybe he is concentrating his efforts on releasing a backlog of music by Lee Morgan, The Jazz Messengers, Sonny Clark and others. Maybe.

Early in the New Year, on January 13th, 1962, Lion arranges another recording session for Grant Green with Sonny Clark on piano and Sam Jones back on bass. He is putting Art Blakey on drums, another of his favourite musicians because he thinks, with him on board, sparks will fly. He is right.

If the first session of Green and Clark produced smooth flowing melodic bop, the next session provides something else. If Lion thought Blakey would take immediate control of the rhythm section, he guessed correctly. As the group fly into 'Airegin,' Green is grooving. His single-note lines sparkle, and this guitarist rarely plays chords. Sonny Clark spurs him on with fluid piano, often anticipating where the guitarist is going before he knows himself. This track sizzles from the first bar. Blakey stokes the fires as Grant improvises easily on the melody. The drummer keeps him on his toes with his trademark press rolls and spurring fills. Sonny is comping joyfully; it is on tracks like this that he can truly repeat that the pleasure he gains from comping is equal to his enjoyment of playing solos. His solo on piano sets off sparks of swing and rich melodic content. Blakey's solo is pure rhythmic fireworks. Green takes it out with none of the intensity of his first solo missing. Blakey guides him to a rousing conclusion.

Sometimes, at a gig, jam session or recording date, something magical occurs. This is one of those moments. Grant begins 'It ain't Necessarily So' in straight ahead, relatively conventional manner. But his singing single notes begin to take on a special musical magic as his extended solo builds slowly, inexorably. Blakey is driving him fiercely, setting and keeping the medium tempo to perfection. As Sonny takes over in solo mode Blakey is beginning to growl and grunt into his microphone, occasionally shouting out 'Wow' and 'Woo-hoo,' along with other mutterings. Clark is by now as much in charge of the time as Art. His invention is inspired. As he moves towards the end of his solo and prepares to hand over again to Green, Blakey yells out, 'No, don't stop, go on, go on.' Sonny grins and begins a fresh chorus. He is as much caught up in the moment as Art and realises what is happening.

It isn't difficult to continue playing solo, Clark is well into some of the most inventive improvised choruses he has ever played. To continue fashioning inventive lines is actually a lot easier than stopping and handing the piece back to Grant. He runs on, melodies overflowing with rhythmic thrust as Blakey shadows him fully, grunting and moaning into his microphone all the time. As he comes to the end of a second round of solo choruses and Blakey hands it back to Green with a barrage, Sonny Clark realises he has just taken part in a very special jazz moment. Blakey adds an explosive solo before leaving it to Green to take it out.

It is a great recording all round even if the rest of the tracks do not match up to the Gershwin piece. 'I Concentrate On You' sounds positively relaxed by comparison. Grant swings gently, his single lines singing melodically, as are the following chime-like notes from Sonny Clark. Much the same could be said for 'The Things We Did Last Summer,' where the only departure from straight-ahead ballad reading is Grant's cheeky quote from 'Three Blind Mice.' Sonny ponders the way a band can change so dramatically as it did on the Gershwin track with the substitution of just one musician. Still, when that one musician is Art Blakey... After some remarkably sensitive brushwork on the two ballads, Blakey swings them through 'The Song Is You' at a clean, rapid tempo. Clark's piano solo glides through with ease, the up-tempo thrust taken in his stride.

An ultra-slow meander through 'Nancy' is an almost sleepy performance. Grant improvises solely on the melody and uses, as usual, only single lines. The sensitivity employed by Sonny on his moving, short solo is notable. An unaware observer, listening to this, would likely conclude that the pianist lives a life of peaceful tranquillity if he can produce wonderful music like this.

Unlike the reality of the situation where Sonny goes from a considerable high during the height of the recording session to bleak, almost total despair as he sinks back into grim surroundings. In a dark, damp, grimy, soiled apartment. He has just finished the Grant Green recording and now has only seven days before he returns to Englewood Cliffs to play piano on Ike Quebec's sextet date. Just seven days. One week and yet it stretches out in front of him like a year. When the music flows, he is in paradise. As soon as it stops, he is in hell. Back to chipped filthy sinks, mattresses that stink, rooms littered with debris and unfinished food and drink. Or back to the Jazz Loft which isn't any better; sometimes worse.

Life lived amongst fellow addicts. The younger ones, grey, pallid and with dead eyes staring into nothingness. Scruffy, dirty. The older ones bleaker still in appearance, cold-eyed, stragglehaired, toothless. He shoots up heroin, which is now his only comfort, the only substance that can lift his mood upwards towards temporary equilibrium. Sometimes he can hang out with Butch Warren or Bill Evans. With Grant Green occasionally. Or Bob Whiteside, the bass player who does seem to live a comparatively normal life. Then there is Jimmy Stevenson and his wife Jackie. Those last two though have a respectable home life and don't want him in it. In any event, the meetings almost always end up one way, shooting up heroin and nodding out somewhere sleazy.

It is a long seven days. Although his life is pretty much established now, it is less flexible. Less open to change. The recording scene has begun to open up once again even as his private life out of the studio has deteriorated. He no longer makes any effort. He goes from bar to loft, to seedy apartment, and lives to drink, shoot up and smoke. Occasionally to sleep. In whatever murky space he happens to find himself. Maybe things will improve as he gains more and more gigs and more recording sessions. Maybe.

He has not been near Nica's place for a long time now, aware of his general appearance when not working and reluctant to take more from her and let her down yet again.

Wearing a good check shirt he has had laundered and smart woollen jumper and trousers, he enters Rudy's studio. Van Gelder is fiddling with his control board, as usual, and Alfred Lion is talking to his friend Ike Quebec. Ike's comeback trail is proceeding well, courtesy of Alfred. He has two LPs recorded and out on the streets. This one has a strong lineup with veteran bassist Milt Hinton standing alongside Art Blakey's drum kit. Trombonist Benny Green is also there. Over in the corner, he notices Stanley Turrentine, Tommy's brother, adjusting the reed on his instrument. Sonny smiles. Alfred is ensuring his friend and talent scout has a good solid lineup alongside him.

'See, See, Rider' is pure twelve-bar blues. Jelly Roll Morton claimed to remember it as long ago as the early 1900s. Ma Rainey, the blues singer, was the first to record it. Sonny kicks it off with a blues chord and the three horns play the melody. Slowly. Clark digs deeply into the blues, that time-honoured format that can represent both joy and sorrow. Clark's piano interjections behind Ike's opening solo pinpoint all the pain and deep sorrow of the blues. Benny Green maintains the mood with a sombre trombone solo excursion. Sonny fills in behind him, his lines maintaining the power and deep sadness of this kind of blues. Stanley's solo is more declamatory but just as full of pain and sorrow. Clark is intricate at the beginning of his solo, still digging deeply into the blues; it is the most comprehensive and deeply felt solo of them all.

'Que's Pills' is an easy burner, a medium-tempo romp. Quebec is in swinging, floating mode. Stanley cruises in blues-based style before Sonny takes over and spins out some glittering single-note lines. He introduces some spurring chords and propels himself into another round of single lines.

Blakey drives B.G.'s 'Groove 2' briskly. Medium to up-tempo, it glides along smoothly enough, the soloists cushioned by the clean, insistent swing provided by Clark, Hinton and Blakey. Sonny, on top of his game, cruises contentedly. This is where he belongs; this is home; in a bright studio, at a piano, playing jazz and the blues. He could stay here all night and all the next day as long as he was playing, and his colleagues were with him. He plays a gorgeous short melodic piano segment on 'Easy Living,' following Ike's breathy, cool tenor sax solo feature.

It is all over too soon for the pianist. The session was a success as far as he is concerned, and the others all seemed happy enough with the results. Alfred was smiling. He speaks briefly to Lion who tells him he will be booking him for yet another Grant Green Quartet date with Sam Jones and Louis Hayes. Sonny nods, happy enough, but it will be eleven days until the recording. Eleven more days in the wilderness. He wanders off into the late afternoon anxious to find a bar and some beer.

He has been in New York City for nine years now, nine productive years. He has had his share of club gigs and recordings. The recording situation has been even better than he expected. But still, even now, no recognition from the record-buying public. How can that be? Of course, it would be a lot better if Alfred Lion released everything he's been on either as leader or sideman. Lion has said that the pile of recordings due or overdue for release is growing bigger by the day. When musicians complain, Lion points out that he can only release so many in any given year and many are stockpiled because musicians have requested them to get instant money. For drugs. Sonny is as guilty as most there so cannot complain.

Somehow, he struggles through the eleven days prior to recording. He is in the Jazz Loft now, listening with increasing annoyance to a scratch combo playing on the fourth floor. He hears a baritone sax, most likely Pepper Adams who is often there, a tenor sounding like Zoot Sims, but probably a copy and the house bass and drums. There are some good solos coming up, but the unit is a bit ragged overall, and the pianist is rather bland and predictable. He shakes his head and walks swiftly into the room and is relieved when Ron Free looks up and suggests the piano player take a break now. He's been playing for hours.

Sonny kicks off 'Tadd's Delight,' and they all fall in behind him. As he weaves a tricky line following the theme, he begins to limber up for his upcoming record session with Grant Green. It is by playing frequently in ad hoc bands like this at the loft that he always feels fresh for the next recording session. Particularly when it is only one day away.

Bassist Sam Jones and drummer Louis Hayes are waiting for him in the studio. Green is having a last few words with Alfred Lion before commencing. Clark has made the date just in time. It is tight though. This is a very relaxed session with Green spinning out his melodies quietly for the most part. The band runs through a chunky version of 'My Favourite Things' in melodic fashion and only referencing John Coltrane's recent, popular recording in overall structure. 'Little Girl Blue' is played as the saddest and slowest of sad blue ballads. Everybody plays well and there are good solos, but overall, it is considered by the musicians to be an average set. Only 'Deep Blue Funk' has a blues-based sparkle to it.

None of the Grant Green Quartet sessions will be released by Alfred Lion and neither will Ike Quebec's session. The average, the good and even the excellent will remain in the vaults for many years before being released to the shops.

Sonny has four weeks before his next recording. He has been lined up to play again with Ike Quebec, Grant Green and the Jones/Hayes rhythm section. Clark will continue to live the life of a man subservient to his addiction, rarely surfacing from the murky rooms of a friend's apartment or the loft. It isn't that he doesn't want to, but he appears to have lost the will to try. It is easier to continue as he is, at least while the money from his recordings and occasional gigs lasts. When it runs low, he hustles and scuffles, seeking help from those he has helped in the past. Honour amongst addicts.

The new record, to be released as *Born To Be Blue*, is a feel-good set. Grant and Sonny dig into the blues on the title track and the faster tempi of 'Cool Blues.' The pianist stretches out on this one playing one of his typically inventive, cascading single-note line excursions with a preaching Ike Quebec tenor sax solo following him. It includes lyrical readings of the ballads 'My One And Only Love' and 'If I Should Lose You.' There is melancholy in Grant's guitar on the last-named ballad, but it is played with warmth and feeling as well. Quebec is up-beat on tenor. Sonny spins his solo out in light, easy swinging lines and only a hint at the underlining melancholy. Grant takes it out, retaining his own mood. The band play their own variations of 'Someday My Prince Will Come,' from the Disney film, and end the recording session feeling that it has gone very well.

Sonny departs the studio experiencing the temporary high that playing good music always gives him. He is unaware that he is heading towards yet another spell in the wilderness, that bleak place where there are no gigs or recordings, and the only relief is a shot of heroin. To be repeated frequently.

Grant Green *Nigeria* Blue Note LT-1032 Ben Sidran's sleeve note.

25

THIRTY-SIX MONTHS IN A BAD PLACE THE DARK SIDE OF THE JAZZ LIFE

Sonny leaves Birdland feeling low. He has been listening to a good pianist playing with an average combo. He wishes he had been playing there. It was a very young band, and he didn't know any of them. The manager there was keeping a watchful eye on him all night and he felt most uncomfortable.

His mood does not change as he gets back to the Jazz Loft. Frank Amoss is playing a series of figures on his tom-toms. Sonny is sitting on the piano stool but not playing. He is not in the mood or frame of mind to play. He does find Frank's workouts fascinating and tells him so. He says that they must work together next time he gets a gig. Frank is keen to do that. He admires Sonny's playing very much and would love to play a gig with him. Sadly, for Frank, it never happens.

Word is out from the cats on the street that bass player Doug Watkins is dead. Sonny, shocked, asks a musician he knows quite well how it happened. Watkins, driving through the night to California to join Philly Joe Jones' new trio, had fallen asleep at the wheel. It is a moment to reflect and wonder for Clark. He worked often with Watkins, particularly on record dates, and liked everything about him. He loved his sound and the ever-true notes he played, always accurate. The sort of bass player any soloist loves to have behind him. Sonny shakes his head sadly. Doug Watkins was just twenty-seven years old.

Clark has seen sudden death up close. He recalls a night with Lin Halliday and Gin where they tried unsuccessfully to bring round a young addict in an apartment near the loft. It made him shudder at the time to see a young life snuffed out like that. Just as he now shudders to think of Watkins, tired from playing a late gig and taking a perilous drive to California through the night, only to die in a car crash.

He feels the need to break out of his feelings of despair which crowd in on him far too frequently now. With little or no money after a long spell of inactivity, he frantically collects quarters, nickels and dimes from bottles he is given by Smith at the loft. Over a considerable period of time, he has amassed a comprehensive collection. Nickels, quarters, dimes, the coins all stashed up in boxes or old baking tins and kept in the toilet tank where he keeps the solid parts of his injection equipment,

Smith gives him hundreds of bottles from all over the loft. From all five floors. Once he has a big enough pile, he will cart them down to the grocery for the few coins allowed on returns. It isn't much money in dribs and drabs, but over a long period of time, it mounts up. All the residents at the loft drink alcohol, mostly beer, which is all they can afford. They throw their empty bottles down as they empty their contents, and they can be found all over the extensive building.

Sonny Clark is not fussy or proud. Not in any way. He only comes to life on the bandstand. After a good five weeks in the wilderness, he is ready to move down to the village. He has filled an old, tatty woman's stocking with small value coins. He wraps the top around his hand and carries the long, fully filled stocking with him as he heads for the Five Spot. The stocking, heavy, reaches down to the ground.

Sonny's tee-shirt is dark coloured although it fails to disguise the grubbiness of the garment. His hair is awry, and he is unshaven. Grey slacks are the scruffiest he has worn in weeks.

He goes in, carrying his long stocking, and approaches the bar. He orders a beer and slowly, meticulously counts out the price on the bar from his stocking. He gets strange looks from many of the patrons who are standing around, drinking, chattering and half-listening to Roland Kirk roaring a blues through three saxophone variants round his neck. Another instrument and a tin whistle and flute are attached to him in easy reach of his hands. Kirk is a wild, exciting, highly inventive improvisor despite his unorthodox approach.

The Five Spot is a popular haunt on Cooper Street. Its dark, bohemian appearance is further enhanced by record album covers decorating entire walls of the club. Clark likes it here. He sips his beer and listens to Kirk's rugged blues. He lights a cigarette and blows bright blue smoke out in rings.

Joe Termini, the owner, is watching Sonny carefully. One move towards one of the better-known patrons and appearing to hustle them in any way and he will turf the pianist out on his ear. Unceremoniously. Many musicians live in this area and frequent the club regularly. Elvin Jones and Blossom Dearie are often in. Lester Young was a regular before his sad demise in 1959. Ornette Coleman had a great run at this club in 1959/60 and filled the place to capacity. As Thelonious Monk had done before him. Sonny likes to sit here, and it almost cheers him up when he is feeling low or strung out. He orders another beer and counts out his small change meticulously, taking up much of the bartender's busy time. Termini is watching him closely, a scowl on his face and beginning to edge nearer. Sonny recognises the signs of old, drinks up and walks out to wander along to the next bar with his depleted money stocking, He drinks more beers and makes his way slowly back to the loft. He shoots up heroin carefully, ensuring he does not use too much, and then gets high. He nods out until the next day.

Sonny's general condition is beginning to attract attention. A magazine article has just appeared where the author wrote, 'One of the saddest sights these days is the terrible condition of one of the nation's foremost and certainly original pianists. I saw him several times in the past three months and was shocked to see one of our jazz greats in such pitiful condition.' The writer went on to suggest that the number of record dates he gets only help his addiction become worse instead of better. Sonny Clark was not named as the subject of this article, but there is little doubt in the jazz community. And beyond.

If Sonny knows that he is being talked about disparagingly he shows no sign. He has not worked or recorded now for a very long time, and he exists, from day to day, on beer, cigarettes and heroin injections. He eats very little. Payments from record sessions, royalties, such as they are, and composer credits have fuelled his habit for some time, but they are running low. Constantly redeeming empty bottles provides another very small source of income but only to bolster the other money temporarily. Days spent mostly in the Jazz Loft are primarily for nodding out. Evenings for music. Listening to the good and the great jamming and playing himself when he feels well enough to do so. Far into the night.

If he is aware that he really needs to get himself tidied up and go out to try and hustle up some work, he does not do so. He feels tired and lethargic most of the time. If he goes out and travels any distance, he requests lifts from friends or musicians he has met.

Sonny is heading towards the upstate Hudson River Valley area. He is travelling in a car driven by his friend Jimmy Stevenson. He sits in the front passenger seat next to Stevenson. Sandy, Jimmy's wife, is in the back. Suddenly a police patrol car appears, and they are pulled over. Sonny tries to remain calm; he has not taken any toxic substance for some time and has done nothing wrong. There does not seem to be any reason why they have been stopped, but these things happen. Frequently. They have not broken any law or exceeded the speed limit. It is just that Jimmy is white, and Sonny is black. And they were sitting side by side in the front of a car. With a white woman on the rear seat.

The police officers demand to know who they are and where they are going. For what purpose. They also require identification. Sonny does not have any identity documents but tells the police officers that he has copies of some of his records in the trunk of the car. He collects them from the trunk and shows them LP records with his photograph on the front. The officers seem unimpressed.

Sonny and Jimmy both land up in prison. The policemen had found marijuana in the car. The two friends spend two nights in jail. If the dark, grim police cell is not very different to Sonny's usual accommodation, at least he could leave the Jazz Loft whenever he wanted to. Here he is incarcerated behind iron bars.

The life of a heroin addict in New York City is hard, as it is anywhere in the world. Sonny Clark has spent the best part of nine years as an addict. The brief interludes where he has received treatment and become clean and drug free have been few and far between. He has never found the strength of mind and purpose to rid himself completely of his addiction. If he realises that it has always been his own choices and weaknesses that have placed him in this position, he has often nursed the thought that he could end his suffering by having intense treatment. And the iron-willed determination never to go back. But he has known now, for a long time, that he has passed the point of no return. He is an addict who will remain so until the day he dies. He admires musicians like Horace Silver and the late Doug Watkins, who, it is reported, left the original Jazz Messengers because they hated the constant stops and searches that went on with the police believing they were all addicts. Unlike the other three Messengers, they were not. Sonny might wish that he was like Horace and Doug, but he is not, and he knows he is not.

At times of deep despair, he longs for the chance to work again regularly and record frequently. He has had many chances. Today he is nodding out in the loft and ruminating gloomily on the fact that over two months have gone by without recording and he can't remember his last well paid club gig. It is beginning to seem as though his days as a working, gifted jazz pianist are over. It is always darkest before the dawn though, they say, and now, as he sits watching the cold grey light of a New York morning slowly filtering in through the soiled glass of a loft window, he wonders. What next?

The call from Alfred Lion is unexpected. Sonny thought the Blue Note man had given up on him years ago, but it is not so. Jackie McLean, the alto sax master, has a new recording session set up for June 14th. Jackie made it clear he would like Sonny on piano, and Alfred set things in motion. Kenny Dorham is booked to play trumpet and Butch Warren is the bass player. Billy Higgins on drums. Sonny is particularly pleased that he will be getting together again with that fine rhythm team that played so well on his latest album, released as *Leapin' and Lopin'*.

It is though, on this occasion, much harder to get himself cleaned up. He will arrive at Van Gelder's studio clean-shaven, hair tidy and good clothes, even if they are somewhat crumpled. It has been an almost herculean effort to drag himself out of the mire he has been living in for eleven weeks and present himself at Englewood Cliffs looking respectable. It is a warm sunny morning in the flower district, and if Sonny can shake off his lethargy and clear his brain from dark, fearsome thoughts by this afternoon, well, who knows?

It is a meeting of old friends in the studio. Warren and Higgins he has seen fairly recently but not Jackie or Kenny Dorham. Jackie is planning a blues-based programme which is another reason for Sonny to feel cheerful. As soon as he hits the first chords under the leader on 'Blues For Jackie,' Clark is back doing what he does almost as though nothing had changed since his last visit to Englewood back in March. Jackie is on fine form in his solo and Kenny Dorham has that lightweight, strained blues sound that is so attractive to hard boppers everywhere. Sonny's inventive solo outlines what the modern blues are all about, his lines skipping merrily along with only the faintest hint of an underlying sadness. He is back in business. 'Blues In A Jiff' is even more blue and funky, a slow stroll through the blues changes with McLean in the lead. Sonny's chords underneath him are both strong and percussive. It matters not to Sonny at this moment what he was doing or feeling yesterday, the magic is suddenly back, and he is with friendly accomplices doing what comes naturally to him. A bright, spinning chord introduces his own solo after Kenny. He plays old blues licks, new lines, all spun together into a compulsively swinging solo.

'Marilyn's Dilemma' is an up-tempo romp. Clark gets a rush of adrenalin as he combines with Warren and Higgins to swing this one along, cruising contentedly with his rhythm colleagues. The gift that keeps coming is that he never feels sluggish or jaded after a long lay-off. It is as though he has been playing regularly every day for months. 'The Three Minors' represents McLean peering into the future with a modal line. Soon now he will begin to embrace it more fully. The rhythm section clicks straight into gear and drives a smooth, pulsating rhythmic carpet under the soloists. Sonny's skipping, headlong solo is right in the groove Jackie has set up. It is the greatest feeling ever to be swinging joyfully with these cats.

As the musicians are driven back to New York from New Jersey, after the recording, Sonny feels pleased at having completed another good album but wonders what the future has in store. He is still feeling up-beat from the session. That will fade though and there is nothing to feel cheerful about as he returns to the loft and his usual way of life.

Alfred Lion is planning a record date for tenor saxophonist Don Wilkerson. The man is a blues-based performer who is popular with rhythm and blues enthusiasts. His music is, in many jazz musician's opinions, closer to R&B and Rock 'N' Roll than modern jazz. Alfred, though, has his own ideas. With Wilkerson's catchy blues lines and a prime support band, an LP could be a big seller. His ideal combo would be Grant Green on guitar and his current high profile rhythm section of Sonny Clark, Butch Warren and Billy Higgins.

He wastes no time in setting up a recording four days after the Jackie McLean session and recruits the players he thinks would be ideal. Wilkerson may not be the usual Blue Note name, but an R&B influenced LP could sell well enough to make the company some money.

Sonny is happy to get another recording date just four days after his last. He doesn't mind who with either. For someone who loves accompanying, loves the blues, and just goes for the sheer joy of playing, this is fine. Wilkerson begins with 'Jeannie-Weenie,' a wild shuffle blues which Billy Higgins sets up with a flourish of stickwork. The tenor solo is in rocking style followed by Grant Green hamming it up with blues phrases and a few accents displayed pointedly. Sonny provides blues chords in the section. 'Homesick Blues' is more to the rhythm section and Green's taste. A slow tempo low down blues, Sonny almost parodies himself in support of the tenor man. His blues counterlines spur the saxophonist on. His solo brings out all the cliches and familiar licks heard in blues-based jazz over the years. Grant Green continues in similar manner as he takes the spotlight.

'Pigeon Peas' is the closest to a bop and blues opus on offer. Sonny's solo is crisp, dancing, full of jazz phraseology and blues licks. By this time the musicians are fully immersed in the funky lines that Wilkerson has set up. Billy Higgins sets up 'Dem Tambourines,' along with some whoops and shouts from the rest of the band. A wild exercise in blues, shaking tambourines and shuffle rhythm, this one gets the toes tapping. Don Wilkerson, who has played in many a blues band and was a featured soloist in Ray Charles' unit, is in his element here. 'The Eldorado Shuffle' is a straight-ahead call and response piece.

'Camp Meeting' rocks along compulsively. Basic blues and soul.

It is not the usual session associated with Clark or indeed the other musicians present but is a soulful exercise in snapping finger popping rhythm and blues. Laced with bop solos from Sonny and Grant and shuffle rhythms courtesy of Warren and Higgins. There are smiles all round at the end. The musicians have had a ball and played it up to the hilt. 'Preach Brother' is the title for the album and Wilkerson has certainly done that.

As they collect their money and pack up their instruments ready to return to New York, Sonny is smiling. So is Alfred Lion. If Alfred has heard horror stories about Sonny's private life and descent into a living nightmare, he shows no sign. And says nothing. Over the years and with a few, self-imposed absences, Sonny has functioned as virtual house pianist at Blue Note. If a band needs a pianist, it is Sonny that Alfred usually lines up. Apart from regular personnel units like Horace silver's quintet or Blakey's Jazz Messengers, many leaders assigned a record date have asked for Clark. He has never given anything other than brilliant performances, and nobody has ever been disappointed. He sounds like no other pianist and no other piano player sounds like him. Sonny Clark is unique.

26

DIGGING WITH DEXTER

DEXTER GORDON HAS BEEN MAKING QUITE A COMEBACK IN NEW York. A major player in the early days of bebop in the 1940s. he left to return to his hometown California in the 1950s. If his style of red-blooded bop tenor was out of favour in the more cerebral cool jazz of the West Coast, that would explain why he received so few opportunities to play and record. It was Dexter's long lean period although he did play a couple of gigs in California with a slim, young pianist named Sonny Clark. He remembers the name and how good that pianist was when, back in NYC, he discusses record dates with Alfred Lion of Blue Note.

Dexter's resurgence in New York is highly successful. Lion records him with a good rhythm section he has been playing with in the clubs. He follows that up with a second LP where the tenor man is supported by pianist Kenny Drew, bassist Paul Chamber and Philly Joe Jones on drums.

Lion has another session lined up for Dexter one week after Sonny completes his recording date with Don Wilkerson. Alfred mentions Clark to Gordon, who is happy to use the pianist that he recalls was so good on that distant California club gig. Trumpeter Dave Burns has been booked, along with Ron Carter on bass and Philly Joe Jones at the drums. The band record five tracks including a reading of 'Blue Gardenia' and 'Second Balcony Jump.' Overall, there are rejected titles and a somewhat lethargic feel to the session. There is nothing wrong with the music taped, but somehow it lacks that glow. Lion decides not to release it. It will be many years before it comes out on the Blue Note LT series of previously unissued material.

Dexter is impressed with Sonny's playing and says he would like to have him on some of his club gigs that he is playing currently. The jazz fraternity in New York are enjoying rediscovering Dexter and his gigs are filled with enthusiastic, vocal audiences. And not just the older fans who remember him. New, young Dexter fans are springing up all over the place. Sonny suggests Butch Warren on bass and Billy Higgins, drums. The three of them make up a cooking rhythm section, Clark adds. If Dexter looks doubtful, he still goes along with the pianist's suggestion. He is not disappointed.

The summer of 1962 is a time of joyous music for Sonny Clark. If his private life is still squalid and unpleasant, he can still come alive when playing. He lives for his music now and is only fully functional when playing. There is plenty of work for him this summer. It is August and the weather is bright and sunny, and the gigs are plentiful. A time to immerse himself in his art. A time to shine brightly.

Dexter Gordon is enjoying a wave of love and appreciation for his music. Lost in his own wilderness of heroin addiction in California, he is now back on the scene of his earlier triumphs. A bop titan on tenor sax in the 1940s, he is making a full return to swinging jazz in New York in the hot summer of 1962. Dexter is playing all over New York this month. He has well-attended gigs at The Coronet. He plays a Monday night at Birdland and an afternoon at the Jazz Gallery. There is a concert at the Town Hall and several one-night gigs and one-afternoon recitals. On several of his gigs, he is backed by Clark, Warren and Higgins and the music swings like crazy. Enthusiasm and wild applause everywhere.

The enthusiastic response from the audiences gives Clark a rush of adrenalin. He is bathed in applause and appreciation for all his solo work but understands that the wild enthusiasm of the listeners is mainly for the old lion, Dexter Gordon. It is great to be part of it though. Warren and Higgins share his delight.

As the four musicians enter Van Gelder's studio at Englewood Cliffs, the euphoria seems set to continue. Some recordings produce that special magic. Like Sonny's *Cool Struttin'* and *My Conception* LPs. Like the trio with Max and Duvivier and his own recent *Leapin' and Lopin* dates. Is this yet another special programme of music? It is Monday, August 27th, 1962, and Dexter is getting ready for what he thinks will be just another routine recording session. A good one though, he hopes.

Dexter calls for 'Three O Clock In The Morning,' a stomping blues. The first run through is a disappointment and Dex thinks they can do a lot better. Unlike a club performance where a wrong note sticks out but is forgotten overnight, records are for posterity. They run it through again and then to please Dexter a third take. They have time to get it right. For all time.

Dexter begins slowly, moving from 2/4 to 4/4 time and gradually developing a muscular solo. Sonny's chords are also strong, echoing the leader's approach. Dexter is a big man with a big sound. He is a great improvisor too with that strong but still tender sound. This time the quartet lock immediately into a smooth groove, the music flowing along briskly. Strength with sensitivity but not sentimentality might be a good description of Dexter's playing and the same phrase would suit Sonny. The pianist picks up crisply where the tenor man left off and contributes his own percussive but warm solo. Warren and Higgins ensure the entire unit swings effortlessly from start to finish.

Next up is Billy Eckstine's 'Second Balcony Jump.' Gordon is cruising by this time, his solo showing all the power, warmth and strength he is capable of demonstrating in a single solo. Sonny is percussively elegant as he takes over the solo spot and Higgins is punctuating his lines with spirit. Already the quartet is playing with all the power, swing and blues inflections they developed so impressively in their recent club appearances. Higgins takes a short sharp drum solo and Dexter takes it out.

Dexter tackles a ballad next, 'Where Are You?' His sound is cavernous but with an underlying romanticism. So rich and yet powerful. Once more Sonny keys in immediately with the leader's mood. Gentle, flowing vignettes of piano aid and support the tenor sax to perfection. This session has that touch of magic that Clark experienced with Grant Green on his date with Art Blakey. On this occasion, the magic permeates each and every piece of music.

'Cheese-Cake' is a minor-key opus, and it glides along at a rapid tempo. This one is Dexter's only original written for the date. The quartet are fully engaged now, enjoying every minute of a set where soloist and rhythm section are in complete accord and the music swings easily and endlessly. At any tempo. Clark's solo equals Gordon's for invention, swing and controlled power. They sail through a Latin flavoured 'Love For Sale,' which is the final selection. Higgins and Sonny set it up, and Dexter floats out on their coattails. Looking around the studio at his colleagues and the smiling faces of Alfred Lion and Rudy Van Gelder, Clark has a feeling of joyous euphoria that only comes at moments like this when he is at the piano and playing to his full, considerable strengths. His solo is alive with the joy of the moment, to be captured now and held on record for posterity.

Alfred Lion is so pleased with the result that he wants to record these four again for a second LP. Dexter tells him he is booked to travel to London, England, next week for an engagement at Ronnie Scott's famous jazz club. Well then, in that case, it must be this week. He sets it up for just two days later.

SONNY CLARK - FRAGILE VIRTUOSO

From joyous participation in a near perfect recording session in a brightly lit studio to near despair in a dark, grim loft space, is just one hour away. Sonny Clark playing at Van Gelder's studio and the man sitting in a filthy bathroom shooting up heroin are two different people. They may look the same and have the same build, but the eyes now are dull and lifeless, the body limp and barely moving. Nodding out. Waiting for the fix to kick in and give a temporary feeling of pleasure. Waiting for the next recording session in two days- time which is the only time when he can experience four to five hours of contentment. And be an entirely different person.

Sonny notices the dull look in the eyes of fellow junkies all around him. It is rather like viewing pictures in an abstract manner; he passes them in the corridor or nodding out, but it hardly registers in his mind. He passes Eugene Smith's space and notes that he is busily sorting out his latest batch of photographs. No change there then. There is a man who left a good career, a wife, two children and a stylish house to set up in a sordid loft. To take endless pictures and record every single sound in the building. Day after day, week after week. Ask him why and he probably wouldn't have an answer. Clark nods at him but does not speak. He walks on, heading for the murky bathroom.

He has made the effort. Clean clothes and he has shaved. In Van Gelder's, studio he looks forward to four or five hours of music-making that will give him great pleasure. Quiet and reserved at first, Sonny nods to Butch and Billy as the drummer sets up his kit. Dexter starts to talk to him, but he is strangely reticent. The saxophonist is asking Sonny about his recent gigs and recordings, but he is practically inarticulate. It is only when Gordon starts to give him a rundown of the order in which he wants to play today's tunes that he shows any interest. Dexter looks into Sonny's dull eyes and recognises that look. He has been there himself. Not perhaps to the extent of disillusioned suffering that he sees in the pianist. But close. He reaches the conclusion that Clark has given up on life and has no further interest in living. Many years later, he will express that opinion in public and assert that Monday's recording was the best he ever made.

Now is the time to play though. Sonny sits on the piano stool and perks up immediately. He sits up straight, appears to gain in height, and looks down contentedly at the piano keys. Dexter, in playful mood, chants the title, 'Soy Califa.' Billy hits his kit provocatively and Gordon jumps into a fast samba. Limbs planted firmly on the ground but legs shaking rhythmically, he runs down a few jumping choruses, Billy's live drums spurring him on. Tough, rich but tender tenor on offer here. Sonny's bright chords and fills are nourishing and can only spur him on further. Dexter is improvising on the theme, practically re-composing it. Sonny's piano lines are chime-like, light and melodic as he glides deftly into his solo segment. Higgins hits his tom-toms rhythmically, leading to Dex's final run out. Smiles all round, in the studio and the control room.

Sonny's soft-focus introduction on piano brings Dexter out in warm, bitter-sweet mood. He caresses the Billy Holiday-associated song as only he can and preaches the sadness and sorrow inherent in the melody with choice, blues-inflected lines. Sonny fills all the gaps with ringing piano lines. Sonny's lyrical piano interlude shines out in sympathetic contrast. Clark's tinkling rising notes complete it. 'Don't Explain.'

By the first jaunty bars of 'You Stepped Out of a Dream,' the band are cruising blithely. From Dex to his pianist to his bass man and to Billy's crackling drums, the track is surging at mid-tempo and indicating by the forward thrust that this band, well as they are playing, have plenty more in reserve. Butch jumps in with a charming, bouncing bass solo.

Butch is out front on 'The Backbone,' his own composition. His flexible, spinning bass sets the mood, and Gordon grabs it firmly and invents a strong variation on his mid-tempo surge. Sonny, still provocative but immensely challenging the hornman with his clean, fruity lines and accents, keeps the smooth, comfortable flow moving irresistibly. Sonny nods and then grins broadly. It happened joyfully on Monday, and it is happening again. The music is every note, every chorus, every drum break as great a session as the Monday date. A fraction more refined perhaps, a wee bit less frantic on the up-tempo material but magical improvised, melodic and hard-swinging jazz. All the way. Sonny's solo is pensive at first then glittering with invention and notes chosen like a poet set on finding the only words that will do.

The earthy 'McSplivens' is a catchy Gordon original designed as a blowing vehicle, and the boys make good use of a wild rhythmic romp. Dexter bows up a storm before Sonny rides out a solo that just moves majestically on its own volition under the pianist's guiding hands. As they bring it to a rousing conclusion, everybody is looking cool. They have done it again. Dexter grins broadly, holding his tenor sax aloft. Sonny hunches up his shoulders and bends down towards the piano keys. It is a characteristic gesture but only when a set has gone unexpectedly exceptionally well. Both LPs will be winners all the way, Alfred says, handing out extra drinks to the musicians. No rush to leave the studio then.

Dexter leaves knowing he has left two cracking albums behind. The sidemen couldn't have been improved. Sonny on piano was superb all through, but he worries about the young man's state of mind. Butch and Billy are almost hyper in their enthusiasm for the two recordings. Even an evening in a damp and dirty cold-water apartment will not evaporate Sonny Clark's hyped-up state. Without a fix for half a day too. This is a time when the Lion and the Wolff, as the musicians call them, appreciate their record company most of all.

He departs the studio. For a few days of dark encounters with people who are struggling with the same problem he has.

His life outside the studio is now a round of scoring for heroin, sleeping rough, nodding off in less than pleasant surroundings and trying to keep going. Somehow, anyhow. Perhaps by instinct alone but more likely to try and survive for the next gig. He needs the club and studio gigs for the pleasure of playing, but he also needs them for the payments. Money to buy heroin. He can only keep going if he makes enough money to feed his habit. Payment for a gig. For a record session. Royalties from record sales if he ever sells enough copies to pay back the money he has borrowed against them. Composer royalties for music he has written and recorded. He called the composition 'Five Will Get You Ten' that he took from his friend Monk and recorded on Jackie McLean's date, but now Thelonious has been told or heard the McLean record and knows. Monk has given the piece the title 'Two Timer.' He has not recorded it and he will make no attempt to confront Sonny or challenge him in any way. Perhaps he recognises and sympathizes with Sonny's desperate condition.

Seven days after the recordings with Gordon, Alfred Lion wants Sonny to play piano on two tracks to make up an album he is planning for Ike Quebec. Grant Green will be featured on guitar and Sonny on piano. The rest of the band will be Wendell Marshall on bass, Willie Bobo, drums, and a conga player named Carlos Valdes. Or 'Patato,' as he is known in jazz circles. They play 'Grenada' and 'Hey There,' neither of which will be issued by Lion but will turn up in twenty years' time on a collection of music by Green with Sonny Clark. The pianist contributes a perfunctory solo that glitters with melody and helps the track swing along, but it is not one of the best recordings. 'Hey There' is more like typical Green/Clark material and styling.

A Latin beat from the drummer and conga player whisk it along merrily following Green's medium-clip solo Quebec solos with breathy warmth in his typical ballad style. Sonny is crisply lyrical, his solo sparkling as it glides along. Nothing more is recorded on this day, and Sonny departs knowing he has given his usual supportive contribution. Sonny returns to his normal round of walking the streets, drinking and shooting up heroin. It is the only life he knows now.

Dexter Gordon – *Go*. Blue Note 4112 Ira Gitler's sleeve note.
Dexter Gordon - *A Swingin' Affair*. Blue Note 4133 Barbara Long's sleeve note.

27

GO ON SONNY BEAT IT, GET OUT OF HERE!

JUST THREE WEEKS AFTER THE GREEN/QUEBEC RECORDINGS, SONNY gets the call to play on another Jackie McLean date. He arrives at the Englewood Cliffs studio for the rehearsal to be greeted by Butch Warren and Art Taylor. Old friends. Jackie McLean arrives and gives everybody a run down on what is to be played. Sonny nods, content. He has brought along an original chart called 'Nicely' at Lion's suggestion. The rest of the programme looks promising to him, two originals, two blues and an old popular standard called 'Cabin The Sky,' rarely played these days. Bebop and blues. Should be fine.

As it is when they play Jackie's 'Tippin' the Scales,' which will, eventually, be the title of an LP, Jackie's solo at rehearsal is tart, blues-based and with his trademark hard sound. Sonny's piano solo clips along rapidly, glittering single notes shining brightly. Clark is pleased that this is to be a quartet date. It leaves more room for extended solos by Jackie and himself. Jackie is at his most intensely painfully lyrical on 'Cabin In The Sky.' They run through the two blues at rehearsal, 'Rainy Blues' by Jackie, and Sonny contributes 'Nursery Blues.' The pianist enjoyed working with Jackie on his recent quintet session with Kenny Dorham and Billy

Higgins but is pleased that this is more of a relaxed bop set for just four players.

So, it is something of a surprise when, at the recording session, Jackie is talking enthusiastically about a record he recently taped called *Let Freedom Ring*. On that disc, he says, he got to play with much more freedom, incorporating modal elements and a nod to the music of the future. He is excited by the work of Ornette Coleman, as he states on the liner note to that album. Sonny is puzzled. If Jackie is looking towards playing in the new free-style and has already done so, why is he recording this session with a repertoire of bop and blues? Does it make sense? Well, perhaps because this album may be seen by Jackie, and Alfred for that matter, as a safety album in case his new free records fail to sell.

For the present time though, Sonny intends to make the most of this session. He introduces his ballad, 'Nicely,' leading in Jackie's solo, which is stark and pleasantly blues-based. It is an attractive bop ballad of the sort Clark specializes in. His piano solo sparkles with melody, optimism, full of bright invention. The sound of jazz and the sound of surprise. He can stretch out in a quartet setting and takes full advantage. Tinkling, pretty notes on piano introduce the chosen take of 'Cabin In The Sky.' And Jackie plays an attractive, slightly sombre alto sax solo. Sonny's solo sparkles with warmth and invention, his best on the date. The underlying sadness in it is barely perceivable.

The session is a remarkably relaxed run-through, some new and old material and a fine example of laid-back bop at its very best. But Jackie is into his freedom kick and goes from this date to another free record which will be released with the prophetic title *One Step Beyond*. *Tippin' the Scales* will not be released and will have to wait for twenty years to be issued. Sonny departs from the studio, pleased with the result and blissfully unaware that the record will be shelved for many years.

Now he goes back to the grim life that is all too familiar. He has worked regularly and successfully over the past four weeks and played on some first-rate albums even if many of them will not be released in their time. None of the Grant Green discs he played on will appear, nor the last two he recorded with Jackie McLean. *My Conception*, given a catalogue number as if intended for release, is still in the vaults. He bitterly resents this last one but is still hopeful it will come out. But he knows he is not alone; his friends Hank Mobley, Donald Byrd and Tina Brooks are in the same situation. Brooks told him he has recorded three albums and only one, *True Blue*, has been put out. Sonny would appreciate more support from Alfred Lion.

None of this alters the fact that he is struggling. Scuffling when short of money, nodding out. He shoots up heroin regularly, feeling euphoric one minute and deep in depression the next. Although he has worked in clubs and recorded more than most pianists lately, he still feels inadequate and a failure. Only when the drug kicks in can he feel he has some worth and has achieved anything. The jazz public, who buy the records, are deserting him. Or unaware of his presence even when he makes sterling contributions to other leaders' albums. Like Dexter Gordon recently. At least that album and the second one will be released.

He walks the streets at night, the dim, grey, high buildings that threaten, it seems, to close in on him. He meets up with friends like Butch Warren, Bill Evans occasionally, Philly Joe Jones. Paul Chambers, who has more pus-filled scabs on his arms than Sonny has himself. Meetings invariably end up one way and one way only. The cycle continues unabated.

The streets are dull, dark and grey. Litter and graffiti everywhere. At least the ones he frequents are. Few people are about late at night and those that are there are mainly hustlers. He would like to spend more time in the clubs, but he is unwelcome. His reputation precedes him. Joe Termini chases him out of the Five Spot regularly now. With Monk no longer in residence, the baroness is rarely there now, the one friend with influence he could always depend on.

SONNY CLARK - FRAGILE VIRTUOSO

The bad news on the street is that Eddie Costa, a well-respected, brilliant pianist and vibraharpist is dead. He crashed his car on New York's Westside Highway at 72nd Street. Fortunately, no one else was injured. Sonny discusses it gloomily with a friend. He was only 31, I mean it's no age at all, is it? Sonny pulls a face. Thirty-one. That is his own age now. Another really good player gone. The last few years we've lost Lester Young, Billie Holiday, Walter Page, Basie's bass player, and so many others.

It is a bright Sunday afternoon on St Marks near Tomkins Square Park. Sonny's friend Bob Whiteside, the bass player is working in the Jazz Gallery there. Sonny walks in hoping to have a beer or two and listen to some good jazz. It is a nice club, and he likes it here. He chats to Bob for a while, but the bass player is busy. There is a good-sized crowd inside. Sonny has washed and shaved, but his shirt and trousers are crumpled. He still carries his stocking with dimes and quarters, but it is only half-full and not too prominent. The manager, also the club owner, frowns as he spies Sonny walking in. As the pianist reaches the bar, the owner moves slowly over to where he stands and says, quietly.

'Go on, Sonny, get out of here. Go ahead and beat it.'

'Can't a man buy himself a drink?' Sonny asks just as quietly.

'No,' the manager replies, his tone hardening. 'No, get out of here.'

Sonny walks out of the bar feeling as if he has been stabbed with a knife. He has had similar experiences to this recently. Not quite such a bleak, firm request to leave even though he has done nothing wrong but enough to hurt a fragile ego. He walks to the nearest shabby bar he can find and goes in. He drinks beer, alone with his thoughts. The jazz public do not want to know him and even a good record company like Blue Note have failed to release much of his best work. Now even the clubs where he has played successfully want to keep him out.

Sonny Clark is feeling unwell. It is a cold October morning, the ninth of the month. He is sick. He is shivering. His last fix did not last as long as he thought it would and he is suffering. He is in a sad, bleak place both inside his body and his surroundings. Dirt and grime surround him here and he has nothing to eat or drink. Not that he wants anything, he just needs another fix. He must get through the next few hours feeling much as he does at this moment. Later he is due to appear at the Village Gate in Greenwich Village. It is the night of the memorial concert for the late Eddie Costa. A much loved and respected jazz pianist.

Many musicians have volunteered to appear at this concert to remember Eddie. Some of the biggest names in jazz are lined up to perform. Sonny will play piano in a combo with Coleman Hawkins. Urbie Green is on trombone and Markie Markowitz is the trumpet player. The rhythm section will consist of Sonny, bassist Chuck Israels, and Roy Haynes at the drums. It is quite a lineup, more illustrious than many of Sonny's usual club musicians, but this is a special occasion. He must play well, but then he knows he will. However he is feeling now, when he sits at the piano in the Village Gate, he will be transformed.

It is the waiting, the time between now and then. He wants to do his very best for Eddie and knows that he can, but he will not be feeling good until he reaches the venue. Al Cohn, Art Farmer, Zoot Sims, Clark Terry, Jim Hall, Benny Golson and Charlie Byrd are all lined up to play at this event. It is a long night of music, and the Village Gate is packed. When his time comes to play, Sonny is ready. Coleman Hawkins begins to play 'I'm Confessin'.' Slowly, his tenor sound breathy, warm. Sonny chords gently behind him with occasional little ripples of notes along the keyboard. The Hawk is on good form. Roy Haynes swishes everyone along in his usual tasty, skilful manner. It is a good performance by all but better is to come.

Sonny plays bright, upbeat chords to introduce 'Just You, Just Me.' This time the Hawkins quartet is joined by Markowitz on trumpet and Urbie Green's trombone. Hawkins, who has not been playing that well lately, launches into a well-wrought solo. His tenor is twisting and turning the melody as he stretches out on an extended improvisation. Nourishing chords from Clark are continuous. As they are for Markowitz who follows Hawk. Roy Haynes' accents help the sturdy swing along. Urbie Green is next with his flourishing trombone lines improvising on the melody.

Sonny Clark is fleet, his lines flowing along gracefully now that the momentum of the piece has been established and maintained through three soloists. Full of invention and twisting and turning elegantly, this driving piano solo may well be the best of them all. The pianist certainly never runs out of ideas and maintains sparkling invention throughout. His solo is followed by Chuck Israel's bass explorations. The selection ends with Sonny and Roy indulging in a series of four bar exchanges before the ensemble take it out. Swapping four-bar exchanges with Roy is always exhilarating. Clark has done it enough times at the Jazz Loft and always enjoys it.

Sonny is feeling good, a combination of the effects from an injection of heroin and knowing he has played well in memory of a fellow pianist. The concert was a success throughout and the lively audience most appreciative. And vocal in their response to the music. He will sleep well tonight even if he does not have a bed or even a rough mattress to lie upon.

The spectacle of Sonny Clark walking the grim streets of Manhattan at night is not a pretty sight. He is unkempt, unshaven and has a generally run down, dissipated look about him. His clothes are mostly crumpled. He makes an effort to present himself as reasonably clean and well-groomed before arriving for a gig or at Van Gelder's recording studio. Always. In his leisure hours though, if that is what they can be described as, he makes no such attempt. If he goes out during the day, it is usually to score heroin.

Most of the people he knows or have been associated with him, now avoid him. Record company executives, sales-people, nightclub owners and managers avoid him. He is not welcome in the clubs as a visitor. Most of those people will cross the road to avoid passing him in the streets. Only the jazz musicians, many sharing his addiction, are friendly, they know how great a talent he is. Bassist Butch Warren is a good friend, but he has not seen him for some time now. Warren has a fear of heroin and has occasional mental health issues. He may be incarcerated in a facility for addicts now.

At the Jazz Loft, he is friendly with bass player Bill Takas and drummer Ronnie Free. They are long-term residents of the loft. Eugene Smith nods and even occasionally smiles at him but has little time for conversation. Smith's cat seems to like him and sometimes sits by him when he is nodding out. Or spreads herself across his legs in the passageway.

Sonny remembers all the cats at Nica's house. Dozens of them. In the living areas, the kitchen, the bathrooms and all over the dining room table. It seems a long time ago that he was there.

Only Alfred Lion has not deserted him. He has Sonny marked down as pianist on a recording date to be headed up by tenor saxophonist Stanley Turrentine. It is a strong ensemble with Stan's brother on trumpet, Kenny Burrell on guitar and yes, Butch Warren on bass. Al Harewood is the drummer, a long-time associate of Turrentine's. Clark likes the look of the group and looks forward to the recording session.

As he expected, Stanley and the rest of the cats greet him enthusiastically at rehearsal and the run-throughs go well. Sonny is in good form at the recording session. He is with musicians who enjoy similar music to himself and play in the same general, hardbop style. Playing what will eventually be the title tune, 'Jubilee Shout,' he works up a gospel vamp to play behind Stanley's opening phrases. Turrentine plays a pulsating-blues-based solo followed by a similar contribution from Kenny Burrell on guitar. Brother Tommy's long lines on trumpet are particularly blues-inflected before Clark takes his piano solo. Sonny is now at his peak as a piano soloist. He digs into the blues heartily and flies through a free-flowing, highly inventive solo. Once he has worked through the blues parts, Sonny reverts to springy, single lines that swing along under their own momentum. It is a particularly inventive piece of improvised piano work.

'Brother Tom' is dedicated to Tommy by Stanley. A medium-tempo stomp, Stanley kicks it off with a tasty solo, Tommy playing harmony. This one has an early bebop flavour which Sonny relishes. He does not solo but supports brightly in the section.

Clark is also on top form in his ballad playing. The leader takes 'My Ship' at a very slow tempo, and all Sonny has to do is support with those magical sustaining chords he provides. No piano solo here but his musical presence is felt strongly. 'Cotton Walk' is similarly slow in tempo but stately in interpretation. 'Little Girl Blue' is slow and sumptuous. Exquisite ballad playing by all.

Stanley preaches gently but impressively on tenor sax with punctuating chords from Clark behind him. A down-home reading. Kenny is bluesy in a following solo. Tommy's trumpet lines sing out with restrained clarity as Sonny underlines his solo before commencing his own. As he digs into blues and gospel licks then directs his solo along a casually swinging route, he is absolutely at the top of his game. He hopes there will be many more sessions with similar personnel coming along soon. This, like the two recent Dexter discs, has unexpectedly, turned out to be one of Sonny's best sessions on somebody else's date.

If it had been released on completion this would have been a fine epitaph to the special talent of a remarkably gifted modern pianist. Everybody playing was on top form throughout. Sadly, sixteen years will pass before it comes out on a Blue Note Double LP. Much later it will be released with the original cover art and the catalogue number Alfred Lion assigned to it at the time. Strange are the ways of Blue Note Records in 1962.
Melody And Melancholy—*The Jazz Loft Project*. Sam Stephenson.

28

THE FINAL DAYS

It is 4:45am on a December morning. Unseasonably warm for the time of year. Sonny Clark is feeling sick. He is shivering and can't seem to keep his limbs still for even one minute. Some mornings are worse than others. He will feel a lot better once he has had a fix. The problem now is to find a space somewhere on his arms or legs without scabs, sores or broken skin. If only he could keep still long enough to explore. When he does finally locate a spot that seems relatively unmarked, it is very painful as the needle goes in.

Sonny is admitted to hospital later that day. He has severe pain in his leg that is causing him agony. He has a serious leg infection the doctor informs him, but they can treat it. Over the next few days, he will receive specialist treatment for his leg infection and the staff at the hospital, immediately aware of his condition, will give him pills and various medicines to reduce his craving for heroin and help to restore him to normal life. He is being carefully watched and his progress monitored. The pills he is taking regularly, under careful supervision, appear to be working.

Sonny lies back in bed and sighs. He does not want to remain in hospital, but at least he is in a warm, comfortable bed. The best he has slept in since his last visit to Nica. How long ago was that then? He knows he can't do anything about his situation at this moment so he might just as well relax, lie back and find peace in rest. Now that the pills are reducing his craving considerably, is it possible that he could achieve the impossible and kick his heroin habit? Two weeks ago, it seemed utterly and completely impossible. He was much too far gone.

The days and nights trawl slowly past. Nineteen Sixty-Two dies out and the new year creeps in quietly. Sonny is released from hospital on the 11th January. He walks through town breathing in fresh, biting January air although it is still warm weather overall. He feels good. He has been offered a gig of two nights at Junior's Bar, a jazz piano room in the basement of the Alvin Hotel, on the Northwest corner of Fifty-Second Street and Broadway. It is something to look forward to. Two nights of solo piano with nobody else to worry or concern himself about. Although the bulk of his work is playing in sextet, quintet or quartet format, it is good to have a chance to express yourself fully with not even a rhythm section to worry about.

The gig goes very well, better even than he anticipated. The next day he is up and about and walking along Broadway, enjoying the bright, clear sky and crisp temperature. He meets a man he once did a big favour for, some time ago. The man is gushing in his praise of Sonny and how he will never forget how he helped him. He presses a bag of heroin into Sonny's hand. At first, Clark wants to refuse, hand it back swiftly and keep away, but he reconsiders. Maybe he should keep it with him at all times but never use it. Have the bag with him as a talisman, ready for use if he should need it? He thinks it a good idea.

The second night of the gig is just as successful, perhaps more so. At the end of his performance, he goes to the bar and drinks some beer. Much later, Sonny walks to the men's room carrying his personal bag with him. He is never without it. On a sudden whim, he finds himself preparing heroin on a spoon. He is tired and weary, not having slept at all last night. The drug will give him a boost and make him feel good. Just this once and then never again. Ever.

Sonny injects a severe overdose of heroin into his arm and immediately feels faint. He is sitting on the tiles of the men's room with his head against the wall. He splutters and makes a groaning sound but loses consciousness almost immediately. There is nobody else about. Within minutes, he is dead.

The barman who discovers his body on the floor of the men's room panics, runs to fetch the manager, who also panics. He immediately sets about, with help from his staff, to remove the body to a private apartment just a few steps along the street. They can't have the dead body of a junkie jazz musician discovered on the premises or they will lose their liquor licence and the press coverage might shut the entire hotel down. When the body has been placed elsewhere, they notify the police.

In the mortuary, Sonny's body lies waiting to be identified. Alfred Lion is one of the people who are brought in to make the identification. Lion has brought bassist Butch Warren with him, as the musician was a good friend of Clark's. Butch Warren looks down at the cold, grey, lifeless face of his friend and thinks that he too could be in this situation. He shudders. He foresees his own death. Heroin frightens him, it always has, so he must be sure he avoids it in future. Butch can't wait to get out of the morgue and back to his car where his wife and son are waiting.

When the sad news of Sonny's demise reaches Nica, the baroness springs into action immediately. She telephones Sonny's eldest sister in Pittsburgh to offer her deepest condolences and offers to arrange for the body to be transported to Pittsburgh. She will pay for the funeral and all expenses in shipping Sonny back to his hometown. She is as good as her word and makes all the arrangements. But there is a serious problem of tragic proportions. A man assisting the funeral director in New York where the body now resides says he is sure the man in the coffin is not Sonny Clark. He knows what Sonny looks like.

The dilemma for the funeral director is what to do about it if the man is correct.

If a mistake has been made at the morgue, which seems most likely, and bodies have been inadvertently mixed up, well, what then? Unidentified street death bodies are sent out to potter's field on New York's Hart Island. If a mistake was made in the mortuary and Sonny's body was sent there for burial together with perhaps a dozen other street deaths, there is no way he could be located and identified.

The funeral director does what he is being paid for and transports the body from New York City to Pittsburgh, Pennsylvania. Once there in Pittsburgh, the funeral director and a colleague start to prepare the body for burial. The colleague looks closely at the face of the dead man and says that it is not Sonny Clark. As a locally-born musician, the man has followed his career and knows exactly what he looks like.

What to do? The director decides it would be too agonisingly painful to tell the family what they believe. Besides, he reasons, they can't prove anything. And nothing now can alter the situation. The funeral must proceed.

The funeral of Sonny Clark takes place in mid-January, 1963, in the Allegheny Hills, Sharpsburg, Pennsylvania. In the rural fields of Greenwood cemetery, a gravestone is placed on the wide green pasture, close to trees and bushes in a peaceful setting. The name 'Sonny Clark' is on the gravestone. It is here, in this calm, country setting, that people wishing to remember Sonny and pay their respects to his memory must come to see his gravestone. And remember a brilliant jazz pianist who never received due recognition during his lifetime, although the bulk of his brilliant music is out there forever.

If Sonny Clark's physical body lies in Potter's Field, Hart's Island, New York City, and it most likely does, the final irony is that New York City was the one place that he wanted to get to and remain in. And here it is that his bones will rest, in peace, from now to eternity.

Butch Warren - To Hell and Back- *Jazz Times*.

Sonny Clark Part 2 - Sam Stephenson -*The Paris Review*. January 26, 2011.

Thelonious Monk - The Life & Times of an American Original - Robin D.G. Kelley.

TIME SLIP—JANUARY 11TH & 12TH 1963

EPILOGUE

TRANQUIL INTERLUDE 2

As he approaches the piano in Junior's bar, Sonny Clark hears a spluttering of applause. It is a fair-sized, comfortable room although there are not that many people in. It is early evening, time for quite a few more to stroll in. Some from the street outside and a few from the Alvin hotel above. People staying at the hotel or in there for a meal or drinks may well decide to investigate the piano room in the basement.

It is a good location and many jazz pianists have played solo recitals here. Sonny likes the ambiance of the room even with only a few people in. He loves playing solo piano. Naturally most of his work has been in combos, that is the usual set up. Not that he doesn't like that situation, it is fine, but playing solo piano is special. After all, the greatest of the great jazz pianists all loved playing solo. Art Tatum, Bud Powell. Fats Waller too. He knows he can express himself fully and it is a great feeling to be in a good room, with a fine instrument, an audience listening just to him alone and he can show them just what he is capable of.

Sonny smiles. No bass player to worry about and no drummer to add a multitude of fills and spurs, most of which he doesn't really need. And he does, truly loves playing with all the great rhythm players where the interaction can be, and often is, really something. Just occasionally though, it is a special gig to play alone and be completely in charge of every selection. Every note. It doesn't happen often. He recalls playing solo at Randi Hulton's house in Europe when he was on the Jazz Club U.S.A. tour of America and Europe for Leonard Feather's show. That was several years ago. He remembers that it went well though.

He runs his fingers silently over the piano keys. He hunches up his shoulders, as he has grown used to doing and launches into playing a standard tune. Sounds good. A well-tuned piano and that is more than you can say for many of the jazz clubs in New York City. Some are on the edge, hollow sounding as though they are about to go out of tune any minute. He ends the standard and receives a polite round of applause. A few more people are coming in now. Slowly filling out the big room.

He has not been feeling well for some time now. His health has been failing due to drug taking and bad diet. Sleepless nights. The stay in hospital did him quite a lot of good really, he must admit that. They pulled him off drugs too, and now he really must make a supreme effort to stay off, now that he's been given another chance, one that he thought was lost forever.

Time to play another standard. Yes, get the audience with him, and then he'll play one or two of his originals. 'My Conception' is one he likes playing when in a light, melodic mood. 'Junka' and 'Blues Blue,' when he feels like digging into that format. It's a great feeling, truly satisfying, playing your own songs and finding new melody and harmony within them. Exploring old material and adding a new dimension. Alone.

There are a good number of people in Junior's bar now as he plays his last selection. The applause is loud, spontaneous and that sounds very good indeed, particularly to a solitary soloist.

On the second night of his gig, it is much the same as yesterday. A few people in, a few more trickling in as the night progresses.

If he is feeling slightly uncomfortable, and he is, that will pass as soon as he starts to play. He did not sleep at all last night. He walked the streets, stopped at the automat for refreshments and took his tablets regularly. To stop himself taking anything more lethal. What is wrong with him? It is just tiredness, he decides, just tiredness.

He hunches up, launches gently into his first standard, fingers brushing the keyboard lightly. It is a great feeling. As the music flows his burden of doubt and his feelings of tiredness subside. The tables around the room are gradually filling up now. He plays a pretty ballad at a slow tempo and then begins an investigation of the blues. There is an innate melancholy in his music which is always there if often, barely detectable. He is aware of it himself but only in the sense that it is part of his being, part of his feelings, part of a natural outpouring of the blues. An up-tempo swinger changes the mood, lightens it. But the undercurrent remains.

The longer the gig goes on however, the more relaxed he feels. Once fully and completely into the music he experiences a floating, lightness of mood. It is now, at times like this when he is fully engaged with his music and he senses the audience are listening attentively, that he is complete. A man and a musician although the two are interchangeable. He begins to explore variations on a composition he first played three years ago.

Here we go, another chorus, fingers flying lightly over the keys and producing that familiar, smooth and natural swing. He is playing solo, playing some of his best improvised choruses and enjoying it immensely. Sonny Clark's music is forever. This is what he does.

RECOMMENDED RECORDS

A full discography of Sonny Clark's recordings is available on JAZZDISCO.org on the internet. This is a listing of those considered to be the best of his output overall. Those marked with an * are suggested as very special and two ** are suggested as being indispensable in Clark's output. Readers will, of course, have their own personal preferences. Where to find them? The internet these days appears to be the best bet. Failing that it is always possible to listen to the tracks on Spotify or other digital platforms. I have only listed the first issues.

1. The Buddy De Franco Quartet 1954 Norgran MGM 1026
2. Sonny Clark -Oakland 1955 Uptown UPCD 27.40
3. Serge Chaloff Quartet 1956 Capitol T 742 *
4. Sonny Criss Plays Cole Porter 1956 Imperial 9024
5. Lawrence Marable Quartet featuring James Clay-Tenorman 1956 Jazz West JWLP 8
6. Stan Levey Sextet 1956 Bethlehem BCP-71
7. Sonny Rollins Quartet 1957 Riverside RLP 12-241 *
8. Hank Mobley Sextet 1957 Blue Note BLP 1568
9. Sonny Clark Sextet 1957 Blue Note BLP 1570

RECOMMENDED RECORDS

10. Sonny Clark- Sonny's Crib Blue Note BLP 1576 *
11. Sonny Clark Trio 1957 Blue Note BLP 1579 *
12. Hank Mobley Sextet 1957 Blue Note GFX-3066 Japan first issue. *
13. Johnny Griffin Quartet 1957 Blue Note BLP 1580
14. Lee Morgan Quartet 1957/58 Blue Note BLP 1590 *
15. Sonny Clark Quinet 1957/1958 Blue Note BLP 1592--- Unissued by BN. First issue in Japan Blue Note K18P-9279
16. Sonny Clark Quinet-*Cool Struttin'* 1958 Blue Note BLP 1588 **
17. Tina Brooks Quinet-Minor Move Not issued by BN. First issue in Japan. Blue Note- GXF 3072**
18. Louis Smith Quintet 1958 Blue Note BLP 1594
19. Sonny Clark Trio 1958 Not issued by BN. First issue in Japan. Blue Note GFX-3069
20. Sonny Clark Trio 1958 Not issued by BN. First issue in Japan. Blue Note GFX 3051
21. Jackie McLean Quintet Blue Note BLP 4051
22. Sonny Clark Quintet. My Conception. Not issued by BN. First issue Japan. JFX 3056 **
23. Sonny Clark Trio Time T/ 70010 *
24. Jackie McLean Quintet Blue Note BLP 4089 *
25. Sonny Clark Quintet Leapin' And Lopin.' Blue Note BLP 4091 **
26. Grant Green Quartet + Ike Quebec Not issued by BN. First issue Japan. GFX 3058
27. Grant Green-Nigeria Blue Note LT 1032
28. Ike Quebec Sextet Blue Note LT 1089 *
29. Grant Green Quartet Not issued by BN. First issue Japan GFX 3065
30. Grant Green Quintet Blue Note BST 84432
31. Jackie McLean Quintet Not issued by BN. First issue Japan LNJ 80118. Originally planned as Blue Note BLP 4116 *

RECOMMENDED RECORDS

32. Don Wilkerson Quintet Preach Brother! Blue Note BLP 4017 (Not a typical Sonny Clark type record but interesting. And different)
33. Dexter Gordon Quartet Go. Blue Note BLP 4112 **
34. Dexter Gordon Quartet A Swingin' Affair. Blue Note BLP 4133 **
35. Jackie McLean Quartet. Tippin' The Scales. Not issued by BN. First issue Japan GFX 3062 *
36. Stanley Turrentine Sextet. Jubilee Shout. 1962. Not issued by BN. Late issue in 1978 as Blue Note BNLA 883 *

ABOUT THE AUTHOR

Born in North London, Derek Ansell was educated locally and attended St. Martin's School of Art in Charing Cross Road, Central London. He worked as a commercial artist for a few years before moving into sales in London, before re-locating to Preston, Lancashire where he spent six years. He moved back south to Newbury, Berkshire and is domiciled there today. Although he spent many years as a Sales Representative and Area Supervisor for an international office equipment manufacturer he began writing relatively late in life and published his first novel, The Whitechapel Murders in 1999.

To learn more about Derek Ansell and discover more Next Chapter authors, visit our website at www.nextchapter.pub.

Sonny Clark - Fragile Virtuoso
ISBN: 978-4-82419-701-6

Published by
Next Chapter
2-5-6 SANNO
SANNO BRIDGE
143-0023 Ota-Ku, Tokyo
+818035793528

24th August 2024

www.ingramcontent.com/pod-product-compliance
Ingram Content Group UK Ltd.
Pitfield, Milton Keynes, MK11 3LW, UK
UKHW030813030325
4826UKWH00036B/518